China Fireworks

*How to Make Dramatic Wealth
from the Fastest-Growing
Economy in the World*

Robert Hsu

WILEY

John Wiley & Sons, Inc.

Published by John Wiley & Sons, Inc., Hoboken, New Jersey.
Published simultaneously in Canada.

For general information on our other products and services or for technical support, please contact our Customer Care Department within the United States at (800) 762-2974, outside the United States at (317) 572-3993 or fax (317) 572-4002.

Wiley also publishes its books in a variety of electronic formats. Some content that appears in print may not be available in electronic books. For more information about Wiley products, visit our web site at www.wiley.com.

Library of Congress Cataloging-in-Publication Data:
    Hsu, Robert, 1968–
        China fireworks : how to make dramatic wealth from the fastest growing economy in the world / Robert Hsu.
            p. cm.
        Includes index.
        ISBN 978-0-470-27677-8 (cloth)
            1. Investments—China. 2. China—Economic conditions—21st century. I. Title.
        II. Title: Wealth from the fastest growing economy in the world.
    HG5782.H78 2008
    332.67'30951—dc22
                                                            2008006117

Printed in the United States of America.
10 9 8 7 6 5 4 2 1

For my son, Sean, and
for my daughter, Rachel,
who wants to be an international
money manager when she grows up.

Contents

Preface

Not long ago, *Newsweek* ran a feature article that asked, "Does the Future Belong to China?" If you ask me, the answer is that the future actually belongs to those who *invest* in China. Despite media reports calling China's economy a bubble and TV personalities questioning the sustainability of its growth, many on Wall Street believe that China is the single biggest investment opportunity that the capital markets have ever seen. From the stocks of industrial Chinese powerhouses to the stocks of global companies serving the gigantic Chinese marketplace, investors have a wide selection of investment choices all based on China and its incredible economic development. The key to successfully investing in China is to make the right choices.

I have written *China Fireworks* to show you how to capitalize on this opportunity—right down to the last detail. I refer to China's phenomenal growth and financial success as the "China Miracle." Unlike many other investment strategies, this miracle is well documented. China has, in the course of barely a decade, become the world's fastest-growing economy. It produces more steel, coal, clothing, and toys than any other country in the world. It is on its way to becoming the leading supplier of electronics, ranging from DVD players and flat-screen TVs to personal computers.

China's exports to the United States alone have grown by more than 1,500 percent since the early 1990s.

This is simply an opportunity that investors around the world cannot afford to miss and cannot afford to get wrong. For many, China is a country shrouded in mystery and even secrecy, presenting a front that can be daunting to those seeking to tap into its financial growth. Investing in China's growth can be much easier to navigate and much more profitable when you take a close look at what's actually happening there . . . and when you know what to look for.

That is exactly what you will cover in *China Fireworks*. Fortunes and wealth are being created at astounding rates, and the opportunities and potentials are vast. Over the course of this book, I will take you on a firsthand tour that will guide you through the new and exciting world of China investing. By the time you've finished reading, you will have the skills to build your own wealth from the China Miracle.

Acknowledgments

I would like to thank the team at my money management company—Dr. Fei He, Lucia Caldera, Eric Leibowitz, Ada Lu, Frances Liu and Shao-feng Xu—for their hard work, support and research. I must thank my associates at Investorplace Media for helping me share my ideas and experience with thousands of investors through my investment newsletters. I also want to thank Dr. Andrew Kadar for early encouragement and guidance.

Finally, special thanks to HP Newquist, Chris Marett, and Shannon Miller, who helped make this book possible.

Chapter 1

Introduction to the China Miracle

There is a six-lane bridge being built in Shanghai that connects Mainland China with the island of Yangshan 20 miles offshore. It will ultimately become the largest sea-span bridge in the world. It will connect Shanghai with a new port in Yangshan, a phenomenally huge facility that will double Shanghai's shipping capability—which is already the third largest in the world. Much of the world's clothes, toys, and electronics will be shipped from this location over the next decade.

Just to the west of Shanghai, the largest construction project in the world, the Three Gorges Dam hydroelectric project, is in full swing. Three Gorges is expected to be five times wider than the Hoover Dam and is the biggest construction undertaking since the Great Wall of China was started in 200 B.C. It will also be the largest source of hydroelectric power on Earth.

The Chinese government is able to pay for these projects thanks to the largest foreign reserve fund, and the largest trade surplus, ever seen. Those reserves and that surplus come by way of China's economy, which is growing faster than that of any other nation in history. In five years, China has sped past Italy, the United Kingdom and France in growth and now trails only the United States, Japan, and Germany. Rest assured, China will not be in fourth place for long. It is already the world's leading manufacturer and exporter of goods. No other nation even comes close.

Welcome to the China Miracle.

China is experiencing the greatest boom in the history of the world, which I believe will provide you with the best investment opportunities of your lifetime. No other economy and no other marketplace has ever come close to offering investors so much potential to make money and build wealth. To be sure, stocks in emerging markets such as China tend to be more volatile than stocks in the United States and other global markets. The potential financial gain from investing in an emerging market with sustained growth, however, can also be much higher.

My purpose in writing this book, quite simply, is to show you how to build your own fortune by investing in the China Miracle.

I've been making money for years by watching China's growth and identifying trends that deliver the greatest return for investors. As one of the leading experts on investing in China's economy, I advise people every single day on how a China strategy will truly take them to a new level of investing. And since you and I are going to be spending a fair amount of time together over the course of this book, I think it's only fair that I tell you a bit about myself and my credentials.

I was born in Taiwan and raised in Southern California. I'm an American citizen, even though I share a heritage with more than a billion ethnic Chinese around the world. I've spoken English my entire life, but I speak, read, and write Mandarin fluently.

Being proficient in Chinese is not the reason that I've been able to successfully invest in the China Miracle—although it hasn't hurt. After all, there are more than a billion other people in the world who can read Chinese and have an ethnic background similar to mine. That's obviously not what makes me unique. What sets me apart from other investors is my history of investment success, along with my understanding of what's happening in China.

I started my career as a trader and analyst for a global macro hedge fund and was then hired by Goldman Sachs, the world's premier investment firm. I learned a great deal about every aspect of international markets while at Goldman, and put that expertise to good use. Like many investors, I made a very nice return from tech stocks in 1999. But unlike most tech stock investors, I continued to do well between 2000 and 2002 even though the NASDAQ declined 70 percent. I was able to do this because I listened to the markets and I changed my strategy when the market changed. I was a millionaire by the time I was 29 years old.

I eventually took my knowledge of international equities, interest rates, currencies, and commodities markets with me to start my own firm, Absolute Return Capital Advisors. I have offices in Century City, situated right next to Beverly Hills and Hollywood, and my team and I use global investment strategies to manage private client money. I also oversee Pearl River Capital Management, a private investment partnership that focuses on China.

In addition, I have two investment newsletters, *China Strategy* and *Asia Edge*. *China Strategy*, in particular, has become one of the largest subscription-based services in the United States since its launch in 2006.

In order to stay on top of investment opportunities in China, I employ a team of analysts on the Mainland to keep me up-to-date with information relevant to my current holdings as well as potential new investments. I also read Chinese newspapers and periodicals while at home in California and travel several times a year to visit the Mainland. I firmly believe that getting firsthand information has been crucial to my success.

What else? I live in Beverly Hills with my wife and two children. Even though I've worked and traveled all over the world, I like Southern California for a number of reasons. I like the weather, I like driving my convertible with the top down all year long, I like the exotic restaurants, and I like the energy and excitement that comes with being in a place that is on the cutting edge of everything from food to fashion.

Building True Wealth

Beyond that, I like building my wealth, and I enjoy the fact that my job makes other people wealthy, too. Several years ago, however, I came to a realization: Investing in the U.S. economy was no longer the best way for me to accumulate new wealth. For investors, buying and holding a large basket of U.S. stocks no longer produced real annual returns above 5 percent. Eight years after the start of the twenty-first century, the S&P 500 is still around where it was at the end of 1999. I want more than that, and I'm sure you do, too.

The problems I saw weren't limited to the stock market. The U.S. economy since 2006 has moved along so glacially that it has barely kept us ahead of a recession. The decline of the U.S. dollar during that same time has sunk the value of our currency to previously unimaginable lows.

My investment advice is that now, more than ever, investors looking to build their wealth must look outside of the United States for real and sustainable growth. To attain superior absolute returns in the new century, buy-and-hold U.S. stocks are just not going to deliver the profits that I think every investor should expect. And in looking to make the biggest returns, I've found that the single best place to find great returns is China, where the economy continues to grow over 10 percent a year.

Some people have been skeptical—but only for a moment—of my thoughts on the future of U.S. markets. This is because of two assumptions that have long been drummed into our heads. The first is that the U.S. stock market always goes up over time, and the second is that investment gains in U.S. stocks are stable over time. These two assumptions are less reliable than you might think. There have been long periods of time when the U.S. stock market moved down or sideways, seriously damaging investors' ability to make enough money to fund their dreams or retire in comfort.

For instance, following the market peak in 1929, the Dow Jones Industrial Average fell for four years, and it took a full 24 years to get back to pre-1929 levels. There were also long periods when the stock market went up, but was outpaced by inflation. In the 54-year period between 1928 and 1982, the Dow Jones Industrial Average rose by only 1.9 percent per year on average, while the consumer price index (CPI) shot up by over 3 percent per year on average.

As for assumption number two, we all saw the S&P 500 index fall 23 percent in 2002 and then watched it rise 26 percent in 2003. Obviously, returns are actually anything but stable. It's impossible to predict what any market will do over both long and short periods of time. Thankfully, in this era of globalization, investors have other investment opportunities when the domestic market is weak.

In fact, two things worry me about the U.S. stock market for the next several years: the real estate debacle and aging demographics. The most recent instance of a major stock market being hit with both of these conditions at the same time was Japan in 1990. The Japanese real estate bubble was well documented (at one point, downtown Tokyo was worth more than the entire state of California).

The demographics story is not as well-known, but it had serious ramifications for Japan and its investors. Back in 1990, there were five workers supporting every retiree in the Japanese economy. As the Japanese population got older, there were only three workers supporting every retiree in the system. When Japanese workers retired, the society's economic productivity went down, and retirees took money out of the Japanese stock market to pay for their retirement expenses. Today, the Japanese stock market is still down 60 percent from its peak 17 years ago.

Right now in the United States, there are five workers supporting every retiree. But, as our baby boomers retire, the ratio of workers to retirees will also drop to three workers for every retiree. Does this sound familiar? These ratios do not bode well for the U.S. stock market over the next decade.

This is certainly cause for concern, but the bright side is that there will always be opportunities outside of U.S. stocks to make money, and China's economic emergence is delivering some of the best investment opportunities available. The opportunities have materialized because of two simple economic facts: (1) China has become a mass producer of the world's goods, and (2) China is quickly becoming a mass consumer.

China has an almost unlimited supply of cheap labor, so companies from around the world have been able to produce their goods more cheaply in China. The result is that China has become a leading exporter, with more than half of those goods produced for foreign companies. China's exports soared in 2007 to over $1.1 trillion, whereas imports came in at over $865 billion.

Much of this economic growth is being driven by hardworking entrepreneurs, from small shop owners on the roadsides in Beijing to high-tech graduates forming software companies in Shenzhen.

The importance of entrepreneurs to China's economy has taken many China watchers by surprise, especially most Wall Street analysts who rarely, if ever, visit there. They've been missing the boat for years, and all indications are that they're going to continue to miss it.

The Real Growth Driver

A real middle class is now emerging in China, thanks to the burgeoning private sector, and many Chinese aspire to the consumer lifestyle we're accustomed to in the West. With all of this growth, the proverbial talk of China as a land of one billion consumers is finally coming true. More and more Chinese citizens are finding good jobs or starting their own businesses, and they have money to spend.

The energy and excitement that I like in Beverly Hills I've lately found percolating in China's cities. Shanghai, for one, has gone from being a staid industrial port to being one of the world's most glamorous cities. From restaurants to high-end stores and boutiques, theaters, and arts centers, the same cultural drivers that make cities like Los Angeles, New York, London, Tokyo, and Paris so enthralling have taken hold in Shanghai. Throughout China, other cities are following its lead. There is a dynamism, a momentum, that you can feel in the new China.

I like momentum. I'm a momentum investor. I am not a buy-and-hold investor, and I don't get attached to stocks that aren't delivering me a high level of profits. Momentum is all about what my stocks are doing for me right now. When the stocks lose momentum, I lose the stocks. That's why I invest in China—there is incredible momentum and there are huge opportunities to make money.

This is different from buying stocks for the long term, waiting patiently until they deliver you some preordained number that appears to be acceptable. Then when a stock reaches that number you sell it—even if the company is still growing and has momentum—because that's the way Wall Street tells you it's done.

Momentum investing takes its cue from a company's growth and that of its stock price. As long as those go up, you enjoy the ride. Once they stop, the momentum is lost, and it's time to take your profits and move on. This kind of investing takes a lot of discipline, but it keeps your portfolio stocked with winners because the losers are immediately culled out.

It is my belief that you can't sit around and wait for your investments to pay off. To keep them, they always need to be paying off. The U.S. economy is facing some difficult times ahead as it adapts to everything from higher oil prices to providing health care for aging boomers. We need to be building our wealth now, each and every day. In the long run, it will cost more to live comfortably than many investors expect—or have planned for. Thus, wealth needs to be constantly accumulated. Investors need to focus on building wealth so that things like retirement will take care of themselves.

That's why I'm so enthusiastic about the China Miracle. It provides a myriad of ways for us to improve our financial situations. And the entire market has been truly investable only since late 2002. We're just at the beginning, and there's still a lot more money to be made.

You and I will make this money by investing in companies that are smart enough to take advantage of China's economic boom. Companies that are providing the Chinese government with what it needs and the people of China with what they desire, companies that have improved their bottom lines by taking advantage of China's manufacturing capabilities, and companies that have become fantastic international competitors thanks to the innovation of China's new class of entrepreneurs, can be good investments. Over the course of this book, we will look at commodities, telecommunications, tourism, fast food, health care, and a host of other industries that are exploding throughout China.

In short, you and I will make money by identifying and understanding how to stake the best positions in China. The China Miracle is there for everyone who wants a piece of it, but too many people will never understand how to profit from it. By taking the time to read this book, you will become one of the select few who know exactly how to get rich by investing in China.

The momentum is on your side. Let's get started.

Chapter 2

The China Miracle

"Investing in China" means exactly what it says: You are literally investing your money in the culture, traditions, values, and surging economy of China and its people. Investing in China is more than looking at the financial promise and performance of individual stocks. To really profit from the China Miracle, your investments must take into account the way the Chinese people live and work, the way they structure and develop their businesses, and the expectations they have for becoming a significant component of the global community.

To those who do not understand its history or culture, the China Miracle appears to be an overnight success story. Too many investors perceive China's emergence as a dominant player in global commerce as a recent phenomenon. They think of China as a land shrouded in mystery where factories manufacture millions of products a day and business is conducted by government officials who control every aspect of production and distribution.

Nothing could be further from the truth. The fact is that China has a long and successful history as an economic powerhouse—a history that predates the United States and its singularly impressive economy by thousands of years. It is only now, however, after spending much of the twentieth century in isolation, that China is in a position to join the ranks of the world's preeminent modern economies. While many in China claim that the country is simply reclaiming its rightful status in the world, astute observers note that China's commitment to growth makes its economic might an inevitability.

Because of what appears to be China's rapid rise, investors of all types have rushed to capitalize on it, oftentimes without the proper preparation. Many investors have already been burned by putting their trust in advisers who don't understand the unique dynamics of investing in China: the government, the markets, the lack of shareholder rights, an undeveloped legal system, and other peculiarities of China's markets. I've seen many investment advisers evaluate Chinese companies, or those companies doing business in China, using the same metrics they apply to American or European companies. This is a serious error, because the essence of what makes China the most extraordinary investment opportunity in the world is its uniqueness. China is unlike anything that investors have ever experienced before. Investing in China requires thinking about the drivers of growth in completely new ways.

Understanding the culture is important in identifying which investment strategies will work in China and which will fail. I think it's safe to say that many Wall Streeters go to China, stay in luxury hotels in major cities, meet with whichever high-ranking government and corporate officials are available, and then go out to dinner with their American partners in Americanized restaurants. Their experience in China is little more than that of a tourist with a platinum credit card. They fail to get any real insight into what is going on in the streets and markets around them and thus miss out on the tremendous changes taking place across the entire country. This sanitized exposure to the country means these Wall Street guys never see the real China, and their advice reflects that.

There are several very important elements that you as an investor need to be aware of before ever putting a penny in China. The first is the importance of China's history relative to its current place in the world. Even as it becomes increasingly modern, China embraces and reveres its history, and much of its economic and cultural behavior is based on what the country's relationship with the rest of the world has been over the past 3,000 years.

The second is the industrial spirit of the Chinese people. The Chinese have historically been incredibly successful entrepreneurs. They have developed products and services that are eagerly sought after by the rest of the world, and they work diligently to be the primary competitor in the markets they enter. This is true whether they live in Mainland China or are part of Chinese communities located in other countries.

The third is the influence of traditional Chinese values held in high esteem by the Chinese people. When combined with capitalism and modern business practices, these values have helped the Chinese excel in free-enterprise societies.

Being aware of these elements is crucial to helping you understand why China is so different from every other market on the planet. This is true whether you are viewing China as a producer or as a consumer. These elements apply to China both when it is making goods and when it is buying them.

Investment Essential #1: China's History

China's rich mercantile tradition goes back more than 3,000 years to the era when Chinese traders took their handmade goods to neighboring nations. As the quality of its goods and the reputation of its traders increased, China's trade extended far beyond regional borders, reaching elsewhere in Asia, deep into the Middle East, and across Europe.

Initially, China was known for its gorgeous silk, spun by silkworms and woven using secret methods that were guarded closely. The ancient Romans became significant importers of this silk, referring to China specifically as "Seres"—the land of silk. Other cultures also revered China's silk, using it for royalty and pageantry. Silk has been discovered in the tombs of Egyptian mummies, and pieces of colored silk estimated to be over 3,500 years old have been found in Afghanistan. Even thousands of years ago, China was clearly a country with an extensive trade network and desirable products.

As the country built its relationships with the outside world, trading routes were established that reached from China all the way to Europe. Created some 2,000 years ago, these routes came to be known collectively as the "Silk Road" (see Figure 2.1). The Silk Road ran from what is modern-day Xi'an, in the heart of Mainland China, to ports along the Mediterranean Sea. Its various routes linked China to regions as far-flung as Italy, Persia, India, Thailand, Egypt, Syria, North Africa, and other ancient realms. All told, the Silk Road flourished for more than a thousand years. Trade was brisk and brought goods—and currency—into and out of China; Roman coins nearly 2,000 years old have been found at sites in western China.

The commerce conducted via the Silk Road provided the foundation for many of the European and Asian cities and ports that have evolved into the most important centers of business and finance in our modern world.

When cost-effective commercial shipping developed in the sixteenth century, the Silk Road went into decline. A new breed of seafaring merchants emerged from three coastal provinces in southern China: Fujian, Guangdong (once known as Canton), and Zhejiang (see Figure 2.2). These provinces capitalized on shipping much as other provinces had once benefited from the overland routes of the Silk Road.

China adapted and thrived over the course of many centuries, taking advantage of new distribution methods and the world's taste for its increasing variety of goods, from jade and porcelain to tea. A prime example of Chinese industriousness and entrepreneurial spirit was evidenced by the merchants from the dusty and barren Shanxi province. Because of the poor quality of their land, which was completely unfit for agriculture, the people of Shanxi were forced to conduct commerce in regions far from their home in order to survive.

Shanxi traders traveled with huge caravans of horses and camels through the steppes of Central Asia, selling silk and tea to eager European and Middle Eastern buyers. Shanxi trading houses established comprehensive training programs for young apprentices. New apprentices were taught Turkic, Russian, and Mongolian, as well as accounting and negotiating skills. After a three-year apprenticeship, these merchants were then sent to faraway lands.

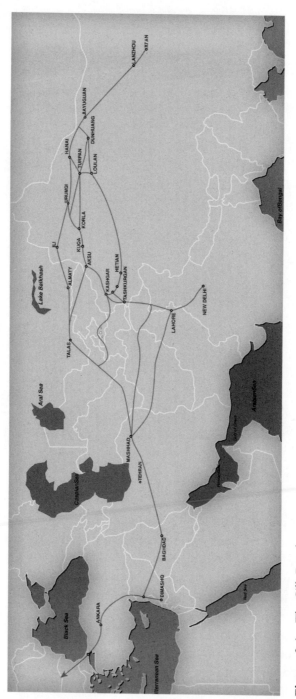

Figure 2.1 The Silk Road
SOURCE: InvestorPlace Media, LLC.

Figure 2.2 Eastern Provinces
Source: InvestorPlace Media, LLC.

Braving extreme weather conditions, murderous bandits, and rugged mountains, Shanxi merchants went through great danger to build their wealth. Many froze to death in mountain ranges where temperatures dropped to 40 degrees below zero. Others died of thirst along the Gobi Desert in daytime temperatures that reached over 110 degrees. Even today, on the road through the Gobi Desert, one can still see the exposed bones of unfortunate merchants who died hundreds of years ago.

Although traders endured incredible hardships to make the journey, the profit potential was enormous. Most of their trades were conducted by barter. Russians would trade a mink for an iron pot, while Mongols were willing to trade a thoroughbred horse for a copper bowl. With the right planning and supplies, a one-year round trip for a Shanxi merchant could generate a comfortable nest egg that lasted for decades.

Even Marco Polo was impressed by this trade practice and opportunity for wealth. The fabled Venetian traveler, who lived in China from 1266 to 1290, wrote about merchants from the Shanxi region conducting business throughout Asia while amassing vast wealth. Their legendary hard work and resulting success transformed the dirt-poor province into the main commercial center of China for 500 years.

As a country, China was protective of its products and mindful of its economy. China's emperors were careful not to allow the country to fall into debt with its trading partners, a strategy that eventually led to a significant trade surplus—mainly in the form of silver. By the early 1800s, the country was trading with partners all over the world, from Spain and Saudi Arabia to the United States, and many of these countries ran up huge trade deficits with China.

China's success as an exporter caused resentment among those trying to sell goods back to China. European trading companies met with significant trade barriers, including high tariffs, strict codes of business procedure, limited access to ports, and a general wariness of European colonial practices. Trade imbalances soared, yet the imperial rulers of China refused to address the trading concerns of its partners. These rulers effectively isolated China, allowing goods to be shipped out of the country, but refusing to import much of anything except the silver that paid for Chinese products like tea and silk.

Trade tensions with Europe resulted in the Opium Wars in the mid-1800s. These wars were an aggressive attempt by China's trading partners, led by Britain, to break down China's barriers and its restrictions on imported goods—notably opium. Despite a ban on opium, many Chinese citizens became addicted to the drug and sought it out on the black market. Trading partners saw a way to right their trade imbalance and began smuggling opium into the country. Even though it was illegal, China's imports of opium increased fivefold from 1821 to 1837. This illicit trade worked in favor of the Europeans: The drugs went in, and silver came out.

Military conflict soon erupted, initiating not one but two Opium Wars. Britain, with superior firepower, prevailed both times, and by the time the second was over in 1860, China was changed forever. The country turned over the critical port of Hong Kong to the British, and China's isolation from the rest of the world deepened.

Dissatisfaction with the emperor, combined with increasing exposure to the West, caused civil unrest throughout the country. Protests, rebellions, and outright civil war wracked China over the following decades. In 1912, little more than 50 years after the Opium Wars ended, the Qing dynasty fell, ending more than 2,000 years of imperial rule in China.

In its place, the Republic of China was created. But from its inception, the country was torn by internal strife between warring factions that included the Kuomintang and the Communist Party. Civil war was a constant during the first half of the twentieth century, with political parties and regional warlords seeking to control the fate of the nation. After World War II, China's internal war intensified, and the Communists ultimately forced the Nationalists out of the country. The Nationalists retreated to the island of Taiwan, establishing a renegade government.

With the establishment of Communist rule in 1949, the newly christened People's Republic of China effectively stopped doing business with the rest of the world. The once-great commercial power had slammed its door on all outsiders.

A little-known fact is that when the Communists came to power, China already had a booming stock market in place. Securities trading within China began in the mid-1800s as unlisted corporate shares and gold-backed certificates were traded among merchants. The first stock market in China was set up in Shanghai in 1891. Despite the political struggles that ravaged the country after the fall of the Qing dynasty, by the 1930s the Shanghai exchange was the largest and wealthiest stock market in Asia, where both Chinese and foreign investors traded stocks, government bonds, and futures. But the prosperity was cut short. When the Communists took over China in 1949, the Shanghai stock exchange was shut down.

For nearly four decades, business in China was effectively shut down. Companies were run by the state—the infamous state-owned enterprises (SOEs) that we'll talk about at length in upcoming chapters—and citizens were told where they could work. Yet soon after the death of Mao Zedong in 1976, Deng Xiaoping pushed the country toward an economy that sought to include both non-state-owned businesses and individual citizens.

Reforms began in 1979, when Deng forced the country to consider modernization at the expense of entrenched ways. For the first time since the Communists ascended to power, Chinese people were allowed to create their own businesses—legitimately—and sell goods and services on an open market. And by opening itself up to the rest of the world, China once again began to assert itself as a global economic force. As a nation with substantial resources, China sought to partner with capitalist nations with which it had long sparred, most notably the United States.

The Chinese entrepreneurial spirit survived almost a half century through Mao's hard-line stance against capitalism and international trade. In the nearly 30 years since reforms began in the early 1980s, the country has grown faster than any other nation—ever.

China reinstated its stock exchanges in 1984, which I'll discuss in a moment. Foreign and government investment in infrastructure, factories, office buildings, and telecommunications drove growth to heights never before seen. During the 1990s, economic growth helped lift 12 percent of China's population out of poverty—during a period of increased poverty worldwide. Today, according to a Human Development Report, industrialization and technology have brought a third of its citizens out of rural poverty.

China's gross domestic product (GDP) growth rate went from −1.6 percent in 1976—the year Mao died—to its current rate of 10.7 percent. Double-digit GDP growth became the norm beginning in 1983, once foreign investment and non-state-owned enterprises were established as staples of the Chinese economy. Growth has been so phenomenal that as of mid-2007 China had a current account surplus with its trading partners of more than $200 billion—the largest surplus in the world. While much has been made of the fact that it has a singularly oversized surplus with the United States, China has done an exceptional job of selling to the rest of the world as well. Exports to Europe, for example, are increasing faster than those to the United States. China also holds more foreign exchange reserves than any other country in the world.

China has benefited from many things in achieving its remarkable rise: inexpensive labor and access to raw materials, modest early expectations, and a national commitment to be competitive on a global scale.

While its recent growth appears to be nothing short of miraculous, history has shown that there is precedent for China producing goods that the rest of the world wants. Once it was tea and silk; today it is electronics, clothes, toys, and appliances.

There is an essential fact here that the careful investor should take note of. All of these goods, from toys to electronics, rely on energy and raw materials for production. They are commodity-based products, and China requires incredible amounts of energy, steel, aluminum, fibers, and other materials to create them. This is a fact to keep in mind as we explore the investment opportunities in China. China needs access to raw materials in order to maintain its level of production, and investors will benefit by knowing how to identify who the key suppliers are. We will certainly cover this important topic in later chapters of this book.

Here is a last historical point to keep in mind as we explore the opportunities in China. The country opened the door to entrepreneurs and industrious citizens in the 1980s. At that time, there wasn't a single business in China of any note that wasn't owned by the state. Today, however, China has nearly 24 million small independent companies, . . . and that number is growing at a rate of 20 percent a year. These are the businesses, and people, that will sustain the China miracle.

Investment Essential #2: China's People

Appreciating China's history is only the first step in understanding what has made China an economic powerhouse that has eclipsed all other emerging markets. The second factor you need to consider is the Chinese people.

As you've just seen, China has a rich history, much of it shaped and built by enterprising citizens like the Shanxi traders of old and the modern business owners of today. There is a unique character shared by Chinese people that is at the foundation of the country's current economic success. That character infuses everything they do.

Let me give you an example of how Chinese people perceive themselves. Over the past several years, the most popular television drama in China was a show called *Qiao Jia Dayuan* (*Qiao Family Courtyard House*). It told the story of Qiao Guifa, a small-time tea and bean-curd merchant who built an international trading empire more than 100 years ago. In real life, Qiao's firm was one of the most successful merchant houses during the Qing dynasty. It bought and sold goods in cities ranging from London in the West to Tokyo in the East.

The Qiao Guifa TV show was the most popular Chinese-made television drama series in years, igniting an interest in Qiao's home. That home is all that remains from Qiao's glory days; it is an extensive Qing dynasty family complex that consists of six courtyards containing over 300 rooms. If you're interested, you can see the house for yourself—on film—as it was featured in Chinese director Zhang Yimou's motion picture *Raise the Red Lantern* starring Gong Li.

As a result of the TV show's popularity, the 250-year-old Qing complex became one of the hottest tourist destinations in China, despite being located near the heavily polluted city of Taiyuan in Shanxi province. After the show started airing, more than 300,000 tickets to visit the house were sold during the May holiday, exceeding in one day the total number of tickets sold during the entire previous year.

Qiao Jia Dayuan is so popular largely because it reminds Chinese viewers of their nation's rich mercantile history and the global scope of ancient Chinese commercial operations. This is a strong source of pride for the Chinese. You have to remember that it was only in the past 150 years that the economy regressed; for most if its history, China was one of the world's great nations of commerce. The TV show's success is an indication of the desire Chinese people have to return to their historic status.

While its commercial history demonstrates that China is not starting over from scratch, the economic and political repression it suffered after the Opium Wars did deliver quite a setback. During a time when the rest of the world was adapting to significant changes in technology and communication, China hardly bothered to keep up. Its industries were antiquated and its people were impoverished. Thus, China's current status in the world is thought of in terms of "an emerging market."

You have to realize that since the 1970s just about every country outside of the G7 nations (Canada, France, Germany, the United Kingdom, Italy, Japan, and the United States) and Western Europe has been called an "emerging market" at one time or another. A friend once commented to me that 80 percent of the people in the world live in emerging market economies. That doesn't mean all these countries have the same potential for investors; some are better than others. I believe the reason for that is the collective industriousness of a people.

For example, for the past 50 years, Brazil has been perennially hailed as the "next big thing." Thirty-five years ago, my older cousin Wen Hsu left Taiwan for Brazil to search for a better life. A civil engineer by training, Wen was well educated and found a nice job with a big international company in São Paulo. With its vast natural resources and relatively educated population, Brazil was widely perceived as *the* emerging economy in the early 1970s. Despite the hype, it never quite delivered. The nation's economy succumbed to hyperinflation, fiscal mismanagement, and other economic crises. Its people remain poor, and violence is common in urban areas.

Brazil is an excellent example of the fate of many emerging markets. Though there have certainly been investment opportunities there, it has never lived up to its potential and has not delivered truly life-changing wealth opportunities for investors.

In contrast, Taiwan's fortunes soared during the same period that Brazil was stifled by economic pressures. From the early 1970s to the 1990s, per capita economic output—gross domestic product (GDP)—in Taiwan increased over 1,000 percent!

The next time I saw Wen was in early 1994 at a big family gathering. After 20 years in Brazil, he had moved back to Taiwan to work as a mass transit system engineer after his nest egg was wiped out in Brazil. Many of his classmates who had remained in Taiwan prospered and made millions from the country's real estate boom.

Why did one emerging market thrive while the other did not? Most emerging markets follow roads similar to that taken by Brazil. They get their first taste of growth, and almost immediately inflation and gross mismanagement derail their promise. Here's a statistic that may surprise you: In the past 40 years, aside from members of the Organization of Petroleum Exporting Countries (OPEC), only four out of 90-plus emerging market economies really "emerged" into the ranks of developed economies (as defined by having an annual per capita GDP of $15,000 or more). Those nations are Hong Kong, Singapore, South Korea, and Taiwan.

What's even more amazing is that each of those four—formerly nicknamed the "four Asian economic tigers"—has a relatively small population and little in the way of natural resources. Yet, these economies went from being poor to being prosperous within the span of one generation.

What made them different? In contrast to the multitude of economies that have not quite "emerged," all four of these nations that have gone on to economic success share a common characteristic: They are dominated by traditional Chinese values and culture.

Immigrants Impact Growth

Earlier I mentioned some of the provinces that grew up as centers of commerce after the demise of the Silk Road. People from these provinces—Fujian, Guangdong, and Zhejiang—had access to seaports and ships that took them around the world to sell China's goods for hundreds of years. Many of them decided to set up businesses or go work in some of the countries where they sailed. As a result of large-scale migration off the coast of China, a huge number of ethnic Chinese are now scattered around the world. Nobody knows for sure how many of these overseas Chinese there are, but a good guess is probably in the neighborhood of 60 million to 80 million. It is a diaspora to which I am proud to belong.

Early settlers from Fujian moved to Taiwan, Malaysia, Indonesia, and the Philippines in large numbers over the past 400 years, and the tradition of seeking their fortunes in faraway lands continues today. Most of the new immigrants into American Chinatowns are from Fujian. For example, if you have Chinese food delivered in New York, chances are the deliveryman is from Fujian.

People from Guangdong (aka Canton) were among the most adventurous Chinese immigrants. These people left their homes and populated Hong Kong, Macau, and Chinatowns throughout North America. Guangdong's proximity to Hong Kong and the rise of special economic zones and favorable tax status, such as Shenzhen and Zhuhai, have helped make Guangdong the wealthiest province in China.

Zhejiang province contains coastal cities such as prosperous Wenzhou and charming Hangzhou, which Marco Polo described as the greatest city in the world. Businessmen from Zhejiang rose to prominence in the wake of the Shanxi merchants and became the most successful entrepreneurs in China. Ports were built to export Zhejiang's tea, sending Chinese sailors all over the world. Today, Zhejiang is the fastest-growing province in China and is now more prosperous than ever—a thousand years after its birth as a major commercial center.

Millions of ethnic Chinese minorities live not too far from their homeland in Southeast Asian countries such as Thailand, Indonesia, Malaysia, and the Philippines. Although they are far outnumbered by natives, their commercial skill, work ethic, family values, and emphasis on education allow them to dominate the economy in these countries.

This is a key point that I can't stress enough. The real force behind the China Miracle is the Chinese people. Unfettered by the shackles of the old system, Chinese citizens have unleashed their boundless entrepreneurial energy and superior work ethic. They've done it for decades in other countries, and now they're once again doing it in China itself.

To prove this point, many studies have been done and a number of books have been written showing that as an economic entity, ethnic Chinese living outside of Mainland China generate more wealth than any country in the world except the United States and Japan. Many of us are thriving, and some are incredibly wealthy.

Ethnic Chinese are very proud of their heritage and make a strong effort to pass it down to future generations. Unlike Americans, the Chinese define their national identity largely by ethnicity as opposed to where they reside.

For instance, if you don't look Chinese, those of Chinese ancestry won't regard you as Chinese. Even if you were born in China and know the language and culture better than most natives, you still would not be considered Chinese. Ethnic Chinese might be impressed by your language skill and knowledge, but ultimately you are not one of them. Chinese believe that ethnicity carries with it a shared history and set of values that cannot be appropriated by other cultures or ethnicities.

This is why it is important for international corporations that set up operations in China to hire a fair percentage of local managers. Many non-Chinese who try to fit into company outposts by behaving like "Mr. China" end up disappointed. You can marry a Chinese spouse or become a close friend of a Chinese family, but most Chinese would still not think of you as Chinese. It is something you are at birth— you cannot become Chinese simply by adopting the language and the trappings.

There is another side to this tradition of being truly Chinese, and it helps to link overseas Chinese with the country itself. My young son, Sean, just recently started learning Chinese and has been to Mainland China only twice. When we last visited China, several tour guides lectured me about the importance of teaching my son Chinese. I remember their exact words: "No matter where you live in the world, your son should never forget that he's Chinese, and his ancestors came from China."

Even though Sean has never lived in China and doesn't speak Mandarin well yet, he's still Chinese to the Chinese citizens. Fortunately, I can now help Sean prepare for a future in which China is a land of opportunities.

These opportunities have created reciprocal interests among Chinese throughout the world. Chinese living in other countries have developed the capital and expertise to build businesses, while Mainland China is replete with cheap land and labor. Together they make for a perfect business combination. Regardless of the country in which they have citizenship, Chinese have found a way to work together for their mutual benefit. It has been estimated that up until 2004, overseas Chinese accounted for nearly 70 percent of total foreign direct investments in Mainland China. The Chinese government welcomed back these overseas Chinese, and their money, with open arms.

Compared with other emerging economies, China's vast and prosperous overseas population is a huge advantage. India, for instance, is just now seeing the beginning of a successful overseas population that can ultimately help establish successful businesses back in the homeland. However, India does not have overseas population numbers commensurate with China's.

In addition, India is culturally much more fragmented than China. For instance, over 80 percent of all Chinese speak Mandarin, but less than 40 percent of all Indians speak Hindi, India's most common language. The cultural, language, and historical bonds between ethnic Indians are typically not as strong as those shared by ethnic Chinese. This comparison applies to the people of many emerging markets, such as Russia and Brazil.

I believe the vast experience and resources provided by overseas Chinese are perhaps the biggest edge China has over other emerging market economies. Many of the top businesses in China were started by ethnic Chinese have returned to the land of their ancestors. In some cases, the global perspective and entrepreneurial expertise acquired by overseas Chinese have given their businesses an advantage—over companies

formed by local entrepreneurs. This is because the reemergence of
private business in China is still in a nascent stage in many regions.

The presence of the Chinese spirit is—and will continue to be—
undeniable. As the Chinese people seek to succeed in business, those
of us who invest in their determination will be rewarded for our
understanding of their critical role in the China Miracle.

Investment Essential #3: China's Values

The third factor that differentiates China from the rest of the world's
emerging markets is the influence of traditional Chinese values. Specifically, it is how these values are instrumental to the success of Chinese
businesspeople in a free market economy. These traditional Chinese values were developed centuries ago to promote social stability and personal
integrity. Today, when individuals combine these values with capitalism
in their business endeavors, these values have proven to be instrumental
to Chinese success in free enterprise societies all over the world.

Many Chinese traditional values were based on the teachings of
Confucius, the fifth century B.C. philosopher who focused on promot-
ing social harmony through respect for authority, strong interpersonal
relationships, emphasis on education, and moral integrity. Other Chinese
values, known as "traditional virtues," include thriftiness, hard work, and
personal honor. Taken together, these are in many ways very much like
the values practiced by the early settlers of America.

For 2,000 years, authoritarian rulers in China promoted Confucianism to help preserve the status quo and maintain social stability.
As the world changed, however, the emphasis on social stability led
to economic stagnation, and China—as I've pointed out—has lagged
behind the rest of the world for the past century.

That state of existence is now changing. In the past decade, the
term *ru-shang,* or "Confucian merchants," has been widely used in
Mainland China and among ethnic Chinese societies overseas to
describe scholarly businesspeople who adhere to traditional Confucian
teachings. Governments from Beijing to Seoul have endorsed Confucianism as a stimulus for economic development, because many aspects
of Confucianism correlate to success in modern capitalist societies.
A strong work ethic, acceptance of hierarchy, emphasis on education,

and moral integrity are all conducive to developing large-scale modern businesses in the Information Age.

Confucius is one of many Chinese philosophers and teachers whose words have meaning and resonance in today's business. One of my favorite books of all time is the *Tao Te Ching,* also known as the *Book of Tao.* The text was written over 2,000 years ago by the ancient Chinese sage Lao-tzu, and it spawned the Eastern philosophy known as Taoism, also called the Study of the Way. Taoism is one of the most influential schools of thought in China.

Like other prominent philosophy texts, the *Book of Tao* explores many different themes and life lessons. One of the book's central themes—the one that I use most in my own life—involves how to interact with one's surroundings. Taoism is about finding the best ways to deal with life's problems. I don't know anyone who doesn't want to find a better, more efficient way to deal with the challenges that life throws our way.

This particular Taoist lesson can be best summed up in the famous phrase "go with the flow." Many people associate this notion with laziness; they think that going with the flow requires no thought or work. But this isn't the case at all.

Instead of advocating laziness, this concept addresses the value of working smart over working hard. Going with the flow increases productivity with less effort by working in the direction of big-picture change. For example, you can go far without exerting much effort just by sitting on a boat floating downstream. By contrast, rowing a boat upstream requires lots of work just to stay in one place. Many people don't realize that the hardest part of any job or endeavor is determining which way the water is flowing, and then pointing your boat in that direction.

Working with the forces of the world, not fighting them, is exactly what I've done in my life. In my career, there were two main trends I spotted early and jumped on with satisfying results. The first was the emergence of the hedge fund industry during the 1990s. I first entered the hedge fund business 17 years ago, before most people knew what hedge funds were. Today, assets under management and revenues in the hedge fund industry total $1.5 trillion, generating $70 billion in fees a year. That's nearly 50-fold growth since 1990!

The second major trend I jumped on was the economic emergence of China. Not too long ago, I gave a talk to MBA students at the University of California at Irvine's Paul Merage School of Business. One student asked me for specific career advice. I told him to "go East, young man," and spend time in the Greater China region. China is where the economic flow is going, and the best course of action is to follow it rather than to ignore it or work against it. The phenomenal growth that we're seeing in China right now represents one of the great all-time wealth-building opportunities. The portfolios that I've created for investors and subscribers have made impressive gains since I recognized this trend, and I believe there are even more profits to come in the years ahead—as long as investors commit to understanding how China works.

Final Thoughts

After reading this chapter, I hope that you now have a basic understanding of how China works. In the following chapters, you will see how these three "China investment essentials" will be part of the foundation of every investment you make in the China Miracle. They may not always be obvious, or even readily apparent, but at some level they are part and parcel of amazing opportunities in China.

History, people, values—they will make the China Miracle an unstoppable force over the foreseeable future. China's rich mercantilist traditions, productive traditional values, and large and prosperous overseas population give it a big advantage over other emerging markets. It has been a long road back, but the Chinese people are increasingly free to pursue their own economic success.

The re-emergence of this great nation gives us a unique opportunity to build our own wealth as well. By investing in the dominant themes of the China Miracle, I created a portfolio that in 2006 alone saw 84 percent of its stocks increase in value. That's a number I doubt few other investors matched, especially in China-based stocks. I say that not to brag, but to point out that profits come from identifying those opportunities that take advantage of trends in China, be they cultural or economic. It is a practice that has served me well time and time again.

Next we'll look at the current state of affairs in China and how you can best take advantage of the growth occurring there. And I'll begin by giving you the one rule you must always remember when getting ready to invest in any segment of the China Miracle: It is not a matter of buying stocks based solely on corporate performance, as Wall Street too often does. It is a matter of buying those companies that are essential to what China needs and what China desires.

In the following pages, I'll identify for you the industries that make for attractive investments as part of the China Miracle. Within those industries, I'll introduce you to many of the companies that have made money for me—many of which I expect to keep making me money for a long time. I'll also introduce you to companies that I've avoided along with some that made me money before losing their momentum.

A great deal of the information I'm going to give you will be about how to avoid the traps that are all too common in China investments. Because Wall Street views China as a huge investment opportunity—without always understanding why—there are a lot of myths and non-sense that get circulated as supposed "investment wisdom." In fact, giving you advice about how to stay away from poor investments may in many cases be just as important as pointing you to great stocks. One of the things I want you to gain from this book is a sense of what is good, sound advice and what simply sounds good but masks a really bad strategy.

As I discuss various investment scenarios, I want you to think of how to apply the lessons learned from these stocks to other competitors (and opportunities) in the China market. Eventually, some of the companies I discuss will lose their steam and I'll sell them off. That's the nature of the market. But new stocks are always waiting around the corner, and my goal is to help you to be ready to snag them—not just today and tomorrow, but for years to come.

Chapter 3

The Golden Rules

Most investment advisers—indeed, most investment books—seek to answer all the questions of who, what, when, where, why, and how you should invest your money. I have a more defined goal in mind. It is my intention in this book to explain simply the why and where of investing in China.

The other questions are easy to answer. When should you invest in China? Right now. What should you invest in? Those companies that take advantage of, and profit from, participating in what China needs and desires. Who is investing in China? Investors worldwide, although many of them are ill-informed. How can you profit from the China Miracle? By making well-informed decisions and understanding that the rules for investing in China are unlike those for investing elsewhere.

That leaves the why and the where, the two questions that form the essence of this book. Over the course of the following pages, I'll be explaining why certain industries, companies, and stocks are worth investing in. I'll also show you where these companies are in China, and how you can find others like them for years to come.

It is my guess that if you've picked up this book you already have a sense of how to invest prudently. In addition to the rules of traditional investing, getting your share of the China Miracle requires that you understand China's myriad investment peculiarities. It is this latter aspect of investing that I will help you with. I don't think you need me to tell you how to be careful with your money or how much of it you should invest at any given time.

That said, I believe the idea of how much of your money you should put at risk is a basic concept that is among the most misunderstood subjects in investing today. Every time you buy a stock, you are putting your money at risk. How much of your money is at risk is a direct function of how much stock you buy. Nothing is more important for an investor than assessing his or her tolerance for an acceptable level of risk. One of my goals in writing about the China Miracle is to help you find the balance between acceptable risk and sizable rewards.

I have some golden rules—perhaps *golden guidelines* is a more accurate term—that I often use when discussing levels of risk and expectations of reward with investors and subscribers. It all boils down to cutting risk to the bone and running up profits as long as you can.

Think of it this way: In a game where the probability of winning is 100 percent, the best strategy is to bet everything you've got. However, when the probability of winning drops down to 90 percent, if you still bet everything you've got every time, you'll eventually lose it all. As a rule, the better your odds, the more you should bet (but not bet it all if the odds are less than 100 percent). The crux of playing the investment game successfully is to strike an optimum balance between the two—risk and potential reward.

Every investment requires that you make some fundamental decisions about how much you can risk—specifically, the amount of money you're willing to invest—and then ask yourself two key questions: How much should I invest in a given stock? And how many stocks should I own?

The decision of how much to invest in a stock is based on your particular financial situation and goals, but let me give you a general guideline: Do not put more than 25 percent of your money in any given investment theme, be it a single stock or a group of stocks in the same industry. I tell investors and subscribers to control their risk by investing equal dollar amounts in the stocks I recommend.

The number of different stocks you should own involves a separate set of calculations and analysis. There are two types of risk I analyze when recommending a stock: market risk and individual stock risk. Market risk involves a variety of circumstances not related specifically to stocks, such as inflation, consumer sentiment, and the general direction of the markets. Individual stock risk, in contrast, can be reduced through diversification or by having multiple holdings in your portfolio.

Many mutual funds take this concept to an extreme and have as many as 100 stocks in their portfolios. This is a mistake; research on modern portfolio theory (MPT) by Nobel Prize winner Harry Markowitz shows that the benefits of diversification go down when you have more than 20 positions. Based on my experience, you only need to own between 15 and 25 strong stocks to achieve maximum profits with minimal risk.

The key to superior risk management is to have multiple investments that will not go down in unison with each other or with the overall market. This is the key most investors miss. Building a portfolio that takes full advantage of the China Miracle will entail including U.S. stocks, Chinese stocks, and other international stocks in various industries. It would be a rare day when all of these diverse investments were losing money at the same time.

While investing can and should be fun, it is much more than a game and shouldn't be left to chance like a Las Vegas casino game. In particular, I don't like to make bets when the odds are against me. But I know that the market offers some stellar rewards, so I don't want to sit on the sidelines. Instead, by carefully assessing risk and reward, constructing portfolios intelligently, and concentrating on only the best opportunities, I tip the odds significantly in my favor. Throughout this book, we will tip these odds together as we explore the opportunities in China.

Finding those opportunities is critical to determining where you want to invest your money. You do not want to invest in everything that is branded "Made in China." You have to find the ones that offer the best potential for returns. Assessing potential based on what we believe the best return will be is something we do in our lives all the time, ranging from where we buy our homes to the schools we choose to the jobs we take. My favorite example of getting great returns, though, comes from the world of sports.

Pick Your Pitch

Many years ago, I asked an enormously successful trader to recommend an investing book for me. He told me that he had asked Warren Buffett the same question, and that Buffett had given him a baseball book. It's called *The Science of Hitting,* by legendary Red Sox slugger and Hall of Famer Ted Williams and John Underwood (Simon & Schuster, 1971; rev. ed. 1986).

I bought the book and right away found that Williams's first commandment of hitting—"Get a good pitch to hit"—is as relevant to investing as it is to baseball. In fact, it's a fundamental part of my answer when people ask me how I've been able to make money in down years (like 2002) as well as up years.

Each time you make an investment, you are by definition putting your money at risk. Therefore, it's crucial to always make sure there is enough upside potential in each stock to justify taking a risk. Just like the baseball slugger who waits for the fat pitch, you must be opportunistic and wait for the right opportunity.

Believe me, it works. I made handsome returns in 2002 by simply staying out of the market in the second quarter when stocks fell nearly 30 percent. I waited until a selling climax in late July and then bought stocks aggressively. I did very well that year, while the S&P 500 fell 23 percent.

The lesson is that it pays to be patient. There's no faster way to strike out than swinging recklessly at any pitch that comes your way.

But you have to look at a lot of pitches to know which one is going to work for you. That means examining the performance of different markets as part of your strategy. While I never ignore the U.S. market, I knew that I needed to find other investment opportunities when the U.S. market was underperforming and flat. The U.S. market "pitches" were unacceptable, so I had to look at other pitches for their potential. It became clear to me that solid and profitable investment strategies had to take advantage of market opportunities in the fastest-growing economies in the world—and China was at the top of that list. It has since become a pitch that I know has all the potential I'm looking for.

Knowing When to Buy

If you'll indulge me and my baseball metaphor for a moment longer, there's something else to consider when looking for that fat pitch. That is to make sure you swing when the time is right—and not before. You need to hit that pitch when the investing conditions are optimal. To ensure that my investments are well thought out and properly executed, and not the product of being overeager or impatient, I am a strong advocate of setting buy limits, which serve as relatively low-risk entry points. Buy limits are predetermined prices that you set in order to keep from making irrational or impulse buys on a desired stock. You wait for the stock to drop to that price point, or lower; you do not dive in when the price is above your buy limit.

Because stocks in emerging markets often tend to be momentum-driven, some will move past the buy limits I set very quickly. A lot of China-based companies have moved up very rapidly, which is great for those investors who own the stock, but frustrating for those who are trying to get in.

By being patient, I can usually jump in at a favorable point since fast-moving stocks frequently pull back temporarily. Then when I see a stock has entered a new, higher trading range and that the risk of a sharp pullback is reduced, I will often raise the buy limit.

I encourage investors to be patient when there's a stock that is worth owning, but which is priced higher than our comfortable buy limit. They may be chomping at the bit to get in, but I encourage them to not chase stocks. We're focusing on building wealth over time, so we can afford to be patient and wait for the prices we want. (Remember, we're patient with the market, not with stocks we already own that are languishing and don't deliver us the profits we expect.) We want the momentum of a stock to be building so that we can maximize the reward and minimize the risk of high-growth, emerging market stocks like those related to China.

Unfortunately, too many investors are prone to making broad generalizations about emerging markets that are usually incorrect. One of the worst mistakes an investor can make is assuming that all emerging market stocks are the same and lumping them into one basket.

To discuss the ne'er-do-well economies of other developing nations and the world's fastest-growing economy in the same breath is ludicrous.

Be Wary of the Crowd

During the mindless selling that took place on Wall Street in the spring and summer of 2006, investors failed to make any distinction among the two dozen or so emerging market countries in the world. They simply bailed out of all of them. They didn't consider that Egypt's economy is radically different from that of India, which in turn is driven by an entirely different set of growth dynamics than China. When they wanted to get out of emerging markets, they sold everything indiscriminately without differentiating among the individual economies. It was nonsensical, but so is a lot of the trading on Wall Street.

Fortunately, such irrational and poorly thought-out behavior leads to opportunities for those who have taken the time to understand the fundamentals of the market they're playing. As long as there is no change in the long-term fundamental trend, panic sell-offs tend to be great buying opportunities for investors like you and me. A perfect example of taking advantage of these opportunities came in the wake of the Tiananmen Square protests in 1989.

I think most of us remember the scenes from Tiananmen Square that year. Thousands of Chinese took to the streets in Beijing to demonstrate for democratic reform. As the world watched on television, the Chinese government brought in military troops that clashed with the protesters.

I remember watching in shock as tanks rolled across the square. I was a senior in college, and two American friends of mine were studying Chinese in Beijing at the time. I was deeply concerned for their well-being. The incident marked the initial clash between the old planned economy reactionaries and young free-enterprise reformers. Although the old guard prevailed on that dark day, many college students who came of age during that era eventually prospered as entrepreneurs and professionals—forming the backbone of what is now the China Miracle.

The tragedy at Tiananmen Square led to a massive loss of confidence in China on the part of international investors. Many investors believed that the government crackdown after the protest would return China to its old hard-line ways. As a result, Hong Kong's stock market plunged over 30 percent within a month amid panic selling, and numerous global companies scrapped China-related investments altogether.

Four years later, by the end of 1993, Hong Kong stocks were up an amazing 400 percent from their low in June 1989. Smart investors, those who understood how China and Hong Kong really operated, made incredible amounts of money. Patience in the face of panic created great wealth for these people.

Buy Parameters

Patience, coupled with opportunity and potential, forms the basis for my investment strategy in China. That's my market strategy. When it comes to selecting individual stocks, however, another set of elements comes into play. As a professional money manager trained in market and stock analysis, I layer a well-defined set of rules over my own knowledge, analysis, and boots-on-the-ground research to help me identify the winners and avoid the losers. I believe this differentiates me from other financial advisers, especially those who have never been to China or haven't taken the time to understand the country and its unique characteristics.

When picking specific China stocks, there are five key parameters I look for. In addition to my golden rules, I recommend that you utilize them for your own investments.

1. *Strong earnings and sales growth.* I want companies with double-digit earnings and sales growth. There are too many good opportunities out there to settle for less.
2. *Defensible market position.* I look for situations where it's difficult for potential competitors to enter an industry or replicate a particular company's success. This is especially important in China, which is notorious for copycats.
3. *Leadership position.* I invest in companies that are either number one or number two in their industries, or the fastest-growing firm in its industry. These stocks usually perform best anyway, but China

wants to create world-class companies and does all it can to make the leaders even stronger.

4. *High profit margin.* China is not only the fastest-growing market in the world, it is also the most competitive. This leads many companies to try to compete on price and sell their goods for razor-thin margins. However, those that can sustain double-digit operating margins are much more likely to produce big profits over time—for themselves and for investors.

5. *Entrepreneurs over state-owned enterprises (SOEs).* I have no doubt that private businesses will win out over government bureaucracie as China becomes a more overtly capitalist nation. This is already happening, and I have already seen great profits from great entrepreneurial companies. There are only a few SOEs that are good investments, and those are ones that are well run with dominant market shares in heavily regulated industries—companies such as China National Offshore Oil Corporation (CNOOC) (NYSE: CEO); China Petroleum & Chemical Corporation, also referred to as Sinopec (NYSE: SNP); China Aluminum (NYSE: ACH); China Mobile (NYSE: CHL); and China Life (NYSE: LFC). I'll talk about them in upcoming chapters.

I analyze many other factors as well—including those that specifically address China's consumers and the needs of the nation—but these five foundational guidelines have served me well in managing investors' money and my own investments. I always check my investments against these criteria. Always.

This strategy led me to recommend in my two subscriber services (*China Strategy* and *Asia Edge*) 3 of the 10 best-performing large-cap stocks traded on the New York Stock Exchange (NYSE) in 2006. On top of that, of the 12 China initial public offerings (IPOs) floated on the NYSE and NASDAQ in 2006 and 2007, half made money and half were losers; the five I had recommended in the past—New Oriental Education (NYSE: EDU), Mindray Medical (NYSE: MR), Home Inns (NASDAQ: HMIN), JA Solar Holdings Company (NASDAQ: JASO), and Trina Solar (NYSE: TSL)—were the top gainers.

Note that growth is my top priority, and growth equals momentum. Because China is the world's fastest-growing economy, I focus on growth over value. My goal is to find and invest in the next wave of great growth companies—like Microsoft (NASDAQ: MSFT) and Cisco Systems (NASDAQ: CSCO) were in the early 1990s—by identifying the best opportunities in China.

But the companies I invest in have to continue to perform as the best available opportunities. I get out immediately if they cease to be great. Back in 2000, when economic growth slowed down, many growth mutual funds made a serious error by holding on to their no-longer-growing stocks and then proceeded to watch them dive. That is hardly what I would call growth investing. When growth slows in any company in your portfolio, you should sell it and shift your money into better opportunities.

It can be wrenching to pull out of stocks that you've held for a long time or for which you had greater expectations. Oftentimes, that leads to an attachment that prevents you from getting out when you should. Investors wrestle with this all the time. It takes discipline, and a commitment to growth, to get out of stocks that aren't delivering the goods the way they should.

One of the most frequent questions I am asked is whether I recommend using stop losses to get out of opportunities that cease to deliver what I expect from them. Stop losses are limit orders set with your broker that automatically sell a stock when specific triggers, like a certain price or a percentage move, are hit.

As with any strategy, stop losses can help you or hurt you. If a stock reverses its upward trend, a stop loss can protect your profits and get you out before the price falls further. However, you can find yourself selling a stock too soon, only to see it bounce back up and continue moving higher.

Stop losses work best for investors who know their own risk tolerance. There is no single formula for setting stop losses that applies to everyone, which is why I don't recommend them across the board or even for most investors. Instead, I tell investors and subscribers to concentrate on earning big gains by focusing on the long-term potential of China stocks and the unstoppable trends that are driving them. As long as those trends remain positive, the best strategy is to ride out any short-term volatility in exchange for bigger profits over time.

However, if you are interested in employing stop losses as an integral part of your investment strategy, let me share three strategies that you may find helpful.

1. After you make 30 percent on any given position, consider setting a stop loss to protect your profit and to make sure that position will not turn into a loss.
2. After earning substantial gains on a position, use a trailing stop—one that automatically adjusts with the stock's upward movement.
3. Trailing stops should be at least 14 percent away from the recent high so that you don't get bounced out on normal volatility.

It is important to remember that advanced techniques like stop losses will not turn bad ideas into profitable investments. The best strategy for building wealth is always to invest in the right investment themes and stocks with momentum.

The Danger in Mainland Exchanges

As I said at the outset of this chapter, my goal is to help you understand the vagaries of investing in China. Not only does that mean guiding you to the opportunities with the best potential, but it also means pointing out some of the pitfalls you should beware of. For instance, the difference between China's stock markets and America's stock markets is a big concern of mine, and it should be for you, too. Investing in China doesn't mean investing in a Chinese exchange. In fact, investing in a Chinese exchange could actually be one of the least profitable ways to participate in the China Miracle.

The Chinese stocks that American investors should follow and invest in are stocks that are traded on American exchanges. The regulations that govern American exchanges provide for a high level of transparency that allows investors to examine and monitor the companies in which they invest. For all its shortcomings, the Securities and Exchange Commission (SEC) runs a pretty tight ship, and securities fraud is generally kept in check. Most investors find themselves playing on a level playing field that protects all those involved.

The same is not necessarily true of exchanges in other countries, including China. Due to decades of isolation, state-run monopolies, and rampant cronyism, China's stock market still suffers from an inability to open itself up to the same kind of scrutiny we routinely demand of American markets. That being the case, when I recommend the stock of any Chinese company, I prefer that it is traded in the United States or in both the United States and Hong Kong, where regulatory standards are higher. Shares of these companies trading in the United States frequently benefit from the high valuations they command in Chinese exchanges like the Shanghai Stock Exchange. Again, good examples have included China Life, China Aluminum, and Sinopec.

Not only are China's stock markets difficult for analysts and investors to navigate on their native exchanges, but they are by and large closed to foreign investors. Until recently, there were few options available to American investors that directly profited from the exchanges in Mainland China. Short of navigating extremely tortuous rules for foreigners, you could not invest in Chinese companies listed only on Chinese exchanges. In recent years, several funds have opened that allow Americans to buy portfolios that contain companies listed on China's stock markets, and I'll discuss them in an upcoming chapter.

I'm always amazed at how many investors—and their advisers—are willing to put money in China without taking a good hard look at exactly what they are doing. Are they investing in companies with growth potential? Are they investing in companies that practice good governance? Are they buying shares at a reasonable price to ensure big profits and negligible risks? Some of this may seem like Investing 101, but when you invest in China, you need to remember to apply fundamentals as well as the essentials that are unique to China. Too many investors forget one or the other.

Once you're committed to employing both, you're ready to start building your wealth in China.

Chapter 4

The Lay of the Land

Peter Lynch, widely considered one of the great investors of all time, said that you should invest only in what you understand. That same ideal underlies my approach to investing in China, and is crucial to building wealth from it.

When you invest in China, you are investing in an economy. You are making profits from those companies that have established their own beachheads in China and that have found a way to capitalize on China's needs and desires. In order to identify those companies that are doing this successfully, you as a thinking investor have to understand what it is that makes China's economy tick.

Investing in an economy is similar to investing in a company. You would never invest in a company without knowing what it produces, who its executives are, what its business practices are, who its competitors are, and what the market for its goods is like. This same diligence has to be applied to investing in an economy. In China's case, you must understand what the Chinese economy runs on, what and who fuels it, and how it compares with other economies.

First and foremost, this means analyzing the consumers who are propelling every segment of that economy to new heights. As is the case in the United States, consumers—what they buy, what they want, where they work, and what they hope for—are the fundamental engines of the economy. But when it comes to China's consumers, you can't take a one-size-fits-all approach; the country is too large and diverse. I have learned this through my family heritage and my on-the-ground team of analysts, and I experience it every time I visit China.

Many Wall Street analysts don't realize the importance of tracking the various types of Chinese consumers, which puts those analysts at risk of falling into the trap of believing that every investment in China is typically no different from the next. But if you, as a committed China investor, learn to identify the core differences in consumer culture and consumer habits, you can use that knowledge to your advantage.

American money managers and analysts are guilty of having lumped China and its various markets into one basket before. I remember back in 1998, when China's economy really started to pick up steam, Coca-Cola (NYSE: KO) supporters salivated over the possibility of 1.3 billion Chinese drinking a can of Coke every day. The stock was hitting new highs every month. Now, a decade later, Coca-Cola's stock price is down almost 50 percent, and the company still has not been able to get the Chinese people to drink that daily can of Coke.

In truth, I never thought it would happen. Why? It's because the Chinese don't drink soda like Western consumers do. Soda is popular in select areas of China, but not throughout the land. This fact was an elemental and essential piece of the investment process that all the financial and media hype never took into account.

The can-a-day model was, and still is, further flawed by a simple fact of economics and demographics: Of the total population in Mainland China, only 20 percent actually have meaningful disposable income.

You can see how that small percentage would affect companies that are building a sales strategy based on reaching every person in the population, or that hope to sell products repeatedly to a majority of the population. Despite the growing income of China's people, achieving that level of sales is not yet a workable proposition.

Smart investors will quickly see that there is a positive way to view this percentage; you just have to flip it around. While 20 percent of the population may not sound like much, it is 20 percent of 1.3 billion people. That 20 percent comes to 260 million people in China who actually have disposable income and are spending money. Those 260 million are equal to nearly 85 percent of the total U.S. population and enough to make China number two in consumer spending behind the United States . . . for the time being. With more and more of the Chinese population rising out of poverty—the untapped 80 percent are experiencing income increases across the country—you can see how much room there is for growth as the China Miracle unfolds and how much money is to be made by investors like you and me.

But that untapped 80 percent is in the future. Let's get back to those who are currently spending money. The majority (71 percent) of the 260 million Chinese middle class are between 15 and 64 years old and live in large eastern cities. Most of them have consumption habits similar to other urban professionals around the world. And like those urban professionals, affluent Chinese consumers aspire to a trendy cosmopolitan lifestyle defined by the modern world. Think *Sex and the City* or *Grey's Anatomy*, and not *Leave It to Beaver* or *The Brady Bunch*.

However, even with affluence taking hold across the country, China is much more geographically, politically, and demographically diverse than most Americans realize. Just like Los Angelenos are different from New Yorkers, people who live in different regions of China have distinctive local characteristics and tastes. In Beijing, the elite tend to show off their wealth more than their counterparts in Shanghai. Beijing hotels have parking lots dotted with shiny new Bentleys and Porsches. At night, men hang out at the hotel restaurants with attractive women the age of their daughters. In Shanghai, there are fewer flashy cars, and guys go out with women who look like their wives. Beijing is the epicenter of often wasteful state-owned enterprises (SOEs), while Shanghai is the nucleus of private businesses.

This dynamic changes even more dramatically as you venture out to other cities and provinces. That's why people usually ask one another when they first meet in China, "*Ni lao shiang zai nah li?*" ("Where are you originally from?") This question helps people size each other up, and gives them a base level for cultural interaction and comparison. It is used in both business and social settings as an initial means of dealing with each other.

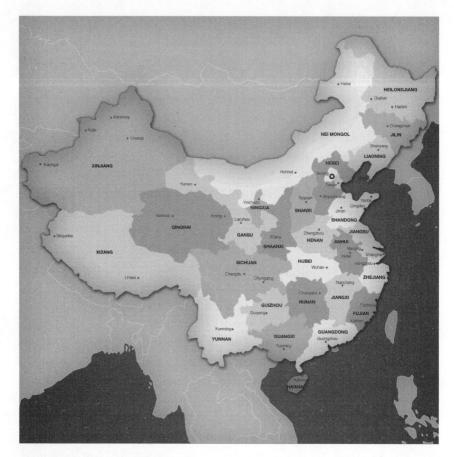

Figure 4.1 China's Provinces
SOURCE: InvestorPlace Media, LLC.

Every one of China's 21 provinces and 5 autonomous regions has its own set of regulations, customs, and local political bosses (see Figure 4.1). Each one requires the use of different sets of business practices and marketing campaigns, to an even greater degree than selling into the United States, which requires an understanding of the local customs, traditions, rules, and regulations of each state. Targeting California is different from the way you would target Mississippi or Maine. Targeting Louisiana is different from New York or Massachusetts.

Investors and businesses have to realize that profiting from the 1.3 billion customer market involves understanding at least a dozen different markets with their own unique regulations and preferences. In order to give you that base level for comparison, I'm going to walk you briefly through Mainland China's major regions, as well as Hong Kong, to provide you with a sense of how their consumer spending habits differ and what that means to building an investment strategy in China.

The reason for this is so that you understand China geographically—and to some degree, culturally—by its regions. It will provide you with a subtext that you can't get from just pinpointing a location on a map. I equate it with understanding where companies and industries are located in the United States.

Know Your Province

When you think of corporations headquartered in Manhattan, typically you expect hard-charging, high-profile, aggressive businesses in finance, media, and international commerce. Think of companies headquartered in, say, the American Midwest, and agricultural, manufacturing, and transportation businesses top the list. You know that the Northeast is a haven of technology and media, the Midwest is the heart of agribusiness, the South has mining and heavy industry, the Pacific Northwest has technology and timber, and the West Coast has entertainment, technology, and research. These are all sweeping generalizations, of course, but they help put commerce and culture in the United States into a thumbnail perspective. The more you consider a specific region, the more you get a picture of it in your mind. It gives you a means for comparison from state to state and region to region.

This is also true of consumer trends. New York, Los Angeles, San Francisco, Chicago, and Miami are the loci of popular trends that eventually spread to the rest of the United States. We look to these cities to see what's hot and cutting-edge in electronics, fashion, entertainment, communications, travel and lodging, and retail. We can then follow their evolution across the country to the second-tier adapters—cities like Philadelphia, Boston, and Dallas—and on to third-tier adapters in smaller cities, large towns, and ultimately rural areas across the United States. The growth of such diverse businesses as cable TV, high-speed Internet, and boutique hotels are prototypical examples of tiered growth and expansion.

Similarly, when we see significant investment in infrastructure and technology in cities or states where we typically don't expect to see it—such as Kentucky or Vermont—then we know that something is going on that, as individual investors, we should probably be paying attention to.

The same generalizations can help those of us who live more than 6,000 miles away from Mainland China. When we see that a company is located in a northern province, or that an event is being hosted in central China, we can get a quick sense of the differences.

Beijing: Where the Waters Run Deep

I'll start with Beijing. Founded as the capital of Kublai Khan's Yuan dynasty in 1267, Beijing has since become China's political and cultural center. The people of Beijing know this, and are proud of their cultural sophistication and proximity to the nation's seat of power. It is no coincidence that Beijing is the capital of modern China. As evidence of its pre-eminence, all clocks in the country—which has five entire time zones—are set to Beijing time.

Here is an example that illustrates how Beijing and its residents—regardless of economic strata—view themselves in relation to the rest of China. I travel often to both Beijing and Shanghai. When I am in Shanghai and ask the hotel staff to do something for me, I always tip them. They are quite efficient at carrying out the requests and are always happy to accept the money.

On my most recent trip to Beijing, I asked a hotel maid to help me with laundry and offered her a tip of 20 yuan—about $2.50. She said she wouldn't accept my tip, but that she would be glad to help me nonetheless. I mentioned to her that every hotel employee I met in Shanghai liked to be tipped, and she proudly said that was the difference between the people of Beijing and the people of Shanghai.

She was right. Everything in Shanghai, as China's commercial center, revolves around money. In Beijing, however, life centers on power and status, as well as gaining political goodwill. In Shanghai, people try to get rich first and then use their money to gain power and influence. In Beijing, the focus is on acquiring political power and then using influence to amass wealth.

Over the course of 800 years, Beijing has built different levels of clearly defined social strata. Traditionally, the imperial family and high-level government officials close to the emperor occupied the apex of Beijing society. Although the titles and names have changed, Beijing's upper class is still dominated by the politically powerful and their families. China is clearly changing as it becomes increasingly worldly and capitalistic, but at least for now, these families can still use their power and influence to get very rich.

Because Beijing millionaires often have both significant political power and spending power, they are not afraid to flaunt their wealth. At high-end establishments in Beijing, the parking lots are filled with far more expensive cars than at comparable places in Shanghai. Beijing's Mercedes-Benz and Bentley dealerships are the biggest in Asia. The Sunday brunch buffet at the Shangri La Hotel is $60 per person, more expensive than similar buffets in Shanghai. The place is packed with local Chinese on Sundays, because Beijing has more Chinese millionaires than Shanghai, while Shanghai has a bigger middle-class population.

Beijing is also the nucleus of China's numerous state-owned enterprises. As you might expect, many of the people who run the SOEs are politically powerful in addition to being wealthy. Historically, high-level Chinese government officials were never paid high wages, but they used their political power to amass private wealth. This came in the form of financial favors; if you were able to get something done politically, someone else was willing to provide you with the appropriate quid pro quo or reward, from apartments to land to jewelry to bank accounts.

This is still the case today. In Beijing, society and government are intertwined and both are extraordinarily hierarchical and status conscious.

At the apex of Beijing society are the powerful government officials and their offspring—also known as *taizidong*, or princelings. Many of these princelings are the heads of SOEs, while others are in private business and government posts. Beginning in the 1980s, well-connected children of government leaders were sent to top universities in the United States. After completing their American-based education, a large number of them returned to Beijing and entered the business world.

Today, many princelings control assets in excess of $1 billion through SOEs. Yet because of the murky commingling of assets among senior management, the government, and various shareholders, it is difficult to tell whether SOE assets belong to the boss or the company. You will rarely see the names of these bosses on the lists of China's richest people, because there is no way to prove that the money they control belongs to them. That is a huge reason why I tell investors to avoid investing in most SOEs. There is little transparency, and it is hard for American investors to determine who is in charge, let alone who the biggest shareholders are. Even though this would raise flags and set off alarm bells in any American company, Chinese SOEs remain the misguided investment of choice for many on Wall Street.

Some princelings are not at all afraid to use their connections to build their personal wealth. Many of them are very bright, serious executives who are committed to their businesses. One such princeling, Zhou Yunfan, the cofounder of KongZhong (NASDAQ: KONG), built himself a $110 million personal fortune by the time he turned 30. While his accomplishments are notable, most Westerners would never know that Zhou is the nephew of China's prominent central bank governor, Zhou Xiaochuan. Without a doubt, Stanford-trained Zhou Yunfan is a brilliant entrepreneur with a great business, but having a powerful uncle certainly helped.

The model of using political power to build wealth is not just effective for certain individuals; it can be very profitable for businesses, too. China's most powerful state-owned monopolistic enterprises have mastered this model. Investors need to be careful, however, because on a level playing field, SOEs are increasingly losing out to the drive, ingenuity, and smarts of private entrepreneurs. That's why I recommend that individual investors avoid most SOEs and seek out opportunities among the best entrepreneurial companies.

There are a select few cases in which an SOE's power gives it a big advantage specifically because the playing field is tilted in its favor. Only a small group of SOEs combine the political clout, monopolistic power, and respectable management necessary to make an attractive investment. When they do all this, they are well worth buying. I'll talk more about them in Chapter 5.

There is a popular saying among Taiwanese expatriate circles in China that "the water is deep in Beijing." This means that there are lots of things going on beneath the surface. The rich in Beijing are often armed with unlimited expense accounts thanks to the SOEs they work for. If I were to open a business in Beijing, I would offer luxury goods and services for high-end consumers who use these expense accounts. It's also a big reason why Focus Media (NASDAQ: FMCN), which advertises luxury goods on monitors in Beijing's office buildings and other public spaces, has had such a remarkable run over the past several years. Know your market, and then capitalize on it. This is as true in business as it is in investing.

Shanghai: Optimism Rules the Day

For the past several years, Shanghai has held the spotlight as the fastest developing city in the twenty-first century. Known many years ago as the "Paris of the East," it is the most cosmopolitan city in China, as well as the epicenter of finance and commerce. Shanghai was established as an international port in 1842 after the first Opium War, quickly becoming the world's primary entry point to the Mainland. Shanghai thus has a long history of Western influence, more so than any other city in China. This is why the people in Shanghai tend to be friendlier to Westerners. They are very proud of their worldliness, which often causes them to be viewed as snobbish by Chinese from less cosmopolitan regions.

In my personal dealings with people from Shanghai, I find them to be efficient and business-oriented, yet very calculating. Chinese from other parts of the country tend to focus on developing relationships, whereas Shanghainese like to get down to business right away.

Shanghai's unique history as a city created only recently—at least from the Chinese perspective—means that many of its established families and businesses have been in place for little more than a century instead of hundreds of years. Many of them came during the late nineteenth and early twentieth centuries from other parts of China to take advantage of Shanghai's position as the West's gateway into China. With China's economic emergence accelerating since the beginning of the twenty-first century, Shanghai is again attracting fortune seekers, adventurers, and retirees from across the world. For example, there are more than 500,000 Taiwanese immigrants—over 2 percent of Taiwan's population—currently living in Shanghai.

Contributing to the culture in this city is the fact that there are more young middle-class professionals in Shanghai than in any other city in China. In fact, Shanghai is the home base for Chuppies—the new generation of "Chinese yuppies"—who set the trend for middle-class consumers all over the country. More than two million Chuppies and their family members live in Shanghai, attracting global companies that often set up their first Chinese outpost there in order to test the Chinese market.

The remarkable effects of the world's greatest construction boom, which has taken place in Shanghai over the past 10 years, are everywhere you look. With over 4,000 skyscrapers and 40 percent of all the construction cranes in the world, not to mention the world's fastest Maglev train—with a top speed of over 270 miles per hour—Shanghai is perhaps the most exciting city on the planet right now.

I can't help but be energized when I see the Shanghai skyline, especially the stunning night view from the world's highest bar at the Grand Hyatt in Pudong. Signs of China's economic growth and the enormous potential for smart investors are everywhere. I have noticed that at trendy new restaurants local customers outnumber outside visitors because they now have the money to spend eating out. On my most recent visit, almost all the well-known restaurants at a nearby shopping center were completely packed and had long waiting lists. I had to wait two hours before seats became available for dinner—the first time I had ever experienced that!

Whereas consumers in Shanghai don't have the kind of money that SOE bosses and senior managers in Beijing have, they can afford to save, and they do buy luxury goods. Instead of big-ticket items like an expensive car—the accoutrement favored by the wealthy in Beijing—Chuppies buy smaller high-end goods such as cell phones, electronic gadgets, and purses. Shanghai's Chuppies are also more Internet savvy and more likely to travel than others are in China. I find the confidence and optimism of Shanghai locals infectious and encouraging.

There are also lots of tourists from other parts of China in Shanghai. The fact that so many more Chinese citizens can now afford to travel within the country is another strong indicator of increasing affluence. Many of the people I see in Shanghai are young, hip, and looking for fun in this most cosmopolitan of Chinese cities.

Other Regions: Finding the Real China

Having described these two best-known and highest-profile regions in China, I want to take a moment to describe why China is so much more than the politics of Beijing and the commerce of Shanghai. Beijing and Shanghai will definitely continue to be the consumer epicenters of Chinese investment for the foreseeable future, but the growth they are experiencing is only the beginning of what will be a long-running China Miracle. It will be fascinating and, I expect, very profitable to watch growth in other areas of the country. This will be especially true for investors who view the big-picture integration of China's economy with its geography.

Wall Street can't see any further into China than Beijing and Shanghai—although it does have an affinity for Hong Kong—but the rest of the country is almost completely off the investment radar. This is understandable, since China is new territory in the investment world, but it underscores how shortsighted Wall Street can be.

I realized how off the mark such an approach can be—no matter where you are—when I met with a prominent real estate developer from Shanghai. During our discussion of various investment vehicles in China, the conversation turned to Los Angeles, where I've made my home for years. The developer told me that Los Angeles is just like Shanghai: There are Chinese restaurants and stores everywhere, and he didn't need to know English to find his way around.

It was immediately clear to me that his impression of Los Angeles resulted from staying in the San Gabriel Valley section of Los Angeles, which is dominated by Chinese. I told him that the rest of L.A. is dramatically different, and invited him to visit other areas to get a real sense of the City of Angels. Even after showing him around, I knew that unless he became fluent in English, my friend would always feel more comfortable in San Gabriel than in the rest of Los Angeles, or in the thousands of miles outside of L.A. that make up the real America.

The same is true in China. Most foreign visitors stick with cities like Beijing and Shanghai, which are cosmopolitan, interesting, and exciting. Yet this does not accurately describe most of China, and visitors who avoid the smaller interior cities form misconceptions about the real China. Beijing and Shanghai have 35 million people between them, yet other cities with 500,000 or more people have a combined population of 320 million.

Most foreign investors and businesses in China are based out of Shanghai and Beijing because they feel comfortable there. Yet the rewards of understanding China's second-tier and smaller cities can be tremendous. Taiwan-born American entrepreneur Roger Wang amassed a $1.1 billion fortune in 10 years by building a retail and real estate empire in second-tier cities along China's eastern coastline. Wang's understanding of Chinese culture and language allowed him to move beyond the typical foreign investor comfort zone into lesser-known cities with huge potential and less competition.

By the way, there are approximately two dozen cities the size of Chicago or bigger that make up China's second-tier cities. These second-tier cities would dwarf the capitals of many nations. In the past five years, many foreign businesses have made moves into China's second-tier cities, but they have yet to venture out into the less advanced third-tier through fifth-tier cities in a big way. There are more than 300 of these lower-tier cities, and they have a staggering combined population of 234 million. These smaller cities account for as much as 43 percent of China's gross domestic product (GDP)—five times the contribution of Shanghai and Beijing.

Shanghai and Beijing are reaching saturation in both resources and population, but smaller cities are growing much faster. Businesses that know how to develop, design, sell, and distribute for inland urban consumers will profit enormously from this opportunity.

Local Chinese companies understand these smaller cities better than their foreign competitors do. In the coming years, it will be essential for businesses to expand into smaller interior cities as part of a successful China strategy. I see equally exciting potential for investors in this next phase of China's historic growth.

A friend of mine has already shown me how to take advantage of this growth. A charming and articulate Southerner from North Carolina, Mark is frequently ahead of the business curve. He first visited China as an exchange student in the early 1980s. Even as a college student, Mark was smart enough to realize the economic potential of China and the Soviet Union, so he spent more than a year as a student in the two Communist countries.

After getting his MBA from Harvard in 1989, Mark turned down lucrative job offers from several top Wall Street investment banks to join a fledgling computer software company. He was deeply impressed by the company's newest product and felt that it would revolutionize the world. He was right. The product was Windows 3.0, and the company was a still-growing Microsoft.

His foresight about Russia along with his language skills paid off. Mark became the regional head of Microsoft in Russia, participating in and benefiting from the chaotic economic transition that followed perestroika. As an executive who joined the company early, Mark received significant stock options in Microsoft. Between 1989 and 1999, Microsoft's stock rose over 10,000 percent, making him a multi-millionaire many times over.

Always looking for the next big thing, Mark left Microsoft in the late 1990s and made a second fortune in the Internet boom. He participated as an early investor in, and adviser to, many successful start-ups, including CitySearch and Match.com. In 2000, Mark cashed out of the dot-com boom at the top after IAC/InterActive Corporation (NASDAQ: IACI) purchased both CitySearch and Match.com.

Where is he today? Not in Shanghai, and not in Beijing. Mark has spent the past three years in central China at Zhengzhou, a second-tier city in Henan province. Many of my friends in Shanghai and Beijing frown upon Henan as a small-time backwater, but Mark points out that just about every major foreign investor is looking for opportunities in Shanghai and Beijing. The over two dozen cities bigger than Chicago in central China are largely ignored by foreign investors.

Right now, the best opportunities for American investors are still businesses based in the major cities like Shanghai and Beijing, but the second-tier cities are the next phase in the China Miracle. Many of the best companies that are currently good investments will expand their businesses to these locations, and many new businesses will be created in these regions to serve domestic and international needs.

As investment opportunities arise, investors have to understand that the new realms of Chinese commerce will be markedly different from Beijing and Shanghai, both culturally and commercially. Let me get back to China's diverse regions and describe to you how each of them has its own unique identity, and how they may ultimately play into the future of the China Miracle.

Northern China

Northern China encompasses the area from Shandong province to Heilongjiang province near Siberia. The people there traditionally eat food made of wheat, such as noodles and dumplings, instead of rice. The food has a reputation of being simple and unsophisticated, yet is often filling and tasty.

Like the food they eat, Chinese in the north tend to be a little rough, but they are straight shooters. They are also, on average, taller and larger than people in southern China. If you run into a Chinese person over six feet tall, that person's ancestors probably came from northern China. Because of the harsh winters, northern Chinese consume strong liquors to stay warm and they build relationships over drinks. Doing business in northern China typically requires a lot of socializing; personal friendship often needs to be cultivated before things get done. At the same time, northerners have a reputation for diligently helping their friends in times of need.

Chinese northerners tend to be more daring and unrefined than other Chinese. In business they are often aggressive risk takers. And unlike their counterparts in Shanghai, many wealthy northerners love to show off their wealth by purchasing expensive cars, designer clothes, and watches.

Once the industrial center of China, many northern China cities like Dalian and Qingdao are undergoing tremendous restructuring as inefficient SOEs close their plants. The economic transformation is creating opportunities for local entrepreneurs. Most of these businesses are too small to invest in at present, but they may provide astute investors with good opportunities in the future. I will be watching the business growth in northern China over the next few years, and fully expect to see significant investment potential develop as this region attracts more attention. I suggest that you do the same with your investments.

Eastern China

Chinese from eastern coastal cities like Suzhou and Wenzhou are the most affluent and sophisticated consumers outside of Shanghai and

Beijing. Because of their proximity to the sea, residents from Chinese coastal cities have a strong tradition of trade and commerce. Most Chinese who emigrate to other countries come from these coastal cities. Therefore, many residents in this part of China have prosperous friends and kinsmen in America, East Asia, and Europe. They typically have a very strong work ethic and prosper wherever they go. One of the factors that helps these Chinese succeed is that they are proponents of the Chinese trait of people from the same city helping one another get established abroad.

Many coastal city dwellers have strong local ties and invest in groups. For instance, speculator groups from Wenzhou have become a strong force in property markets throughout China. They've also formed private financing cooperatives to help others from their community expand businesses. Another coastal city, Fuzhou, provides the majority of the restaurant labor force in New York City's Chinatown.

Consumers in these cities have tastes similar to Shanghainese. Although there are more millionaires in eastern China than in the north, successful entrepreneurs there tend to be less flashy than their northern counterparts. Overall, eastern China has the most courageous and skilled small business entrepreneurs in the country. It is also one of the favorite direct investment destinations for foreign investors.

Southern China

Southern China vies with eastern China for the title of most prosperous region in the country. Economically, southern China is dominated by the province of Guangdong (once known as Canton), which borders Hong Kong and Macau. The latter city, once a major Portuguese port, is now the hub of gambling in China—essentially China's version of Las Vegas and Atlantic City rolled into one.

The main difference between the prosperous southern province of Guangdong and eastern provinces like Zhejiang is cultural sophistication. The south lacks many of the cultural refinements and historical traditions found elsewhere. Southern China's tacky prosperity is epitomized in Shenzhen, a city of seven million bordering Hong Kong that was built over the past two decades. It was created as a special economic zone for business, and young workers flocked to Shenzhen in search of better lives. This makes Shenzhen demographically the youngest city in the world, with an average age of just 29. But the city has not had time to develop much in the way of its own unique culture. Instead, Shenzhen and other southern cities like Guangzhou appear hell-bent on copying Hong Kong. They thus lack the originality or modernity of rival Mainland cities like Shanghai.

Interestingly, people in Guangdong province tend to be more commercially oriented than the rest of China. They also speak Cantonese, unlike 90 percent of China, which speaks Mandarin. For instance, I speak Mandarin, but not Cantonese. Because people move to Guangdong primarily for business and work, the region has a strong commercial flavor to it. Many Hong Kong and Taiwanese businesses have invested heavily in manufacturing facilities located in Guangdong over the past few decades. Bustling Chinatowns around the world represent the flavor of old Guangdong.

Goods that cater to energetic youth with disposable income tend to do well in Guangdong. For example, a lot of people in Shenzhen like to instant message and download Cantopop music, so companies like online and mobile service provider Tom Online (Hong Kong: 8282.HK) benefit. China's largest dance club is also located in Shenzhen. Businesses that capitalize on trends popular in Hong Kong also do well in this region.

Central China

Central China has not become a major commercial center since economic reforms took off. Much of the region has lagged eastern and southern China economically. Although the ancient capital of Xi'an has reinvented itself as a world-class tourist destination, and other cities like Chongqing have attracted considerable foreign investments, much of central China is still mired in poverty.

The pace of life is much slower in central China than in the coastal cities. Instead of flashy skylines and nightlife venues, cities are more understated. For example, Sichuan is famous for its mah-jongg, as millions play it daily as part of their regular routines.

There are still relatively few middle-class consumers here, and the sparse high-end boutiques in cities like Xi'an cater to relatively small groups of regular customers. At an upscale mall in Xi'an featuring high-end designer boutiques, I saw fewer than five customers in the entire shopping center. The saleslady at Piaget told me that the store has only a dozen regular customers.

Western-style consumerism, however, is beginning to catch on in some areas. On my most recent visit to central China, I saw a 25-minute wait outside the Pizza Hut in downtown Xi'an. Pizza Hut and Kentucky Fried Chicken (KFC) are both popular throughout much of the rest of China, and their emerging popularity in central China shows that even in the hinterlands, growth is inescapable.

In Sichuan and Hunan provinces, people favor spicy foods. After eating extremely spicy food regularly, locals in these regions often lose interest in milder food. I have a Taiwanese friend who made a fortune in Shanghai opening a chain of pastry shops. He decided to expand his operation to Chengdu, the capital of Sichuan. The locals, who were used to fiery hot-pot stews, found my friend's cakes and breads too bland for their tastes. As a result, his bakery in Chengdu folded less than a year after its grand opening. Others, however, have learned to adapt to, and even conform to, local tastes. For instance, KFC outlets in Sichuan have put spicier offerings on their menus in order to attract local customers. I believe this kind of localization is important to every franchised business's success in China.

Many of the country's 200 million migrant workers come from central China. These people are often from poor rural villages and are generally not well educated. A large number also work in China's notorious coal mines. Because of the developing nature of the economy, central China has the greatest potential for growth but also presents a much greater risk for investors. The main risks come from three factors: Common business practices are not up to international standards, there is an inferior infrastructure in place, and there is lower consumer income. These factors should be taken into account when considering direct investing in this region right now.

Now you should have a sense of China's different mainland regions and the differences between consumers and businesses in each. That leaves us with one big region left to deal with, and it is something of an 800-pound gorilla when it comes to international finance, trade, and investing. That is Hong Kong.

Hong Kong

With a population of seven million, Hong Kong barely counts as one of the largest cities in China, yet it holds a unique position in China's unprecedented economic development. The former British colony acts as the primary link between China's Communist regime and Western capitalist powers.

After World War II, while Great Britain moved toward increasingly socialist policies, Hong Kong developed a fervently capitalistic system that was so successful even the Communists were impressed. In 1949, when the Red Army took control of southern China, Mao Zedong ordered the troops to leave Hong Kong alone. Mao believed that Communist China needed a nexus point from which it could deal with the West, and Hong Kong would play that role. He was right.

Located off the southern tip of China, Hong Kong quickly became a major shipping and commercial destination for goods entering China. During the Korean War and the Vietnam War, when economic sanctions were imposed against China, large quantities of Western goods entered the mainland through the city.

The freewheeling mercantile culture continued after Britain turned control over to the People's Republic in 1997. Under Beijing's "one nation, two systems" policy, Hong Kong retained its highly regarded legal and civil service structure from British colonial days. And China's Communist leadership has promised that Hong Kong can continue its autonomous practices until 2047—a 50-year period dating from the 1997 transfer of power.

By 1997, the residents of this tiny, overcrowded region with no natural resources had achieved a level of income one-third higher than the residents of their former British ruler. Today, Hong Kong is the richest city in China and a major international center of finance and trade. According to data collected by noted economist Milton Friedman, the average per capita income in Hong Kong rose from 28 percent of that in Britain to 137 percent in the 40 years that preceded its return to Chinese rule.

With its own currency and central bank, Hong Kong has a per capita GDP over $30,000—making it number two in Asia and roughly on a par with Japan—and is a successful showcase of free enterprise economics. Hong Kong also has one of the flattest and lowest tax rates among developed economies as well as the highest concentration of billionaires per capita. Now that the Communist government has opened the door for private enterprise, the entrepreneurial spirit of Hong Kong is helping drive the economic miracle taking place across the harbor in Mainland China.

Due to its superior legal and financial systems, the entire Hong Kong region has benefited hugely from China's economic emergence. There is every indication that this continued growth will continue well into the future. With Hong Kong's history and its longtime role as the gateway to China as the foundation, there are three specific trends that investors should be aware of in order to profit from Hong Kong:

1. *Excellent growth.* China's growth rate is amazing at approximately 10 percent; Hong Kong is not far behind. GDP grew by an impressive 7.3 percent in 2005, on top of an 8.6 percent surge in 2004. Exports grew by 11.2 percent and imports by 10.2 percent. According to a December 28, 2007, article on *Forbes.com*, "For the 11 months to November, the value of total exports of goods rose by 9.3 percent over the same period last year. During the first 11 months the value of imported goods increased by 10.3 percent." This strong merchandise trade reinforces Hong Kong's status as a gateway for goods going into and out of Mainland China.

   In addition, the tourism industry in Hong Kong is booming. The total number of tourists arriving in Hong Kong has increased by 17 percent in 2007. This is mainly due to an exponential increase in the number of visitors from Mainland China. Because of lower duties, Mainland Chinese tourists love to shop in Hong Kong and, on average, spend more money shopping than do tourists from more affluent locations such as the United States, Europe, and Japan.

2. *Windfall profits.* Hong Kong's dollar is pegged to the U.S. dollar, so Hong Kong generally follows U.S. monetary policy. When the Federal Reserve hikes interest rates, Hong Kong tends to do the same. Until China's yuan becomes a free-floating and fully convertible currency, it works to Hong Kong's advantage to stay pegged to the dollar because it keeps the region tied to global financial markets.

   Hong Kong's free currency exchange status also makes it a magnet for attracting billions of dollars of speculative capital seeking to profit from the yuan's likely multiyear appreciation. I believe the yuan will appreciate significantly in the coming years, and companies that operate in the yuan could see profits boosted on the order of 50 percent just because of currency appreciation alone.

Hong Kong reaps profits because global currency speculators park money in Hong Kong by purchasing financial assets and trading on the Hong Kong exchanges. These investments in Hong Kong help the local economy.

3. *Strong ties to Mainland China's explosive growth.* Hong Kong's financial markets have become the top choice for quality Chinese companies to go public because of its reliable legal and accounting standards. Large global investors also place a higher level of confidence and trust in Hong Kong's financial system, and many of the companies I invest in are traded on the exchanges there as well.

Hong Kong experienced a brief recession in 2003 caused by the severe acute respiratory syndrome (SARS) crisis, an outbreak of a highly contagious pneumonia-like disease that originated in Asia. However, afterward Hong Kong bounced back strongly. The benchmark Hang Seng Index has doubled since the summer of 2003—more proof that sell-offs are almost always good buying opportunities when the long-term fundamentals haven't changed.

To help speed up Hong Kong's economic recovery after the SARS crisis, Beijing enacted the Closer Economic Partnership Agreement (CEPA) in June 2003, which further integrated the economies of Hong Kong and Mainland China. CEPA allows Hong Kong–based professional service businesses, such as banks and law firms, to gain access to Mainland China's huge market. Tariffs were also eliminated on goods originating from Hong Kong and going to the Mainland. In addition, China removed restrictions on travel to Hong Kong that same year.

About the same time, an interesting thing started to happen. A decade earlier, back in the 1990s, people in Hong Kong who spoke Cantonese instead of Mandarin often viewed visitors from Mainland China with disdain. The wealthy especially disliked Mainlanders even as Hong Kong business leaders tried to develop good connections with the powerful government officials in Beijing.

Things changed after the SARS crisis. As Mainland Chinese tourists became increasingly affluent, an economically weakened Hong

Kong changed its attitude toward Mainlanders. During a trip there in 2004, I discovered that the staffs at most hotels and restaurants had learned to speak Mandarin, whereas English had long been the preferred language between the service sector and their clients.

Thus, Hong Kong—long the capitalist standard-bearer of China— has made its own concessions to the economic power of the newly vital Mainland. The growth of consumer culture and the increasing importance of international commerce across China's various regions have had a stunning impact on the way that Hong Kong itself perceives the long-dormant People's Republic. This perception will continue to create ever-closer ties between the two, making Hong Kong and Mainland China one of the most formidable business combinations on the planet.

You've now gotten some insight into what all of China's regions have to offer, and we've completed our quick tour across the world's biggest economy. Now let's see how we're going to get our profits.

Chapter 5

The Entrepreneurs versus the SOEs

For decades, China's industries have been dominated by the country's state-owned enterprises (SOEs). These businesses are still ubiquitous in China, but with rare exceptions they are not the places where investors will make money. More to the point, investors should stay away from almost every SOE stock they encounter. This is because private businesses have already become the most important drivers of China's growth, displacing the inefficient and wasteful state-owned enterprises.

The strength of entrepreneurial businesses is evident to those investors who know what the numbers in China really mean: China's 2005 growth rate of 9.8 percent included all of the nonmonopolistic SOEs, which collectively lost money. They were actually a drag on the economy. Yet, American mutual fund managers and exchange-traded funds that are investing in China continue to put most of their capital in these SOEs. We'll cover more of the dangers awaiting investors who buy "China" funds in later pages, but for now, you should know that funds that are heavily weighted in SOEs should be avoided.

The reason so many fund managers and Wall Streeters focus on SOEs is that they were the dominant industrial force in China for four decades. That is no longer true, and by knowing this you will set yourself apart from the millions of investors who will put their money in danger by putting it in SOEs.

The real force behind the China Miracle is the Chinese people and the new age of entrepreneurs. They are, and will continue to be, the long-term stewards of corporate and future economic growth in China. In the process, they are creating entirely new industries that are servicing long-suppressed needs on the part of both consumers and businesses.

You should understand a bit about the role of state-owned enterprises versus private entrepreneurs. To that end, I'm going to walk you through the SOEs and the rise of China's entrepreneurial class. The existence of these two business factions underlies the China Miracle—for better and for worse. They also provide us with a way to differentiate the old way of doing things in contrast to the new era of private sector commerce. The old way is epitomized by the SOE and the creation of China's exchanges, while the new era is defined by entrepreneurs—individuals who are creating companies so big and profitable that the money they are generating is eclipsing the performance of America's best-known entrepreneurs.

Let's begin by talking about the SOEs. These strange businesses came about as a direct result of a centrally planned economy as the official policy in China. Central to the planned economy's basic philosophy was the creation of large companies that were owned and operated by the government. Every significant means of production—factories, power plants—was controlled by the state. Private enterprise was for all practical purposes eliminated and disappeared between the 1940s and 1980s. The concept was that all production belonged to all the people, and that everyone would benefit equally from shared interest in the creation of goods and services. That was the stated goal, anyway.

Each SOE had its own territory and covered its respective area of production. Party bureaucrats were put in charge of these facilities, usually as a result of their status in the Communist Party. Ability to manage was not a skill required for these jobs; party loyalty was. Many of these bureaucrats enriched themselves regardless of how well their businesses were run, and corruption ran rampant. Cronyism, graft, fraudulent accounting, nepotism, and outright theft were part and parcel of the SOE managerial mind-set.

By the mid-1980s, there were 300,000 SOEs responsible for about 80 percent of China's gross domestic product (GDP). When reforms began in the late 1980s, it became apparent to government leaders that these businesses were bloated, unwieldy, and unprofitable. In the face of substantial gains by free-market businesses, SOEs were systematically merged and shut down. By 2003, SOEs were greatly reduced in stature and generated barely 30 percent of GDP.

Today, after two decades of market reform, there are fewer than 100,000 SOEs remaining, and the biggest of them have been consolidated into 157 primary central business units. Yet because SOEs still control about half of the country's industrial assets, the government has kept many of them artificially alive by infusing them with capital.

To its credit, the Chinese government recently took a tougher stance on the SOEs' business practices by demanding that they become self-sufficient in the near future. To demonstrate that the government is serious about this, China's State-Owned Assets Supervision and Administration Commission (SASAC) has reported that some 2,000 SOEs will go bankrupt before 2008, subject to government approval. After that, all remaining SOEs will have to adhere to a national bankruptcy code and fend for themselves.

Despite the changes and reforms, SOEs are still generally not well-run businesses. There are many policies that linger from the Mao era, including poor accounting and little transparency. Typically, SOEs are not subject to much regulation or scrutiny. Many of them are unprofitable due to management corruption and waste, and they rarely return the kinds of profits to the government that are required to expand and maintain the country's rapidly growing infrastructure.

Another effort employed to try to straighten out these SOEs has been to list them on stock exchanges. It's too bad for the Chinese government that in many cases making them public companies has had little effect. The vast majority of these SOEs are, and probably always will be, bad investments. Corporate governance is characteristically nonexistent, and management still likes to reward itself before it rewards stockholders. Most SOEs don't stand a chance competing against the much more nimble and effective private businesses run by entrepreneurs who have a burning desire to succeed.

On a brighter note, improvements are being made to align the interests of a few SOE managers and their shareholders. In the past two years, some of the better managed publicly traded SOEs went through management compensation reforms. Senior managers are demanding an equity stake through company shares to better profit from their work. As an investor, I want to see more SOE compensation policies that tie pay to performance, which would benefit these companies by giving their management incentives to work hard.

The reason I'm going into so much detail about SOEs is that several of the remaining SOEs control China's biggest businesses, notably those in communications, energy, finance, and materials. These are some of the industries that you'll want to look into when investing in China. Within them, there are a very select few SOEs that have the proper combination of political clout, monopolistic power, and respectable management necessary to make an attractive investment. This comes from market advantages they enjoy specifically because the playing field is tilted in their favor. And quite honestly, these SOEs that are exceptions to the rule are excellent candidates for a strong China Miracle portfolio.

The China National Offshore Oil Corporation, better known as CNOOC (NYSE: CEO), for instance, has been given special power by the government: monopoly drilling rights for the entire South China Sea, which contains perhaps the greatest untapped underwater oil and gas reserves in the world. The huge natural gas discovery there in June 2006—which potentially contains enough gas to supply China for four years—is likely to be just the tip of the iceberg.

Due to its favored status, CNOOC gets a 51 percent interest in any gas and oil discovered in the region, no matter who finds it. And this SOE doesn't have to put up a penny to finance the costs associated with the exploration. To date, over 75 oil and gas companies have signed agreements with CNOOC to explore in the South China Sea, and all CNOOC has to do is sit back and wait for the profits. To me, this special status makes companies like CNOOC the best investment opportunities in the world today.

Several other SOEs enjoy similar status. China Mobile (NYSE: CHL) is practically a monopoly as the world's largest provider in China's exploding wireless industry. Sinopec (NYSE: SNP) is the biggest seller of gasoline in China and will benefit as the government allows gas prices to increase. Huaneng Power (NYSE: HNP) is the largest power producer in China. China Aluminum (NYSE: ACH) is the largest producer of primary aluminum in China and the second largest in the world. China Life (NYSE: LFC) is the leader in China's heavily protected life insurance industry.

What sets these SOEs apart from the rest of the pack? They have superior management, operations in high-growth and heavily regulated industries, and special support given them by the government in Beijing. I'll talk more about these companies in the next few chapters, because they are among only a handful of SOEs that you should even consider looking at as holdings in your China Miracle portfolio.

The businesses that should attract your attention are those companies run by entrepreneurs who are building incredible companies on their own merits and profiting from doing business in a free market. Coupled with international businesses that are making money in China, they will form the basis of long-term profits for investors ready to get rich from China's historic growth.

Case Study: China Aluminum and China Southern Airlines

Even though I think China Aluminum is a strong long-term China play, I sold my early stake when the initial momentum stalled (see Figure 5.1). This doesn't mean I won't get back in, but as I've mentioned, I tend to look for new opportunities after I've sold my stake in a particular company.

Here's the reasoning on why I took profits when I did. China Aluminum's tight grip on the aluminum market ensured that it would have market share and profit potential for years to come. But based on the point at which I bought the stock, the

---

(Continued)

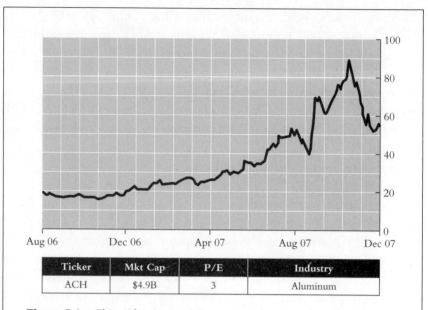

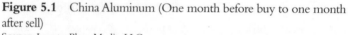

Ticker	Mkt Cap	P/E	Industry
ACH	$4.9B	3	Aluminum

Figure 5.1 China Aluminum (One month before buy to one month after sell)
SOURCE: InvestorPlace Media, LLC.

momentum associated with that timing had evaporated. What happened was that Chinese Premier Wen Jiabao unexpectedly postponed the Qualified Domestic Institutional Investors (QDII) pilot project that would allow Mainland Chinese individual investors to invest directly in Hong Kong stocks. (See box at the end of Chapter 6.) He said that Beijing needed to do more research and planning before allowing this to proceed. This announcement put a brake on the continued upward momentum of the state-owned companies that Mainland Chinese individual investors love to buy. Over the long run, more Mainland Chinese money will continue flowing into Hong Kong because of institutional investment, but in the short run, the psychological aspect of preventing more direct investment into these SOEs was enough to slow their momentum. That included China Aluminum.

With that momentum stalled, I sold my position for a 285 percent profit. I'll take that level of return any day of the week.

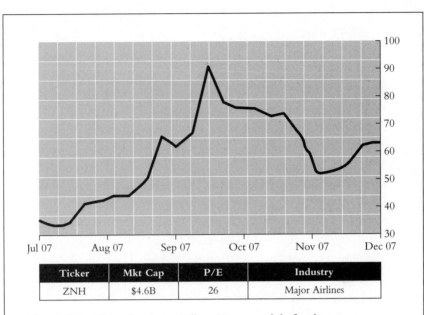

Ticker	Mkt Cap	P/E	Industry
ZNH	$4.6B	26	Major Airlines

Figure 5.2   China Southern Airlines (One month before buy to one month sell)
SOURCE: InvestorPlace Media, LLC.

It was the same announcement by Wen Jiabao that prompted me to take my profits from China Southern Airlines (NYSE: ZNH). (See Figure 5.2.) Another one of the strong SOEs, China Southern Airlines—along with Air China and China Eastern Airlines—controls about 80 percent of the nation's domestic aviation market and nearly all of its overseas passenger traffic. China Southern Airlines provides passenger, cargo, and mail airline services throughout Mainland China, Hong Kong, and Macau, as well as in Southeast Asia and other parts of the world. The company operates approximately 30 percent of the country's total aircraft, and its flight network covers a large majority of commercial and economic centers in Mainland China.

And the future looks great for Chinese airlines. Normally, aviation grows at 1.5 times a country's GDP growth rate, but the airline industry in China has posted a growth rate of nearly double GDP. The country's commercial airline fleet has more

(*Continued*)

than doubled over the past 10 years, and there are 147 airports in operation. That number is set to rise to 190 by 2010. By then, nearly $20 billion will have been spent on building and expanding airports in China, because the country has ambitious plans to create three international hubs in Beijing, Shanghai, and Guangzhou.

When I recommended taking a position in China Southern Airlines, the airline had pushed through 2007 with strong ticket sales and the appreciation of the yuan against the U.S. dollar. It had momentum. But Wen's announcement threatened any further increases in the stock price. I decided to take my gains immediately, which were a very nice 50 percent in only 90 days. If the country puts its investment program back in place, the affected stocks could regain their momentum. Or, should I say, they could gather some new momentum. It's important that you understand that I buy and sell based on the momentum that a stock is experiencing at a particular point in time. Stocks can build momentum many times over the life of a company: right after an IPO, after the awarding of a lucrative contract, while riding a wave of industry-wide growth, and so on. Drops in momentum are opportunities to take profits and invest in other stocks that are experiencing their own momentum.

If you are so inclined, it is worth monitoring the performance of a strong player even after you've sold and collected your profits. If all the fundamentals that attracted you to the stock the first time are still in place, it is quite possible that it will experience another surge of momentum that will benefit your portfolio.

Be Wary of New IPOs

The best privately owned and operated companies are thriving and taking market share away from the big, state-owned manufacturing companies left over from the centrally planned economic model. Under the old planned economy system, the purpose of SOEs was simply to provide employment and churn out products, so they were never concerned with the bottom line. This is an unsustainable model in a genuinely free market.

Because the best private companies in China have enjoyed such tremendous growth, many are now big enough to be publicly traded, which is exceptional news for investors. However, I must warn you again that a growing number of smaller Chinese companies are getting listed, many doing it through less reputable means such as the Pink Sheets (I'll give you a complete discussion of how China's stocks are listed in Chapter 6). These companies are very risky, and I recommend you stay away from them. You should invest only in recognized and established Chinese industry leaders. This not only minimizes your risk, but it also focuses you on where the best opportunities are. China's climate favors big businesses, and it is simply smart investing to stick with those stocks that are number one or two in their respective industries.

The Foundation of Great Companies

It might surprise you to learn that many of the new crop of big companies were created by people who had little more going for them than an idea and determination. They are not products of SOEs, nor are they foreign investors. They are people who grew up in China under economic repression, and some of them were mere children when Deng Xiaoping began instituting reforms. Their success reveals the true nature of the China Miracle: The entrepreneurial spirit of the Chinese people is driving this boom. I stated this at the outset of the book, and I want to give you examples of just how true this is.

Consider this: *Forbes* magazine's most recent list of the world's richest people includes 66 Chinese billionaires. China now has more billionaires than any other country except the United States. Just one year ago, there were only 16 billionaires in China. Something else to consider is that six of the world's 10 richest women entrepreneurs are Chinese. In fact, the richest person in China is a woman: 26-year-old Yang Huiyan, who holds the majority of stock in Country Garden (Hong Kong: 2007.HK), a real estate development company founded by her father. Yang went to school at Ohio State University, returned to China, and is now worth five times more than Donald Trump.

The roster of self-made Chinese millionaires and billionaires who have built great companies in just the past decade is astounding. Even more astounding is the variety of industries in which they've succeeded. From power to paper to the Internet and advertising, they have changed the entire dynamic of China's economy by using the free market system to their advantage. I'll talk about many of these people and their companies in the following chapters, but let me introduce a few of them to you now.

Dr. Shi Zhengrong left his home in Wuxi to study physics and solar energy at Australia's University of New South Wales. After receiving his PhD, he returned to China with $200,000 in savings. In 2001, with some additional venture capital, he started Suntech Power Holdings Co., Ltd. (NYSE: STP) to produce solar power products. Today, just seven years later, Suntech has a market capitalization of $11 billion and Shi is a billionaire five times over, making him one of the wealthiest men in China.

Michael Yu's parents were both farmers in a rural Chinese village, and his father built a pen for their pigs from rubble and stones. Yu taught himself English as a teenager, and then left his village to attend Peking University. Upon graduation, he took a job teaching English for $12 a month. After failing to get a student visa for postgraduate studies in the United States, Yu started a test preparation school for other Chinese students who also desired to study abroad. He founded New Oriental Education & Technology Group (NYSE: EDU), the leading English test preparation company in China, and today 45-year-old Yu is worth more than half a billion dollars.

Huang Guangyu, 36, grew up poor in Guangdong province and spent his childhood selling plastic bottles to make money. At the age of 16, he went to Beijing and set up a roadside stall. There he sold electronics that he bought cheaply from factories in his hometown. That stall led to the creation of GOME Electrical Appliances (Hong Kong: 0493.HK), which is now one of China's leading electronics stores. Huang is now worth more than $2 billion.

The founder of advertising firm Focus Media (NASDAQ: FMCN), 34-year-old Jason Jiang, is worth close to $1 billion. This Shanghai native started out as a literature student at Huadong Normal University, and then saw the potential for selling advertising on video screens placed in strategic locations like grocery stores and elevators. He created Focus Media to do just that, and now more than 90,000 of his company's screens are found in nearly 100 cities in China.

ZhangYin is the richest self-made woman in the world. She was born in Heilongjiang province during the Cultural Revolution, the daughter of a soldier. She eventually moved to Hong Kong and started a company that bought waste and recycled paper, much of it from the United States. Her company, Nine Dragons Paper (Hong Kong: 2689.HK), used the paper to manufacture cardboard boxes for use by Chinese companies. She's now worth more than $6 billion.

Zhu Jun is the entrepreneur behind The9 (NASDAQ: NCTY), one of China's innovative online gaming companies. In 2004 he acquired the rights to operate the world's most popular multiplayer game—World of Warcraft (WoW)—in China. The success of WoW has made Zhu a wealthy man. At the age of 41, he is worth an estimated $300 million. Zhu is also the owner of a professional soccer team in Shanghai, and is known for offering his players cash incentives to encourage them to play better.

James Liang won China's first national computer programming contest at age 13, and then headed to the United States to attend Georgia Tech. He worked for software giant Oracle before returning to Shanghai and founding travel company Ctrip with three former classmates. Using a $250,000 investment, Liang built Ctrip into China's leading online travel web site. Today, he's worth more than $200 million.

These entrepreneurs, and thousands more, have driven China's economy to unprecedented heights. Most of them don't talk publicly about themselves, but I can tell you that they all share very similar traits that make them different from other businesspeople, especially those who do little more than manage companies.

I've found that there are four types of businesspeople that you'll find running businesses in China today. I categorize them as bureaucrats, multinationals, technocrats, and cowboys. Bureaucrats are common in SOEs, which still operate like cumbersome government bureaucracies rather than for-profit businesses. Multinationals are managers trained overseas in large foreign companies who then come to China, often as expatriates. Technocrats tend to be engineers and programmers in technology-related businesses. And cowboys are the aggressive and opportunistic local entrepreneurs who understand the fast, Wild West–like environment of Chinese business today.

Most of China's successful entrepreneurs are cowboys or technocrats. Few of the bureaucrats and multinationals have the requisite passion to make their businesses succeed in a China's growing economy. In addition, bureaucrats and multinationals are limited by their experience: They are accustomed to operating in safe environments where they are protected by the sheer size of government organizations or huge corporations. Succeeding in China requires vision, flexibility, nimbleness, and dedication. Those traits aren't nurtured by lumbering megacorporations.

In marked contrast to American or European entrepreneurs, you don't hear much about China's new breed of rich entrepreneurs. That's because, on the whole, Chinese culture values the hard work, not the fame. As such, these remarkably successful entrepreneurs keep a low profile and let their accomplishments, and the return to their investors, speak for themselves. They are hardworking—even after they've made their fortunes—and are passionate about their companies.

Their determination has heaped substantial rewards on those investors who understand how essential the entrepreneurial spirit is to the China Miracle. Investors looking to make their own fortunes by putting money into government-run businesses that care little about sharing the wealth—yet are favored by so many uninformed investors and analysts—are looking in the wrong place.

Chapter 6

Unraveling the Exchanges

S mart investors understand that the China Miracle is built on the country's booming economy. Thus, smart investment opportunities take advantage of the country's growing consumer class, its increasing participation in global commerce, and its need to keep fueling its engines of growth.

This is a simple strategy, but it takes time and patience to build the kind of life-changing wealth that these opportunities ultimately offer. This process includes doing some basic research and monitoring stocks over time so you can jump in—and out—at those points where you can maximize your profits.

The best way to do this is to track individual stocks based on the trends that best capitalize on the China Miracle. You should know that I'm a firm believer in buying individual stocks. When you invest in individual companies, you can gauge their performance and decide on a case-by-case basis how well they are doing relative to your personal investment strategy. The same can't be said for collective stock plays like mutual funds, where you buy a basket of stocks and hope that they all perform well . . . or that the strongest ones offset any weak members of the group.

In order to monitor individual stocks, you need to be invested in companies that are traded on exchanges that require high levels of financial transparency and reporting from their listed companies. As far as I'm concerned, that means Western stock exchanges, primarily the New York Stock Exchange (NYSE). Because of the stringent regulations enforced by the Securities and Exchange Commission (SEC), companies that are listed on the NYSE and other American exchanges are more forthcoming about their financial performance, their executive compensation, and their overall governance than some of their corporate brethren listed on Asian and other overseas exchanges.

Because it is so important to have up-to-date and accurate information on your investments, I always steer investors to companies making money in China that are listed on American exchanges. But I regularly get asked why I don't just skip the American exchanges and go straight to China's exchanges, where the valuations of China-based companies are often much higher than they are on the NYSE, NASDAQ, or American Stock Exchange.

It's a good question, but not a simple one to answer. In fact, the notion of investing directly in Chinese companies listed on Chinese exchanges creates a lot of confusion among investors. Too many investors wanting to get into the market think that "investing in China" means investing in stocks listed on China's stock exchanges. Nothing could be further from the truth.

First of all, Chinese exchanges don't afford the level of shareholder protection that we all have come to expect from American exchanges. You and I expect the companies in which we invest to report accurate financials, whether it is sales revenue and profit numbers or write-offs and one-time charges.

Chinese companies in the planned economy era had no such inclination to report accurately and honestly, and many of them are still not comfortable with the notion of disclosing all their financials. This is partly because many of the executives at state-owned enterprises

(SOEs) are enriching themselves, and also because they fear losing their jobs in those cases where their businesses are losing money. There is also no universally applied auditing mechanism that forces all Chinese companies to employ a standard accounting system.

Perhaps it is even more important to you and me that just trying to figure out how to navigate China's exchanges is extremely confusing. There are several classes of stocks, trading is based on various currencies, and there are restrictions based on whether investors are residents of China. In most cases, American investors either cannot purchase shares listed on Chinese exchanges or must work through a tangled web of regulations and pay high fees in order to place their money in them.

But in order to be a well-informed China investor, the vagaries of China's exchanges are worth knowing about. At the very least, this will give you a sense of how investments on American exchanges compare with similar offerings in China. In some cases, they do not compare at all—and in fact, can't be compared—but I'll get to that in a moment.

There are four primary share types offered by Chinese-based companies that you need to be aware of. They are A-, B-, H-, and N-shares. Let's work through them alphabetically.

Mainland China: A-Shares

Companies incorporated in Mainland China can issue A-shares that are listed on the two Chinese Mainland exchanges, the Shanghai and Shenzhen exchanges. A-shares are technically available only to Chinese citizens, although there are some convoluted ways around this restriction for institutional investors. The point is that they are designed to be bought and sold within China by Chinese residents. A-shares are priced in yuan (specifically, the renminbi, or "people's currency" that is the official currency of the People's Republic).

Mainland China: B-Shares

B-shares are offered by companies incorporated in Mainland China, but they are dollar-denominated securities traded in U.S. and Hong Kong dollars. Like A-shares, they are listed on the Shanghai and Shenzhen exchanges. B-shares were primarily a vehicle to give SOEs a place to go public and raise money from outside of China before the country joined the World Trade Organization (WTO) in late 2001. Thus, they are available to foreign investors and also to Chinese residents with foreign currency. There are only 114 companies listed on the B-share market, and less than half of these companies are actively traded. The B-share market is, for all intents and purposes, a dinosaur; it hasn't had a new listing in over six years and is highly illiquid. Many China observers expect it will become completely obsolete in the next few years.

Hong Kong: H-Shares

H-shares are offered on the Hong Kong exchange by companies incorporated in Mainland China. This is easy to remember, because the "H" stands for Hong Kong. Shares are denominated in Hong Kong dollars, which are pegged to the U.S. dollar. The shares are typically offered by higher-quality companies than those found on the Mainland China exchanges, including some of the better-run SOEs and companies headquartered in Hong Kong. H shares are available to foreign investors, but are very difficult for Americans to purchase, as I'll explain in a moment. (For more specifics on the Hong Kong Stock Exchange, go to its web site at www.hkex.com.hk/index.htm.)

New York: N-Shares (ADRs)

N-shares stand for New York Stock Exchange and NASDAQ shares. There are more than 65 companies based in Mainland China that have listed their shares on the prestigious NYSE and technology-focused NASDAQ. They are growing in number rather quickly because a successful U.S. listing is viewed as a stamp of international approval. There will be over a dozen new listings in 2008. Specifically they are known as American depositary receipts (ADRs). High-quality Asian companies seeking U.S. capital are frequently listed as ADRs. Because of the NYSE's regulations and requirements, ADRs have to adhere to higher standards than they would on their homeland exchanges. This means that the cream of the national crop usually finds its way to the NYSE.

For many of China's top technology companies, such as Internet online travel giant Ctrip (NASDAQ: CTRP), the NASDAQ is the preferred stock exchange.

You should be aware that there are some smaller Chinese companies listed on the American Stock Exchange, the London Stock Exchange, and over-the-counter (OTC) listings like the Pink Sheets. Be forewarned that most of these companies are small and highly speculative. I recommend you avoid all of these stocks because they are much too risky and volatile.

These are the four primary types of shares offered by Chinese companies. In a moment, I'll tell you why the first three are not places where you want to invest your money. Ultimately, they are distractions—and confusing distractions, to say the least—that will take your eye off the real China Miracle opportunities.

Two Tiers Equate to Double the Difficulty

As investors, it's hard not to be drawn to the spectacle of China's huge initial public offerings (IPOs). Both SOEs and private businesses—like PetroChina (NYSE: PTR) and Alibaba.com (Hong Kong: 1688.HK)—have made big names for themselves by going public on Chinese exchanges over the past couple of years. In fact, they have turned Asian exchanges into IPO hotbeds. But valuations on China's exchanges are often wildly out of proportion to listings in New York and Hong Kong. There's a very good reason for this, and it's based on China's experience with running its exchanges during the 1980s and 1990s and the way in which SOEs initially were traded.

As we've discussed, in 1984 the government decided to reinstate Chinese stock exchanges, which had thrived prior to the Communist takeover. Chinese companies, mainly SOEs, began issuing shares and corporate bonds in Shanghai and several other cities. A trading counter was established by the Industrial and Commercial Bank of China two years later, in 1986.

Unfortunately, many SOE executives and officials viewed the stock market and the unsophisticated investing public as a means to bail out companies that were mismanaged and losing money. Many of these listed SOEs went bankrupt because of bad management and huge debts.

As economic reforms gained steam, China's need to develop a viable stock market became obvious, but ideological resistance from the reactionary old guard slowed the process. In the meantime, the Hong Kong Stock Exchange assisted in developing the framework for what would become China's new stock exchange in Shenzhen and revived the trading floor in Shanghai. After much debate and many compromises, both exchanges made their debuts in 1990, marking a big step in China's transition to a capitalist market system.

In an effort to maintain control of publicly traded companies, the Chinese government divided ownership of listed state-owned companies into tradable and nontradable shares. Beijing was concerned about foreign capital dominating Chinese companies, because it didn't want to lose control of its domestic businesses. As a result, China developed a bizarre two-tier stock market system: yuan-denominated A-shares for domestic investors and U.S. dollar-denominated B-shares for foreign investors.

On average, just a third of each company's shares were actually traded publicly, with the majority of shares locked up in government hands. The nontradable shares remained in the hands of a variety of institutional investors that often represented the state.

This two-tiered share structure was a problem for China's stock market. The different classes of shares contributed to a mismatch of interests between small investors and the big (i.e., government) shareholders. Big institutional shareholders that owned nontradable shares had no incentive to support measures that would boost share prices. In addition, company management ignored minority holders of tradable shares because majority control was firmly in the hands of government institutions.

It was this struggle among small investors, government, and institutions that brought the Chinese market to its knees. For a long time, there had been worries that big shareholders, especially the state, would eventually sell their stakes. After a big speculative run-up in the late 1990s and 2000, the Mainland Chinese stock market entered a prolonged bear market.

The kickoff to nearly five straight years of selling in the Chinese stock market occurred in 2001. A number of smaller publicly traded companies in Shanghai and Shenzhen issued both A- and B-shares. Most of the companies with B-share listings were small-time SOEs, the kind that went public to help the regional government officials who sponsored them get promoted to higher positions. Unlike the handful of giant SOEs that have special government-sanctioned monopoly power, most of these companies were not—and still aren't—profitable in their core businesses.

To make matters worse, between 60 percent and 70 percent of the shares in these companies were owned by the government and couldn't be traded by individual investors. As a result, the Shanghai and Shenzhen exchanges became a dumping ground for money-losing SOEs, and short-term traders dominated the market. In marked contrast to China's phenomenal economic growth, the Shanghai stock market was the worst-performing stock market in the world in 2004 and 2005.

Foreigners were, for the most part, shut out of the Mainland Chinese stock market due to restrictions imposed by the Chinese government. In the 1990s, the Chinese market offered B-shares priced in U.S. dollars for foreign investors. Because of the poor quality of these offerings, though, most foreigners weren't willing to take on the risk of investing in them.

The lack of viable investment options for Mainland Chinese investors caused a major rush to the A-share market. Chinese are notorious savers. The average savings rate in China is close to 35 percent, and you can imagine the impact that 35 percent of the annual income of millions of Chinese had on the market. Soon A-share stocks traded at huge premiums of 100 percent or more over their B-share counterparts. It was impossible to arbitrage the two classes of shares because of China's foreign exchange controls. In 2000, the domestic A-share market ran up 50 percent, further widening the valuation difference between A-shares and B-shares. Trading volume in B-share stocks dried up, and foreign investors focused on the higher-quality Chinese stocks listed in Hong Kong and New York.

Interestingly, Beijing originally planned to list a number of Chinese companies in New York as well as Hong Kong. However, because many of these companies were SOEs with questionable business practices, the government decided that listing them in New York was no longer a good option—especially after the stringent Sarbanes-Oxley legislation was passed to increase corporate accountability.

To save the B-share market, the Chinese government changed its policy in 2001 to allow Mainland Chinese holders of foreign currency to invest in B-shares. Investors perceived the change in ruling as a potential arbitrage trade between expensive A-shares and their cheaper B-share counterparts. Investors bid up B-shares, and these thinly traded instruments rallied a cool 200 percent over the next three months. In a classic "buy on rumor, sell on fact" market move, B-shares reached a new high on June 1, 2001—the day that the new policy went into effect. Subsequently, both A-shares and B-shares sold off into a four-year-long bear market.

A Closer Look at the Shanghai Stock Exchange

After enduring this extended down market, the Chinese government realized that it had to make some changes or face the possibility of seeing the domestic stock exchanges go out of business. The authorities took action, implementing a series of reforms to convert the exchanges into a legitimate stock market. A freeze was put on all new IPOs for nearly a year so that officials could determine which higher-quality SOEs should be listed in Shanghai. Over the course of 2005 and 2006, government officials persuaded leading and better-managed SOEs, like China Life (NYSE: LFC), China Aluminum (NYSE: ACH), and Sinopec (NYSE: SNP), to list their shares in Shanghai. These companies had previously been listed only in New York and Hong Kong.

In another move to create a more reliable market, the government made all shares potentially tradable, eliminating the nontradable shares that complicated investor interest. This was by far the most ambitious undertaking Chinese securities regulators implemented. To make the reform palatable to the public, the Chinese government built in lockups that prevented big shareholders from selling their newly tradable shares for periods of one to three years. These reforms were well received, and retail investors returned to the market.

The result was a 124 percent increase in the benchmark Shanghai Composite index in 2006. After this spectacular run, the Shanghai A-share market gained 13.7 percent in early 2007 before plunging 9 percent on February 27, 2007. The drop was largely attributed to speculation that the chairman of the China Securities Regulatory Commission (CSRC—China's SEC), Shang Fulin, was about to leave his post, along with talk of aggressive interest rate hikes in China to slow down the economy, coupled with the possibility of imposing capital gain taxes on Chinese mutual fund investors.

This hiccup was blamed for sparking a global sell-off that lasted into March 2007. But, since then, the Shanghai Stock Exchange has recovered from the sell-off, and is once again reaching record levels. By the third quarter of 2007, the Shanghai market was up an impressive 87 percent year-to-date. These gains pushed the combined market value of the Shanghai and Shenzhen stock exchanges to nearly $1.8 trillion. The listing of PetroChina (NYSE: PTR) and Internet company Alibaba.com (Hong Kong: 1688.HK) in October 2007 raised $10 billion and garnered huge interest for the Shanghai exchange, drawing increasing numbers of investors anxious to get in on the current big thing.

But there are plenty of reasons to be cautious about what transpires on the Shanghai exchange. A few weeks prior to Shanghai's remarkable one-day drop and eventual recovery, Cheng Siwei, vice chairman of the National People's Congress and an influential senior government official, called the huge run-up in Shanghai's A-share market a "speculative bubble." He said that the companies listed on that stock market are still mostly second- and third-tier state-owned enterprises (SOEs) not fit to be listed on U.S. or other exchanges. Plus, the market has run up much too quickly.

Closer examination shows that, as of late 2007, companies listed on the Shanghai exchange are trading at price-earnings (P/E) ratios of more than 40. That's high in and of itself, but half of the equation is earnings. And as we just mentioned, many of these are SOEs with questionable ways of doing business, so I don't trust that the earnings numbers used in the calculation are even accurate. Chances are that many of them are inflated. By contrast, the Chinese companies listed in Hong Kong and New York are trading at an average P/E of 23, which is 40 percent higher than the S&P 500. But the earnings growth in these companies is on average over 100 percent higher than earnings growth in S&P 500 companies. And you can be confident that their earnings reports give us truer pictures of how companies are operating.

Since 2002, the Chinese companies in Hong Kong have rallied in one of the greatest bull markets of the new century, while the Shanghai stock market declined for four straight years. Even after the run-up in the Shanghai A-share index, the Shanghai market is up only 258 percent in the past five years. I say "only" because that pales in comparison to the 500 percent run-up in the Hong Kong Hang Seng H-Share Index, which is made up of Mainland Chinese companies listed in Hong Kong. (Take note of the fact that the Hang Seng H-Share Index is not the same as the general Hang Seng Index, which is made up of large blue-chip companies in Hong Kong.)

Even after the 500 percent run-up in the H-Share Index during the past five years, Mainland Chinese stocks in Shanghai are still 80 percent to 100 percent pricier than those traded in Hong Kong. That is significantly out of proportion, and should be a red flag for investors. Does this constitute a bubble? It might. But there is one extremely important factor I believe will prevent any bubble from bursting anytime soon: There are still very few legitimate investment options available in Mainland China.

China's 35 percent savings rate and the huge capital inflow that created the world's largest central bank foreign reserve have resulted in over $3 trillion sitting in Chinese financial systems. People want more for their money than the 2 percent or 3 percent they would get by simply putting it in a bank—especially since this doesn't come close to beating the rate of inflation. Some investors have been looking to the booming real estate market to make their money; but the Chinese government is trying to prevent real estate prices from overheating, so the only viable investment option for many Chinese is the stock market. Therefore, it is not completely unreasonable for the Shanghai stock market to trade at a huge premium over Hong Kong or New York.

Avoid Mainland Exchanges

Now that you know the history of China-issued shares and China's exchanges, we need to look at why you should pretty much avoid both of them.

Let's start with B-shares, because they are the least interesting to you and me, and we can dispense with them quickly. You could, if you were so inclined as a U.S. investor, buy B-shares. But you have to either go to China and register yourself as an investor—filling out all the requisite paperwork—in order to buy them, or purchase them through some full-service brokerage firms, which don't usually do a huge business in

B-shares. The truth is that B-shares are all but an obsolete investment vehicle—a product of an earlier age of investing in Chinese companies before the H-share market became big. Today, all higher-quality Chinese companies that want foreign capital go to Hong Kong to be listed. Companies wanting to raise domestic capital offer A-shares on the Mainland exchanges. B-shares have been left out in the cold.

The exodus from the B-share market has been such that six years have gone by without a new listing. There are 37 Chinese companies that still offer both A-shares and B-shares, although they are primarily holdovers from many years back.

A lot of Chinese investors today would rather focus on A-shares because of the momentum and liquidity in that market. Thus, much of the speculation in the B-shares market is by people who think that B-shares will eventually merge with either A-shares or H-shares. That may be wishful thinking, because there aren't a lot of well-placed government officials or financial gurus who are advocating for a merger to happen. Not only are B-shares somewhat lackluster, but in order to be merged with A-shares, they'd have to be rebought using the yuan, since they are now traded using Hong Kong and U.S. dollars.

Overall there just isn't enough interest in B-shares to make them an attractive investment vehicle, and they will continue to be an also-ran in the stock marketplace. Now you can put them out of your mind.

That brings us to A-shares. Over the past few years, a huge number of analysts worldwide have been salivating at the run-up that A-shares have experienced on the Shanghai and Shenzhen exchanges. Chinese A-shares are trading at high valuations, which is perfectly logical considering that there is approximately $3 trillion in the banking system that is seeking higher returns. The only viable investment options for most Chinese citizens are real estate and domestic stocks in the form of A-shares. And they've been pouring their money into A-shares at record rates.

All that money coming from Chinese citizens has led to a super-heating of the value of A-shares and a run-up that has them trading at huge premiums over their H-share counterparts. Mainland Chinese listings in 2007 soared to $61 billion, which was more than twice what the Hong Kong exchange raised, $10 billion more than what U.S. listings raised, and $18 billion more than IPOs in the United Kingdom raised.

As a result, A-share offerings on Mainland Chinese exchanges have a valuation so much higher than those in Hong Kong that it's easy for investors to get the impression that A-shares are where the action is. Again, this is more perception than reality.

The first problem with the red-hot A-shares is that, as foreign investors, you and I are restricted from investing directly in them. A-shares are designed as Chinese stocks from Chinese companies traded on Chinese exchanges by Chinese citizens. The second problem is that A-shares have benefited primarily from the Chinese people not having outlets for their cash. Thus, the boom in A-shares is due in large part to the fact that it's the only game in town for Chinese investors.

And finally, the premiums that A-shares command are frequently due to their scarcity. Even for large companies, there may not be as many A-shares offered on the open market as you would expect. Many of China's publicly traded SOEs keep a significant percentage of their shares off the market in order to retain them in the hands of the government and individual executives. Thus, the laws of supply and demand kick in: With so few shares available, the price rises astronomically as investors fight for individual shares.

Disparities between the A-shares market and other stocks have distorted valuations on Chinese exchanges. Take, for example, the comparisons that have been made between PetroChina and Exxon Mobil Corporation (NYSE: XOM) since late 2007. Newspaper headlines, business journals, and financial program hosts have been shouting about PetroChina becoming the world's biggest company, dropping Exxon Mobil into the seemingly inferior number two slot. The media played this story for all it was worth. Even today, you can find tens of thousands of stories about Exxon Mobil losing its vaunted position to PetroChina if you Google the words "Exxon Mobil," "PetroChina," and "biggest."

When PetroChina had its IPO on the Shanghai exchange in November 2007, it raised $8.9 billion and reached an aggregate market valuation (based on share prices in Shanghai) of a trillion dollars, the first company to ever reach that level. After its first day of trading, it was worth twice as much as Exxon Mobil—not to mention being worth more than the entire Russian stock market.

But all the screaming headlines and the references to a trillion dollars omit some very important facts. First of all, Exxon Mobil is nearly twice as profitable as PetroChina, with net income for the first half of 2007 of $19.5 billion compared to PetroChina's $10.9 billion. And PetroChina's revenues are only a quarter of Exxon Mobil's. Those two numbers alone would raise red flags about valuation to most investors.

Even more important in assessing the real impact of PetroChina's valuation after its IPO is taking into account the number of shares each company has out on the open market. Only 13 percent of PetroChina's shares are available to investors. This is less than 30 billion of its estimated 183 billion total shares. The remaining 87 percent is still held by the Chinese government and PetroChina's SOE parent, China National Petroleum. In contrast, there are some 5.4 billion shares of Exxon Mobil available to the investing public—nearly all of the company's existing shares. Market cap comparisons are not meaningful when the percentage of free float of one competitor is minuscule and thus the opportunity is too small for investors wanting to get in. With fewer shares out there, there is less to buy and shares inevitably get run up.

The most important fact is this: You really shouldn't compare the two oil giants based on market valuation, because investors who can buy one can't buy the other. PetroChina's $1 trillion market capitalization is based on its valuation on the Shanghai Stock Exchange, but by and large only Chinese investors can invest in that exchange. And the almost supernatural strength of the restricted Mainland China markets is immediately evident when you learn that PetroChina's A-shares were selling at roughly $6 a share in Shanghai after its IPO, but at only $2.53 in Hong Kong. The premium that the Chinese Mainland assigned to PetroChina was more than double what the company got from the Hong Kong exchange—a much more internationally attuned marketplace.

Exxon Mobil's valuation, in contrast, is based on NYSE shares traded outside of China, and Chinese investors are not allowed to put their money in the New York exchange. Thus, putting a value on the two companies becomes a classic apples-to-oranges comparison.

It makes you wonder how they would fare if investors were able to fairly invest in them side by side and weigh their individual benefits. But since that's not possible, any valuation is not representative of an open and free market environment. And it proves that following the numbers posted by the media and analysts with minimal information can create the wrong impression—evidence yet again that, as an investor, you always want to dig deeper than the headlines.

With A- and B-shares out of our way, next on our list are H-shares. H-shares are traded in Hong Kong dollars, and their value is more closely aligned with U.S. currency. In addition, companies offering H-shares must adhere to higher standards of financial reporting. These shares give you a better indication of how companies in China are actually performing, but again, you face substantial obstacles to getting H-shares. Surprisingly, what stand in the way of American investors getting their hands on H-shares are not government restrictions, but the brokerage firms.

Local Hong Kong brokerages don't want to deal with small American investors when buying or selling H-shares, because there is too much administration and overhead involved in trading the shares. U.S. reporting requirements for capital gains and other taxes bog down the process in a maze of complexity, making it a regulatory headache for most brokerages. Seeking to simply avoid the bureaucracy, Hong Kong brokerages aren't inclined to help out U.S. citizens who want to trade in H-shares. Large, global, full-service firms that will offer H-shares often require high account minimums, sometimes into seven figures. Even then, I've seen reluctance on their part to even bother with the trades.

Interestingly, there is no reluctance to trade H-shares for citizens of other countries where tax laws regarding the sale of stocks are less onerous. These investors can easily set up accounts at Hong Kong brokerage firms to trade in China stocks, and the brokerages are happy to have them.

The result is that brokerage bottlenecks and high minimums are keeping the average U.S. investor out of Hong Kong's H-shares. That said, however, H-shares comprise an attractive market, because it gives investors who have access to it a bigger universe of Chinese companies to choose from. And unlike A-shares, I think H-shares are less in danger of falling prey to investor exuberance or any kind of investment bubble anytime soon. H-share companies—those worth investing in—are actually making money and growing their earnings rapidly (not something you found in bubble companies like those during the Internet boom of 2000). I also think that well-run H-share companies, even when trading at a premium, are likely to grow into their valuations, because they have organic earnings growth and the currency appreciation of the yuan in their favor. Like other China Miracle opportunities, they're worth paying a premium for.

If you are in a position to convince a brokerage to take your money for H-shares, then you'll find great opportunities and a great deal of money to be made. I have done very well investing in H-shares. But for the average American investor, getting H-shares directly is not an easy task.

Before consigning H-shares to the investment equivalent of a "maybe someday" file, I'd be remiss in not mentioning that there has been regular talk in the investment community (and in some political circles) of merging A- and H-shares in order to take the burden off the Mainland China markets and give Chinese residents access to Hong Kong. Again, this is partly wishful thinking. There is no mechanism in place to make the shares fully convertible since they are valued in different currencies. Extreme adjustments would have to be made to account for the premiums that A-shares trade at over H-shares. In addition, the Chinese government, for all its capitalistic tendencies, is still concerned about allowing the Chinese yuan to become a fully convertible currency, which will be necessary to arbitrage the two markets. Don't hold your breath waiting for A-shares and H-shares to somehow become more appealing and more available as China plays.

The A-, B-, and H-shares are all specific to the Shanghai, Shenzhen, and Hong Kong exchanges, and as you can see, aren't user-friendly to individual investors outside of China. That's why I focus investors on finding Chinese companies that offer N-shares—specifically, American depositary receipts (ADRs) trading on the New York Stock Exchange. ADRs trade like the other stocks offered on the NYSE, and adhere to the same levels of reporting and governance required of all NYSE-listed stocks.

I like the fact that individual ADRs on the NYSE are tied to corresponding H-shares in Hong Kong. ADRs are initially priced based on the underlying shares offered in Hong Kong, and then typically track the price trends of the H-shares.

There's no reason to make this more complicated than it is. Quite simply, buying individual ADRs is the best and safest way to invest in actual Chinese companies. They can each be monitored, bought, and sold based on your investment strategy.

Now, as I said, I like to invest in individual stocks because of the control that I have over each one. The NYSE and the NASDAQ are great places to do that. And because I prefer individual stocks, I don't typically recommend baskets of stocks like mutual funds. But for those investors who really want to get a piece of what's transpiring on China's exchanges, I can point you to a couple of places that might just satisfy your interest. But you're going to have to buy in bulk, so to speak.

Chinese Exchange-Traded Funds

The vehicle that might interest you is known as an exchange-traded fund (ETF). ETFs are portfolio funds that group stocks together and track a specific index on a particular exchange. For example, iShares MSCI Hong Kong Index (NYSE: EWH) is an ETF designed to mirror Hong Kong's Hang Seng Index, which is comprised of H-shares. This ETF has benefited from a heavy weighting in China's sizzling banking sector. Its top holding, however, is Hutchison Whampoa Limited, a massive conglomerate involved in many businesses like ports, property and hotels, retail, energy, infrastructure, finance, and investments. Hong Kong billionaire Li Ka-shing, the wealthiest man in East Asia, controls Hutchison Whampoa. Many investors have made their fortunes riding his coattails, and the iShares MSCI Hong Kong Index is the only way Americans can tap into his business ventures.

Morgan Stanley has an ETF called the China A Share Fund (NYSE: CAF), which was the first U.S.-registered investment vehicle to invest principally in A-shares. The fund is primarily made up of A-shares from Chinese companies listed on the Shanghai and Shenzhen exchanges. However, it has reserved the right to add B-shares to the portfolio in order to improve returns or reduce its exposure in the A-share market. It is highly speculative because it's a closed-end ETF. Closed-end funds trade just like stocks, but are often thinly traded and subject to more volatility than open-ended mutual funds—once closed-end funds have raised their initial capital, no new shares are floated.

The value and risk of this ETF is that it is based on A-share stocks. Yes, they're highfliers thanks to domestic Chinese investors, but as individual companies the components of such funds are not always the most secure or profitable investments. Remember, even with high valuations, A-shares are issued by many of China's companies that haven't performed well enough to venture into the H-share market.

There is also the iShares FTSE/Xinhua China 25 Index Fund (NYSE: FXI). This ETF is made up of 25 SOEs, and was structured by the official press agency of the Chinese government, the Xinhua News Agency. If you examine it closely, you'll find that it is little more than a public relations move to get some of the second-tier SOEs in front of Western investors by using PetroChina (its largest stock component) as bait. And for all the reasons that most individual SOEs are bad investments, you should stay away from funds like this that group them all in one place.

You can buy these ETFs just as you would buy any collective investment or grouped fund. But you can't separate out the stocks, so you buy and sell the entire fund based on the performance of the index, not the performance of the stocks (although their performance in aggregate affects the way the index moves).

So now you have the fundamental story on investing in Chinese companies and China's exchanges. The fact that you've made it through this chapter means you understand the various options and share variations better than many so-called Wall Street experts. All you really have to remember from this information is that many of the best opportunities for buying China-based stocks in the immediate future are the ADRs listed on the NYSE and the NASDAQ. Everything else requires too much work and doesn't give you enough control over your investment dollars.

However, if I still haven't convinced you to stay away from the overly risky alphabet soup of options that feature SOEs, ETFs, A-, B-, and H-shares, always keep in mind this key point about getting in on the China Miracle: Not every good China play is a China company, and not every China company is a good China play. The smart China plays come from companies capitalizing on China's economic trends, not simply from companies that have the word "China" in their names.

Qualified Domestic Institutional Investors (QDII): An Overview

Up until 2006, Chinese financial institutions and Chinese individual investors were prohibited by the China Securities Regulatory Commission (CSRC) from buying foreign stocks. The domestic Shanghai and Shenzhen stock markets were the only markets open to them. There were some exceptions to the rule—there always are—but by and large, Chinese investors were bound by the government to keep their money in Chinese investments.

Due to the amount of capital in China, though, the government had to do something to release pent-up demand. The Qualified Domestic Institutional Investors (QDII) program was started by China's government in 2006 and expanded in 2007. It allows brokerage houses to create mutual funds that invest in foreign stocks. The Chinese government's goal with this move was to cool down its sizzling-hot stock market by diverting some of 35 trillion yuan ($4.6 trillion) of savings to overseas stock markets.

Based on the new program, Chinese commercial banks could invest as much as 50 percent of the funds in the QDII program in overseas stock markets. Individual investors needed to invest a minimum of 300,000 yuan ($39,000) for such financial products. Meeting these limits meant that Chinese investors could buy professionally managed stock funds with overseas listed companies. Most of the money would obviously come from institutional investors, but an impact from individual investors was to be expected as well.

Dual-listed Chinese stocks in Hong Kong, which trade at huge discounts to their Mainland China shares, were to be the biggest beneficiaries of the policy. Because Chinese bankers are familiar with the Hong Kong market, it was to be a natural starting point for the Chinese foray into overseas stocks.

But in November 2007, Chinese Premier Wen Jiabao unexpectedly announced that Beijing needed to do more research and planning before allowing Mainland Chinese individual investors to invest directly in Hong Kong stocks. This announcement slammed the brakes on the continued upward momentum of many state-owned companies that Mainland Chinese individual investors love to buy. Since it affected the momentum of these companies, I took my profits from many of the SOEs that I was holding at the time and exited the positions.

Over the long run, more Mainland Chinese money will continue flowing into Hong Kong because of institutional investment, but in the short run, the announcement was psychologically damaging to stocks that had run up so much in anticipation of the program.

The premier's announcement affected the pilot program only as it pertained to individual investors. The announcement revealed that Beijing prefers to let money flow through institutions to Hong Kong instead of allowing individual investors to do it themselves. The money will still reach Hong Kong, but it will do it through mutual funds instead of individual direct investing. On the institutional front, China's QDII equity fund program has continued and prospered.

Chapter 7

Buying What
China Buys

As I said at the outset, when you invest in China, you are investing in an economy. And right now, there is no more voracious and high-energy economy anywhere. China is the world's largest consumer of steel, cement, aluminum, copper, gold, and even meat. It is second in consumption of oil . . . for now. It is buying up as much of the world's scrap metal as it can on the open market along with textiles and silicon.

As a result of this incredible demand, countries around the globe are increasing their shipments of raw materials and commodities to China. U.S. exports to China, for example, have risen 400 percent, while those from the European Union have grown by 600 percent. China's appetite for basic resources has never been stronger.

And like any growing entity, it needs to be fed. Constantly.

Two things are driving this growth. One is the government's determination to pull China out of its third-world and emerging-market status and position it as a global superpower in everything from commerce and research to space exploration.

The second is international investment. As companies all over the globe outsource manufacturing and production to China, the need for factories and transportation networks has increased dramatically. In order to meet this demand, China has had to build new and more efficient factories and improve its roads, railways, and shipping centers.

All of this has required that China build, build, build. It needs commodities to continue its infrastructure growth because without raw materials, the wheels of production—as they say—grind to a halt. This option is not acceptable to either the government or the legion of worldwide business partners who rely on China's low-cost manufacturing and distribution.

China consumes virtually all of the raw materials it produces, notably coal, timber, and iron ore, yet this is still not enough to satisfy its domestic demand. Despite the fact that China covers a physical area larger than the United States, it is a land of limited resources. Hence, it relies on the rest of the world.

China has no choice: It must buy commodities.

Therein lies the first opportunity for investors in the China Miracle: buy what China needs. Those businesses and industries that produce the goods China needs will be the sources of lucrative investment opportunities for many years to come. The beauty of this strategy is that you can benefit from China's explosive demand for materials and energy, yet not invest directly in a China-based company or find your way to a Chinese exchange. Because commodities are globally traded, those energy, mining, and metal companies with a keen understanding of the new China-driven paradigm have been able to return significant value to their shareholders.

There are companies within China itself that are worthwhile for investors as they have been granted near-monopoly status by the government and have used their favored positions to reap huge profits from the demand for metals and energy. To get you thinking about where you should be looking for great China plays, let's consider the following statistics:

- China has been the world's leading consumer of steel since 2003. It imported an estimated 325 million tons of iron ore in 2006, and nearly 15 percent more than that in 2007.

- In the first eight months of 2007, China imported 110.4 million tons of crude oil, a net increase of almost 20 percent from the previous year. During the same period, China's domestic production reached 124.7 million tons, up 1.3 percent from the previous period. China ranks second only to the United States in oil importation.
- China is both the world's largest consumer and largest producer of aluminum. Since the year 2000, China has accounted for 67 percent of world demand growth and 72 percent of world production growth. Much of this has gone into new construction.
- China has been the world's largest consumer and producer of cement since 1985. It represents more than 40 percent of world cement production, a figure estimated to be more than six times what the U.S. uses.
- China's consumption of beef has jumped 31 percent in the past five years, spurred in part by the introduction of fast-food hamburgers. China is now the world's third-largest producer of beef.
- For much of the past four years, China has been building cities the size of Philadelphia at a rate of one every six weeks.

These are astounding numbers, and they barely scratch the surface of everything that China is consuming. When you add commodities as varied as textiles, nickel, pork, vanadium, or copper, the list of China's raw materials needs is seemingly endless. And while the country has long produced a huge amount of everything from steel to livestock for export, more and more of what it produces will be used internally. As that becomes the norm, China will need to supplement domestic production used for domestic consumption with outside sources.

Domestic consumption of these commodities helps sustain the support structure that ensures that commerce keeps running at a fast clip. This support structure is given little thought in fully modernized countries where economic growth typically fuels an expansion of existing infrastructure, not the creation of new infrastructure. In a great number of places throughout China, however, infrastructure simply doesn't exist. Brand-new cities need energy plants to handle brand-new demand. They need highways for transporting raw materials and finished products, schools for children whose families are moving to urban and industrial centers, water systems for new housing and office developments, bridges, tunnels, waste management and removal, public buildings, and on and on.

If you've tried to put a shingle on your roof, pour concrete, drive a nail, or hoist a two-by-four in the past year, you've been in direct competition with a 1.3-billion-strong China powerhouse growing at an annual pace firmly in the double digits. In short, you—and the rest of the world—are competing with a country that is building much of its infrastructure from scratch. And I do mean "from scratch"; in 2005, China unveiled plans to build 300 entirely new cities. As a result, prices have soared. Copper, nickel, iron ore, aluminum, coal, and especially oil doubled, tripled, and quadrupled in price in 2005.

Those are impressive increases. To hear the talking heads on television and a lot of analysts on Wall Street, you would believe that making money in commodities is easy. But all of my research and analysis indicate the easy profits have, in most cases, already been made. The time when you could buy any diversified natural resources mutual fund and make 25 percent a year is over.

That's partly because the initial buildup in China is leveling from its near-frenetic and chaotic early days, but also because China is changing rapidly. New domestic capabilities are likely to create a future glut where once there was a shortage. For example, the concrete and bitumen being poured for China's new superhighway system have been drastically downscaled. I personally saw evidence of this in rural Xi'an where road workers were using little more than hand tools to build roads; they were not using concrete trucks or road graders. This firsthand observation is confirmed when we look into China's import figures for concrete: China has drastically cut back cement imports and ramped up domestic production.

As an investor, you have to look at what China needs going forward, not at what it has snapped up in the past. Moving forward translates to momentum. Looking back does not. From my research, I believe the most dangerous investment of all right now is one that many investors are still pumped up about: steel. China is building up its low-grade steel capacity so fast that it could create a slump in the global market at any moment. Overcapacity has already cut China's internal steel prices in half, and exporting this steel—the next step for China—could create havoc among steel producers. The wisdom here is that when, and if, China can produce needed materials itself, it won't need foreign suppliers. Steel's momentum has stalled.

Find the Scarcity

But as China continues to grow, new shortages will inevitably appear, providing us with several excellent opportunities. For you as an investor, the entry point into what China needs is to ascertain which companies either are selling high percentages of scarce commodities into the country or control the supply of those commodities. These are two different barometers. The first barometer might include a company like Tyson Foods (NYSE:TSN), one of the world's largest producers of poultry products. Almost 10 percent of its exported chicken business goes straight to China. The second barometer, by contrast, would be a company like state-owned CNOOC (NYSE: CEO), which is entitled to up to 51 percent of all oil and gas discoveries in Chinese waters. That's what I call strong control of a commodity.

The strategy is to find those companies that fit either of these criteria and track their performance. You do this on stock exchanges, not commodities exchanges. Even though we're focusing on the movement of commodities into China, this is not a commodity play. Trading in commodities themselves is a far different endeavor than buying corporate stock. Just because China is one of the world's largest consumers of pork, for instance, doesn't mean you should put all your money in pork-belly futures. You don't want to be fretting over whether the commodity markets are pulling back or whether there is a worldwide commodity bull market.

No, what you want to do is invest in those companies that are actually serving and meeting *China's* demand for those commodities and invest in those companies that make products that China must have regardless of the price. Specifically, I'm talking about commodities that are in high demand and in low supply. I'll walk you through examples in several industries and share my experience with some of the companies that fit these criteria now.

Infrastructure Investing

Perhaps most critical to China's sustained growth is the availability of mined metals. These materials are needed for everything from electrical wiring to air-conditioning ducts and skyscraper support. Metal is essential to China's massive construction projects, which are mind-boggling in scope.

In the early 1990s, for example, the city government of Shanghai took a swampland east of the Huangpu River called Pudong—which literally means east of Huangpu—and declared that it wanted to transform Pudong into the Manhattan of the Orient. The result was the greatest construction boom in human history. For over a decade, more than 25 percent of all construction cranes in the world gathered in Pudong, building hundreds of skyscrapers and gleaming office towers. The tallest building in Pudong is the Jin Mao Tower, one of the tallest buildings in the world and the location of the luxurious Grand Hyatt Hotel, which boasts the world's highest bar.

Right after the turn of the century, Beijing spent more than $30 billion to build out its roads, hotels, stadiums, convention centers, and infrastructure as the city prepared to host the 2008 Summer Olympics. Constructing it all is one thing; maintaining it all will be an ongoing process for Beijing, its neighboring cities, and commodity companies.

China is also preparing to host World Expo Shanghai 2010, which will certainly prolong the country's desire to put on a presentable face to the outside world . . . and result in even more construction.

It is all of this construction, and much more, that has made China the fastest-growing aluminum market in the world. Since 2003, China's demand for aluminum has skyrocketed 70 percent. And yet, annual consumption of aluminum is less than nine pounds per capita. The United States uses an average of 66 pounds per person each year. With much of China's aluminum going for industrial use, there is a huge upside to aluminum's eventual use in consumer products such as beverage cans, household appliances, and automobiles.

One of the biggest beneficiaries of this boom is China Aluminum (NYSE: ACH), the largest producer of primary aluminum in China and the second largest in the world. It is China's only producer of what's called alumina. Alumina is a raw material refined from bauxite through a chemical process and is the key raw material for producing aluminum. China's growth is expected to drive alumina demand up another 15 percent annually.

Most interestingly, China Aluminum is a state-owned enterprise (SOE) that enjoys a government-granted monopoly. It has thus cornered

97 percent of the domestic alumina market and 16 percent of the aluminum production market. As the only producer of alumina in China, the company enjoys a 20 percent profit margin, a key reason why earnings grew more than twice as fast as sales in 2006, by a ratio of 17 percent to 7 percent.

The company is also growing aggressively through expansion and overseas acquisitions. It increased production capacity of alumina by 47 percent and aluminum smelting by 81 percent during 2007. It also acquired alumina supplies in Brazil, Australia, Vietnam, and old coal mines in China's Henan province.

Given the upswing in China's aluminum needs—and not the aftermath of an overheated market—we can look to aluminum as a business that can deliver profits into the future. Companies like China Aluminum can continue to grow because of the country's massive infrastructure build-out as well as its own privileged status as a monopoly. In my *China Strategy* newsletter, I recommended China Aluminum and made my readers a 280 percent return on it in less than 18 months. This is an excellent place for you to start your investigation of companies benefiting from China's insatiable appetite for raw materials.

Among the other mined commodities in high demand in China, the most important is copper. China is the world's biggest consumer of the red metal, which is critical to the country's expansion of its electricity grid.

Vast new factories, neon-lit cities, and thrilling new skyscrapers all rely on threads of copper wire pulsing with electricity. However, the lack of an efficient electrical grid is a severe problem in China. Prior to 2005, because of power cuts and brownouts, many factories ran a primary shift from 11:00 P.M. to 8:00 A.M. Even factories producing desktop computers are often forced to rely on kerosene lamps and diesel generators to get through a summer daytime shift. Children in Taizhou, one of China's fastest-growing cities, often did homework by candlelight in the summer.

To address this urgent need, China undertook a massive power build-out over the course of 2005 and 2006. During that period, less than 18 months in all, it built the equivalent of Great Britain's total electric power supply—which itself took 150 years to build.

That was just the beginning. China is rushing to build two new nuclear power plants every two years for the next 20 years. Power needs are part of the rationale for the astonishing Three Gorges Dam (for hydroelectric power) and the massive new Yangshan port (for natural gas imports). They are the two largest man-made structures in the world today. To give you an idea, the Yangshan port is the size of 470 soccer fields, and it features the world's longest sea-span bridge, a 20-mile, six-lane highway that connects the island to the Mainland. The fact that the two largest man-made structures in the world are both in China tells you even more about the growth taking place there.

Building power is one thing, but transmitting it is another. No one has ever devised a more efficient way to transmit electricity than copper wire. China is already the leading consumer of copper, accounting for over 20 percent of the world's demand. Due to the need for electricity, China's demand is also increasing 20 percent a year, versus a tiny 1.9 percent for the rest of the world. Approximately 45 percent of China's copper demand goes to generating power, which translates to almost 10 percent of the world's total copper going to China's electricity infrastructure.

Power is so important to China that the government has committed $560 billion for power generation over the next five years. A lot of copper will go into that initiative. Yet, tight supply worldwide and strong demand from China have caused copper prices to jump 40 percent in 2006. And copper is generally pretty scarce. There were 65 copper mine discoveries in the decade leading up to 1970, but there have been fewer than 60 in the 37 years since.

Case Study: BHP Billiton and Rio Tinto

China's need for copper led me to take a strong position in Phelps Dodge (now owned by Freeport-McMoRan), the second-largest copper mining company in the world (only state-owned Codelco in Chile is bigger). It operates six mines in Arizona and New Mexico with three more in Chile. Three of its mines—Morenci, Bagdad, and Sierrita—are the biggest in the United States. The six American mines produce over two billion pounds of copper each year and account for 60 percent of U.S. production.

Strong copper and molybdenum demand pushed Phelps Dodge's earnings up significantly in 2005 and into early 2006. By that time it had returned 37 percent in the six months I'd had it. But the fiscal first-quarter earnings report in 2006 showed that it failed to take full advantage of the unprecedented rise in copper prices. Phelps Dodge hedged its production and decreased its profits. As a result, net income dropped $50 million versus the prior year, even as copper prices doubled in the same period. That was unacceptable. Its momentum was gone, so I took my profits and moved on.

Now, note that I didn't sell because there was a panic or a collapse in the copper market. There wasn't. I sold off because what had once been a great opportunity—in the form of Phelps Dodge—had ceased to be a great opportunity. It was a function of management's choices, not the state of the market. As I said earlier, you can't stick around hoping that a stock will get better when it heads south. You have to get out and find the next great opportunity and invest your money there.

The demand for copper remains strong, but many of the capital markets have shown concern about China's import demand not being as strong as it was just a few years ago—in part because China is trying to increase its own production. Focusing on a potential cooldown, investors have limited the upside potential of the stocks of many of the world's other copper-producing companies. Some of these companies, notably BHP Billiton (NYSE: BHP) and Rio Tinto (NYSE: RTP), had incredible runs selling to China during the very peak of the energy buildup (see Figures 7.1 and 7.2). BHP Billiton, for instance, boosted its sales to China an amazing 800 percent from $371 million to $3 billion within a span of four years. China ended up accounting for 16 percent of Billiton's total sales and close to 20 percent of its profits by the beginning of 2007. This made it a strong China play, well worth investing in while the market was sizzling.

(Continued)

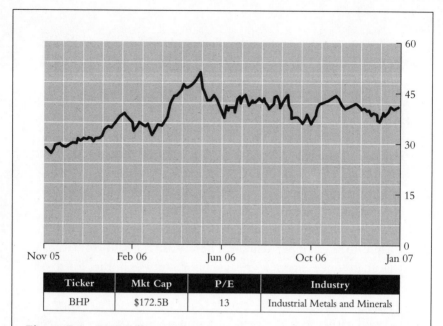

Ticker	Mkt Cap	P/E	Industry
BHP	$172.5B	13	Industrial Metals and Minerals

Figure 7.1   BHP Billiton (One month before buy to one month after sell)
SOURCE: InvestorPlace Media, LLC.

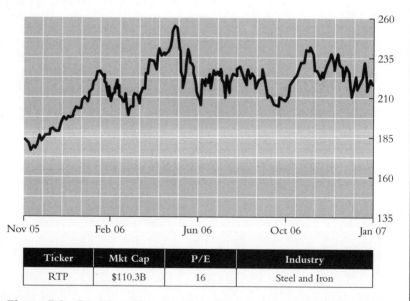

Ticker	Mkt Cap	P/E	Industry
RTP	$110.3B	16	Steel and Iron

Figure 7.2   Rio Tinto (One month before buy to one month after sell)
SOURCE: InvestorPlace Media, LLC.

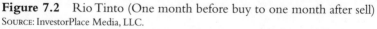

But as demand for imported copper leveled off—despite a robust market—and investors believed a cooldown was inevitable, these stocks were hit hard. Again, the very thing that initially made them great China plays also made them less profitable and valuable in the long term as China's level of demand for their products eased back.

When I started the *China Strategy* newsletter in 2006, two of the companies that I recommended at the outset were BHP Billiton and Rio Tinto, the number one and number two diversified mining companies in the world. They were in a great position to take advantage of China's exploding demand for natural resources and three commodities in particular: copper, iron ore, and coal.

I got us into these stocks just as two important things were happening in China. First, the country was in the early to middle stages of building out its infrastructure, which required immense amounts of copper for electrical conduit, coal to fuel that energy, and iron ore for steel to build buildings and bridges. Second, the demand for these commodities was hyperelevated in Beijing as the city and the surrounding region rushed to prepare for the 2008 Summer Olympics.

As the charts show, the companies were just gaining momentum when I recommended them. They were each increasing their business in China, meaning that the China Miracle was having a direct effect on their growth and their profits. Billiton, for instance, had boosted its sales to China an amazing 800 percent from $371 million to $3 billion within a span of four years. By 2006, China accounted for 16 percent of its total sales and close to 20 percent of its profits. And that percentage was rising.

Both stocks took a hit when the commodities market got knocked around in the summer of 2006, but this wasn't through any fault of company management or strategy; it was a reaction to the overall market. It was evident, however, that while the worldwide commodity bull market had gone on for more than three years, the long-term uptrend had clearly matured.

(*Continued*)

To sell right then would have been a panic play, and panic is not something that guides the smart investor. As you can see, the stocks recovered at the end of that turbulent summer, and headed back toward their highs.

However, the core of their success in China changed as they were emerging from the market's summer doldrums. China's demand for external commodities began slowing as it increased its own internal production and as the huge early build-out phase was completed. China's demand for commodities was not collapsing—far from it—but it was slowing enough to stop the overall momentum. When I saw the data that suggested China's voracious appetite for some of Rio Tinto's and Billiton's core products was cooling down, I knew it was time to take the profits from these companies as China plays.

In both cases we walked away with 20 percent gains in the course of just over a year. And in the year since, Billiton has aggressively pursued a takeover of Rio Tinto, and the subsequent wrangling has buffeted both companies' stocks.

Testing Your Metal

With China expected to produce more of its own copper in the coming years, it leads me to look at other metals the country needs to import. The first obvious one is nickel, which more than doubled in price in 2006 thanks to China's steel use.

Nickel is an enormously useful metal that has many different applications. You're undoubtedly familiar with its role in coins, but nickel's biggest use is producing stainless and alloy steels (mixtures of steels), which are used primarily in industry and construction. Stainless steel accounts for 62 percent of nickel demand right now, and world consumption is growing 6 percent a year.

Chinese steelmakers are driving that surge in demand, as China's nickel use grew from 15.5 percent of the world's total consumption in 2005 to 18 percent in 2006. I expect China to continue to drive demand over the next several years. Consumption there could increase 20 percent annually, compared with 2.3 percent on average for the rest of the world. Also driving nickel demand is its increased use in other application and product areas that are experiencing rapid growth, including aerospace, energy, and rechargeable batteries.

What attracts my attention as an investor is what has happened to nickel prices. For more than a decade, prices stayed very low (about $15,000 per ton), which led to underinvestment in the metal. With demand increasing, however, supply shortages followed.

It's no wonder that nickel prices tripled from $15,000 per ton to more than $45,000 from 2006 to 2007. With no major supply boosts on the horizon, it's clear to me that high nickel prices are here to stay, and that companies that have China as a nickel client are in good positions.

Another investment opportunity comes from iron ore, the core element in steel. Chinese iron ore imports reached 326.4 million tons in 2006, more than tripling from less than 100 million tons in 2002. As a result, iron ore prices increased 19 percent in 2004, 71.5 percent in 2005, and 19 percent in 2006. Prices were up another 9.5 percent by the third quarter of 2007.

Despite steady production growth, China has been unable to keep up with increasing demand. China produced only enough ore to handle 45 percent of its total iron ore consumption last year, down significantly from 72 percent in 1999.

As with nickel, higher-than-expected demand for iron ore, especially from Chinese steelmakers, is keeping supplies tight. Chinese steel production is expected to grow at an average rate of 13 percent until 2012, so demand should stay strong for some time to come. You should also be aware that booming construction in the Middle East is also driving iron ore demand.

Seeking to capitalize on this trend, I found that Companhia Vale do Rio Doce (NYSE: RIO) was a leader in both iron ore and nickel. CVRD, as it's commonly called, is the world's second-largest metals and mining company, just after BHP Billiton. This Brazilian giant has grown enormously from a market capitalization of just $9.2 billion at the end of 2001 to its current market cap of $90 billion, averaging 43 percent growth per year. I like this company's increasing exposure in nickel and iron ore, especially given China's ongoing demand.

In October 2006, CVRD bought a controlling stake in the leading Canadian nickel company, Inco, making CVRD the world's second-largest nickel producer. CVRD now has the world's largest nickel reserve, measuring about 11.3 million tons.

CVRD's iron ore sales to China surged from 15.8 million tons in 2001 to 75.7 million in 2006. That's a staggering 379 percent increase over five years, brought about by latching onto the China Miracle. Sales to China hit $1.3 billion (17 percent of revenues), up 32 percent from the third quarter and an impressive 73 percent from the same period the preceding year.

In addition to being a prime beneficiary of two of the hottest commodities in the world, CVRD is a well-managed company. For the past five years, return on invested capital remains above 50 percent. Earnings grew sixfold in just four years, from $3.8 billion in 2002 to $24.2 billion in 2006. At the same time, profit margins almost doubled from 24.7 percent to 43.7 percent. Total shareholder return (capital gains plus dividends) averaged over 50 percent per year for five straight years. You can see how this company is attractive as a China play: It has the proper fundamentals from the perspective of a traditional investment (good management, dividends to investors) as well as from the perspective of a China-specific investment (the ability to service the specific needs of an expanding Chinese economy).

Finding Profits in Power

Metals are just part of the story of what China needs. The other great investment story is energy. No other global industry has been so thoroughly affected by China's growth. In particular, China's demand for oil and gas has changed the dynamic of what the entire world pays for oil. China's astonishing economic growth has led to accelerating demand for everything from crude oil to refined products such as gasoline, jet fuel, and petrochemicals. On a per capita basis, each person in China consumes an average of only 1.7 barrels of oil per day versus 22 barrels a day for every American. That gap is certain to narrow as the average Chinese consumer begins to spend his or her newly made wealth and more closely mimics the spending habits of consumers in more developed countries.

As the second-largest consumer of crude oil, China's oil imports grew 50 percent between 2002 and 2005. Although that trend flattened out briefly in 2005 because of state price controls, in the long run energy remains an important bottleneck to economic growth. Imports grew 17 percent in 2006, which was very strong but down from the blistering 35 percent growth of imports in 2004. With import demand slowing—in relative terms—it is important to buy select companies with unique competitive advantages.

Because China currently imports 40 percent of its oil, up from 0 percent only 10 years ago, the Chinese government has made it a top priority to acquire oil assets elsewhere. To that end, Chinese President Hu Jintao has conducted regular diplomatic visits to oil-rich countries such as Canada, Iran, Venezuela, and Saudi Arabia to help secure oil.

At the center of this global geopolitical struggle for oil is an SOE with a mandate to acquire and develop oil assets off the coast of Mainland China. That company is, as I pointed out earlier, CNOOC, formerly known as China National Offshore Oil Corporation. Its appeal to investors is that it is a well-managed oil exploration and production monopoly sanctioned by the government.

It's possible that you remember CNOOC's failed attempt to purchase Unocal in 2005. The idea of a Chinese government–owned company attempting to buy a U.S. oil giant caused quite a bit of controversy and generated a lot of media coverage. The bid failed largely as a result of protectionist political sentiment in Washington, but CNOOC has continued to acquire energy assets around the world, more than any other company in China.

As long as China relies on oil imports, CNOOC will play an increasingly important role in the country's energy industry. CNOOC is one of the three main oil and gas companies in China, but what is more important is that it carries the distinction of being the only company permitted to conduct exploration and production activities offshore in conjunction with foreign governments and companies.

CNOOC has monopoly drilling rights on huge undiscovered reserves of oil and natural gas in the South China Sea. Over 70 international oil companies have teamed up with CNOOC to win rights to drill in the area. As I mentioned earlier, CNOOC also has a special government-granted power to acquire up to 51 percent interest in any offshore oil and gas discovery in China's jurisdiction at no cost, even when the discovery is made by a foreign company. With new oil and gas found in the South China Sea by international companies every day, CNOOC gains new energy assets without having to pay a dime.

Talk about a competitive advantage.

Oil industry geologists believe that the South China Sea contains one of the last great undeveloped oil and gas reserves in the world. If that turns out to be true, CNOOC will reap tremendous windfalls once more reserves are discovered. Calgary-based Husky Energy has already discovered a natural gas field in the South China Sea that could be big enough to supply China's natural gas needs for four years. CNOOC gets its 51 percent stake in the discovery without having incurred any of the costs.

There's an interesting side note to the Husky Energy story. Husky may be based in Canada, but controlling interest belongs to Li Ka-shing, the legendary Hong Kong businessman who also controls mobile Internet provider Tom Online, among other companies. He is a great entrepreneur, and his company conducted the exploration, footed the bill, and absorbed most of the risk. Thanks to CNOOC's unique situation, it should benefit greatly from Li's work.

Another gold star for the company is that CNOOC is one of the few SOEs with American-style corporate governance, which means a higher degree of financial transparency and freedom from the corruption that often plagues other SOEs. Its CEO, Chengyu Fu, is a University of Southern California–educated engineer trained as a manager at Phillips Petroleum. Nearly half of the company's board members are outside independent directors, including Ken Courtis, a vice chairman of Goldman Sachs Asia. All board meetings are conducted in English, and the company has a much more open policy than other SOEs.

As an international exploration and production company, CNOOC focuses on upstream operations (supply), meaning its profits are not adversely affected by China's state-mandated gasoline price controls. Instead, CNOOC's profitability is tied to the price of oil and the value of the yuan. Since both have been strong, profit growth and margin are substantial.

Trying to adapt to the constantly changing demands of the entire country—at both the industrial level and the consumer level—Chinese policy makers have been modifying the country's gasoline pricing systems. In China, gas prices are still regulated by the government. That has been good for consumers there, who have been protected to some degree from the soaring cost of oil. But it has been bad for refiners, who are forced by Beijing policies to sell gasoline at a loss. The modification would better reflect high international gasoline prices as well as encourage conservation.

China Petroleum & Chemical Corporation (NYSE: SNP), which is known as Sinopec, is also the top distributor of gasoline and other oil products in China. It is the largest oil refiner in Asia and one of the three giant state-owned enterprises spun out of China's Oil Ministry. The stock is listed in Shanghai, Hong Kong, New York, and London. Sinopec is involved in everything from finding oil to operating gas stations throughout China, making it what is known as a vertically integrated energy giant. Sinopec operates over 30,000 gas stations in China, which is 40 percent of all stations.

Sinopec is also the second-largest producer of crude oil and natural gas in China, after rival PetroChina (probably the world's most famous SOE thanks to its mega-IPO in 2007), and has a reputation for offering higher-quality gasoline than PetroChina (NYSE: PTR).

At the direction of the Chinese government, Sinopec has increasingly focused on midstream and downstream operations such as oil refining and product marketing. The government is having PetroChina focus more on upstream exploration and production of crude oil, and CNOOC is taking the lead in working with foreign governments and companies to find and acquire more oil.

Despite Sinopec's dominant position in Chinese oil products, it loses money selling gasoline in China. Since the government imposes price controls on gasoline, the company's profitability has been capped in downstream operations like retail. When I visited China in 2005, I saw gas stations in Beijing selling 90 octane unleaded gasoline for only $1.90 per gallon. That same gasoline was selling for more than $2.50 in the United States, a full 30 percent higher.

The Chinese government has helped Sinopec with a series of policy maneuvers over the past several years. The company was paid a one-time special reimbursement of $1.1 billion for its losses from selling gasoline. Then, China imposed a new windfall-profit tax on oil producers to help subsidize refinery operations that are losing money.

As the largest operator of refineries in China, Sinopec will receive more in subsidies than its oil production division will pay in windfall taxes. In 2005 and 2006, this amounted to just under $2 billion.

These benevolent gestures are clear evidence to me that the Chinese government favors Sinopec, and I expect the company to be the biggest beneficiary as China gradually reforms its energy market. And despite the fact that it is an SOE, Sinopec, like CNOOC, is well-run and has good corporate governance.

In addition to reforming gas prices, China is also reforming its taxes, which should be good news for many China-based companies. China established a new tax policy that reduces rates for domestic companies from 33 percent to around 25 percent. Both Sinopec and CNOOC paid about 30 percent in taxes in the past. According to my analysis, a 25 percent tax rate would increase their earnings by a solid 4 percent to 8 percent.

Another Energy Play

There is one other energy company that is an exception to the SOE rule: Huaneng Power (NYSE: HNP). The company is 51 percent owned by China Huaneng Group, an SOE that is one of China's five major power groups. As the largest power producer in China, Huaneng Power fits all my criteria for a good SOE: It is well-run; it is operating in a very high-growth, heavily regulated industry; and it is backed by China's government.

The chairman of Huaneng Power is Li Xiaopeng, the son of Li Peng, the leading princeling in China during the 1980s and 1990s. Even though Li Xiaopeng was born into a privileged family, he didn't become chairman of Huaneng based on his connections alone.

In fact, Li Xiaopeng has more than proven himself capable. During his time at the company, Huaneng Power's success has been unparalleled. The company went from an unreliable and relatively small provider of electricity to become a world-class power giant, fueling the energy needs of China's most energy-hungry regions, including much of the country's eastern coastal area. In 2004, power demand surged in eastern China, and most coastal provinces suffered from electricity shortages.

Under Li's leadership, Huaneng built dozens of power plants quickly and efficiently, which solved the problem.

Huaneng is the key beneficiary of China's increasing demand for electricity. China's solid double-digit growth depends greatly on generating power, and that's a need that won't go away anytime soon. Huaneng Power is growing in order to keep up with that demand, and has been expanding its electricity generation capacity by a minimum of 5 percent per year. After adding 15 percent power capacity in 2007, it is determined to follow up with steady double-digit growth in capacity over the next couple of years.

The government is transforming the country's power industry by separating the power generation business from the power distribution business in order to prevent unfair competition. As a result, China plans to sell the electricity generation assets owned by grid operators to SOE power firms like Huaneng Power. This will definitely work in Huaneng's favor.

One thing that Huaneng hasn't done a good job of is generating electricity in an environmentally friendly way. Currently, the vast majority (95.6 percent) of Huaneng's plants are using coal to generate electricity. As the whole world knows, coal to generate electricity produces lots of pollution.

The good news is that Huaneng is aware of this and is trying to clean up its act. The company plans to increase its renewable energy capacity more than 10-fold by 2020, reducing its dependence on coal. That translates to 4.5 million kilowatts of total installed capacity in renewable energy projects, which is a huge increase from its current renewable energy capacity of just 424,000 kW.

Huaneng Power is also moving into the area of nuclear energy. The company has a contract with Tsinghua University, China's number-one institution of higher learning, to strengthen cooperation in the field of nuclear power and nuclear hydrogen production. And it has partnered with China National Nuclear Corporation, China's largest nuclear reactor builder, to build a nuclear power plant in Hainan province in southern China. The project will include four 650,000 kW reactors.

Currently, China has nine nuclear reactors, and an additional six are under construction. By 2020, China aims to generate 4 percent of its power from nuclear energy (up from 2.3 percent right now). In order to meet this goal, China needs to build two reactors a year. Huaneng Power's two nuclear development deals will allow the company to fill China's exploding demand for alternative energy.

Overall, I like the company because of its monopolistic clout, the potential for future assets from its parent company, its substantial presence in economically strong regions of China, and a strengthening yuan. I expect all of these catalysts to benefit Huaneng Power in the years to come.

Cleaning Up by Cleaning Up

No one can dispute China's astonishing increased demand for energy, but one of the problems related to China's energy use that has drawn a huge amount of international attention and debate is its resultant pollution. According to Worldwatch Institute, a Washington, D.C., nonprofit environmental group, 16 of the world's 20 most polluted cities are in China. It's a very serious problem, due in large measure to coal and oil burning. Huaneng Power is a prime example: China needs its energy and can in no way ease back on its requirements without hurting its citizens and its economy. So the pollution increases.

To help combat this, the Chinese government has mandated that the amount of renewable energy (like solar power) more than double from 7 percent today to 15 percent by 2010. With energy prices on the rise and environmental problems related to fossil fuels like oil and coal, the solar power industry is growing rapidly. According to Photon Consulting, solar power industry revenues grew from about $8 billion in 2004 to $12 billion in 2005. That's a 50 percent increase in just one year. The solar market grew by another 50 percent in 2006 to $18 billion. It's projected that solar industry revenues will skyrocket to $72 billion by 2010. That's a 600 percent increase in six years.

In terms of production, solar power will skyrocket from 1.5 gigawatts currently to 12 gigawatts by 2010, largely driven by rising electricity prices around the world, government initiatives, and new distribution channels. That represents a compound annual growth rate of 52 percent.

The problem with the technology is that it is more expensive than traditional means of generating power. But this is changing because, at the same time that traditional energy prices are rising, solar energy costs are coming down—thanks in large part to China's own Suntech Power Holdings Co., Ltd. (NYSE: STP).

The Chinese solar cell industry, through low-cost production, is increasingly making it more cost-efficient for the world to use solar energy. China's solar cell industry is booming because it includes so many highly efficient, low-cost producers. The success of Suntech prompted the launch of more than a dozen other Chinese solar cell companies over the past three years, many of them publicly listed in the United States. A few of them, such as Suntech and Trina Solar (NYSE: TSL), have strong competitive advantages and are quickly becoming major winners in the global solar industry. New Chinese solar cell companies are popping up every month, and they're ramping up production quickly.

Suntech is one of the leading solar cell manufacturers in the world, and also one of the world's fastest-growing alternative energy companies. The company develops, manufactures, and markets solar cells. Its products are used in everything from solar-powered homes and buildings to mobile phone networks to transportation infrastructure (like stand-alone lighting for street lamps) worldwide. It went public on the New York Stock Exchange in December 2005 and was the largest private-sector Chinese company to get listed on the exchange.

Based in Wuxi, China, Suntech is already one of the top five makers of photovoltaic cells in the world. That's impressive, considering the company was founded just a few years ago in 2001 by Dr. Shi Zhengrong, a global authority on solar cell efficiency. I view Shi as part of the new breed of entrepreneurs driving China's economic growth and increasing prosperity.

Shi personally owns over 68 million shares of Suntech, a stake worth nearly $5 billion on paper, making him one of the wealthiest men in China. He was trained as a solar energy expert at Australia's University of New South Wales, which holds the world record for achieving the highest silicon solar cell conversion efficiencies. Shi returned to China and founded Suntech with $200,000 in personal savings and $3 million in venture capital obtained from the city of Wuxi. In 2005, Wuxi sold its stake in Suntech for nearly $30 million in a pre-IPO round of funding led once again by my former employer, Goldman Sachs.

The company is able to reduce costs in a number of ways. First, it takes full advantage of the low-cost engineering talents available in China, giving it a significant competitive edge. Second, Suntech has increased its manufacturing capacity 12 times in the past three years, growing its economies of scale and driving production costs down. It also focuses on higher-efficiency cells that generate more power for less expense.

While demand for solar energy is increasing throughout the world, including Asia, the Chinese solar market is not a significant end market yet. On my recent trip to Xi'an, however, I saw solar panels everywhere, on both homes and buildings. I believe it is only a matter of time before solar energy takes off in China, and I know that Suntech's home-field advantage will give it a huge edge over non-Chinese companies in helping to meet this mandate. This advantage certainly didn't hurt Suntech when it was chosen to supply a solar system to Beijing's Bird's Nest Stadium, the main stadium for the 2008 Summer Olympics.

Suntech is expanding into other Asian markets, most importantly Japan. It purchased a 67 percent majority stake in MSK Corporation, Japan's leading solar cell company, for $107 million in cash. It was a great move because Suntech not only bought out a competitor, it also gained access to MSK's sales and marketing platform in Japan. Japan is the most important market for solar energy in terms of both total installation and production of solar cells and modules. Right now it accounts for 53 percent of the world's solar cell and photovoltaic module production. It is also one of the most difficult markets for foreign players to enter, so it was a groundbreaking deal for Suntech that positioned it even more firmly as the leader in solar cells.

Other governments around the world are also favoring solar energy. Led by Germany, Suntech's biggest market, governments are giving incentives to businesses and consumers who use solar power. In the United States, California Governor Arnold Schwarzenegger approved a new $2.9 billion program that would make my home state one of the world's largest solar energy users. Other states often follow California's lead, so I expect more to adopt solar energy incentives soon, and Suntech stands to benefit. The company began selling its products in the United States in 2006, and demand has been very strong ever since. It also expanded in the United States by building a subsidiary in Delaware.

Case Study: Trina Solar

I first recommended solar-power manufacturer Trina Solar one month after its IPO on the New York Stock Exchange (see Figure 7.3). The stock was doing very well, racking up gains quickly and building on its momentum. However, in short order, the field got very crowded. China Sunergy (NASDAQ: CSUN) made its debut on the NASDAQ, followed by IPOs from LDK Solar (NYSE: LDK) and Yingli Green Energy (NYSE: YGE). From my perspective, these new IPOs brought an oversupply of Chinese solar stocks to the market and would dilute investors' interest in Trina. Not only that, but according to Chinese Renewable Energy officials, China had more than 500 solar makers by the middle of 2007. Increasing competition, coupled with the rising cost of silicon, was evident in a drop in Trina's quarterly report for the beginning of fiscal 2007; operating margins were off 30 percent from the previous quarter.

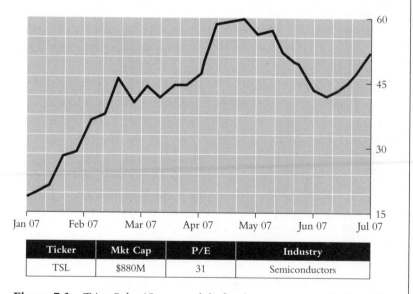

Ticker	Mkt Cap	P/E	Industry
TSL	$880M	31	Semiconductors

Figure 7.3 Trina Solar (One month before buy to one month after sell)
SOURCE: InvestorPlace Media, LLC.

(Continued)

That was enough to alert me that momentum was slowing, but there was more news that I viewed as disconcerting. When I first started investing in Trina, the company was still fresh from its IPO. At the time, much of the stock's float was locked up with institutional investors. But because the six-month lockup period was about to expire, Trina and its shareholders filed for a secondary offering of 5.4 million shares. In my opinion, the new supply of shares would weigh on the stock in the weeks that followed.

Increasing competition, a secondary offering, and other Chinese solar IPOs put a brake on TSL's momentum, so I locked in my gains. After holding the stock for just four months, I took a 63 percent profit.

Trina is a good example of how stock price and momentum can be affected by nontraditional, even unexpected, forces. That secondary offering meant that more individuals were looking to get a piece of the pie, which had already shown impressive gains. Once you have a large number of investors who want to jump in and claim their profits, you're competing with them for your own profits.

And unlike a hugely oversubscribed IPO (like Google's), you have to take into account just what the market will bear based on how high the stock has risen with the initial shares—or if the market will bear it. If the stock is soaring like a rocket, then a secondary offering may mean nothing to your holdings. However, if the secondary offering is triggered automatically (such as after a vesting or lockup period), then you need to be ready in case momentum slows in a flood of new shares.

The Future is with the People

Lest you think the only things China needs are commodities and energy, remember that China's economy depends on its people and its incredible workforce. There are many other things that China needs in order to serve its largest constituency, which is it citizens. The country faces some huge health care issues, especially among those affected by pollution from the incredible growth of factories and energy facilities. It has also faced severe health crises in the form of SARS and virulent flu strains over the past few years.

To feed its people, China imports an incredible amount of food in the form of livestock and poultry. Its farmland has decreased in the wake of factory construction, and there are regular water shortages in the grain-growing areas of the north. Most of China's water is in the south, and even that is being diverted to be used in cities.

Clearly, getting people what they need as individuals presents an entirely new set of investment opportunities. I'll touch on the potential of these other needs in Chapter 11 as we discuss China's 1.3 billion consumers.

So, here's what you need to take away from the concept of buying what China needs.

- *The country is quickly becoming the world's largest consumer of commodities*, and in many cases it already is. That's not going to stop. China will continue to need raw materials and other basic commodities in order to keep growing.
- *A slowdown in growth is unacceptable* to either the government or the many thousands of international companies doing business in China. Acquiring raw materials is of paramount importance to the Chinese, and large international companies will be paid handsomely to service this need. These companies will be excellent China plays—as long as they are selling commodities that are in growth areas. Avoid those that have already had their peaks or are selling into a slowing market.
- *The national infrastructure will continue to build out* for at least the next decade, perhaps longer. Domestic companies that have dominant positions in controlling energy resources are among the very best China-based buys that you can make—even if they are SOEs. Follow the power: Identify regions where new power capacity is being brought online, and determine which company is controlling that power. This will be a strong play for many years to come as entirely new cities are constructed from the ground up.

Chapter 8

Buying What China Desires

For Chinese consumers, it's a brand-new world. China has more than a billion individual consumers who, for the first time, have disposable income. As emerging members of the global community, the Chinese people can afford millions of goods never before available to them. And they're buying a lot of them.

As I've pointed out, it's obvious that not every Chinese citizen in every region of the country is buying the same things. Nor can they all afford to buy the same things. But in those regions where consumers are increasingly affluent, even by Western standards, their purchasing habits are remarkably similar to those found in the rest of the world.

Much of China's newfound consumerism embraces goods and services you and I typically take for granted. This includes cell phone and computer use, leisure travel, and even everyday items like personal stereos and home appliances. China has waited for all of these for a very long time.

Ownership of many items, along with travel, was restricted by social principles during the Mao era—not to mention prohibitively expensive and just plain unavailable. Chinese people had no opportunity to own the kinds of goods you and I buy with our disposable income. Consumerism is really a new phenomenon in much of the country, like the infrastructure build-out I mentioned in the previous chapter. As a result, Chinese people are not buying new cell phones or microwaves to replace their old ones; they're buying them for the first time.

An interesting element of this new consumerism is the Chinese people's appreciation for what is new and exciting. Even when they are buying utilitarian products, they are buying those with the most modern features and appeal. In so doing, they are mimicking the West and appropriating those products that best capture the affluence and trendiness of Western culture. China may be steeped in its own culture when it comes to history and traditional values, but it likes what it sees in Western fashion, style, and entertainment.

China is—as a country—a huge aspirational consumer, looking to buy what its modernized and affluent neighbors and partners already own. This applies to everything from iPods and luxury goods to automobiles. Yet, this aspiration goes beyond personal or household products. After so many years of having their lives regulated, Chinese Mainlanders are finding excitement in their many newfound freedoms. They are vacationing in their own country, they are getting advanced education, they are surfing the Internet, and they are communicating far beyond the confines of their farms and villages.

That means they are enriching the coffers of companies that are selling them what they desire. That is where you need to look for the next set of great investments that have grown out of the China Miracle.

Communication Buildup

Of all of these consumer freedoms, the one that you and I probably give the least amount of thought to is our phones. In the United States, cell phones now rank as the item that most people can't leave home without, just after their wallets. They are a routine fact of daily life. We get new cell phones as a matter of course, either when our old ones die or if a new model has some incredible features (like the iPhone) that appeal to our sense of style and technology use.

In China, the whole concept of mobile phoning has exploded in the past few years as consumers finally get to own these devices. Cell phones are more than utilitarian; they also impart a sense of modernity and keeping up with the rest of the world—a notion that is very important to Chinese consumers.

In a culture where large extended families are idealized and who you know is often more important than what you know, staying connected is one of the highest priorities. This is why many Chinese people now view cell phones as a necessity. Beyond the necessity, they want the latest and greatest features on these phones, despite the fact that an average cell phone costs more than $100. That's a steep price when you consider that $100 is close to half of China's average per capita monthly income. Nonetheless, many Chinese are willing to plunk down a half month's wages for the most sought-after phones.

To give you an idea of how popular cell phones are in China, one of the highest-grossing movies in China in 2004 was a film called *Handset,* which depicted the significance of cell phones in the lives and affairs of urban Chinese professionals. Consumers related to the film's premise on a very personal level.

Chinese people have been lining up in droves to get their own cell phones. China's wireless phone industry now has more users than there are in any other country in the world—more than 500 million people. Cell phone use is growing in excess of 15 percent a year, yet still has only a 30 percent penetration rate. With numbers like this, I expect China's Mainland cell phone market to follow the path of economically advanced, and Chinese-populated, neighbors Taiwan and Hong Kong. In those places, the cell phone penetration rate exceeds 100 percent— there are more cell phones in circulation than there are people. It is not unusual for young women in Taipei to own multiple handsets so they can match them with different purses and outfits.

The big player in China's wireless market is China Mobile. It holds the distinction of being the primary wireless operator in the largest cellular phone market in the world. The company, which is a state-owned enterprise (SOE), has what investors in state-controlled utilities need to look for: excellent growth, reasonable valuation, dominant market share, and even a nice dividend. With a market capitalization of roughly $337 billion, China Mobile (NYSE: CHL) is the fourth most valuable company in the world, after PetroChina (NYSE: PTR), Exxon Mobil (NYSE: XOM), and General Electric (NYSE: GE).

As I've made clear, most SOEs are lousy investments. However, there are a few exceptions—and I mean a very few—specifically when the SOE is respectably run and has a monopoly in, or near-monopolistic control over, a fast-growing sector. Oil giants Sinopec (NYSE: SNP) and CNOOC (NYSE: CEO) fit the bill for investors in the energy sector, while China Mobile is a perfect example in the communications industry.

China Mobile is not exactly a monopoly, as it does have one large wireless competitor—the poorly managed China Unicom (NYSE: CHU). This competition is little more than an irritation to China Mobile, as its monthly rate for adding new subscribers is more than five to one over China Unicom. Month after month, China Mobile continues to gain market share and further cement its monopolistic position.

The company has high penetration in urban areas, and further growth will come from phone and service upgrades in the cities as well as major expansion into rural China. Signs of this are everywhere. According to the company, the number of rural wireless customers increased by over 20 percent in 2006. When I took a group of investors to China in 2006, we confirmed this trend firsthand after we saw numerous bustling China Mobile stores in rural farming towns.

The biggest wireless opportunities will ultimately tie into the country's decision to upgrade its wireless network to the next generation of wireless broadband, known as third-generation technology (3G). The increasing number of cell phone users worldwide has created demand for faster technology that lets people use their cell phones for more and more of their daily activities. 3G aims to meet that demand by providing networks with the ability to simultaneously accept both telephone and nonvoice data, like receiving e-mails and text messages, video, pictures, and so forth. 3G allows faster data transmission than existing 2.5G (second and a half generation) wireless communication, because it moves data at over 2 MB per second or nearly 10 times faster than current technology. That means high-end multimedia gaming, Internet surfing, messaging, and seamless online video transmission all become possible.

The problem is that 3G networks don't operate on the same frequency as current 2G networks, and they're extremely expensive to create. Companies must spend huge sums to build new networks capable of handling these frequencies. In Europe, licensing fees just to get the rights to these networks have run as high as billions of euros.

Asian countries do not want to be left behind in the race to 3G. Many of them, including China, have made developing their technology infrastructures, including wireless communications, a top priority in order to better participate in the global marketplace. China alone will spend more than $24 billion to upgrade its wireless communications network to 3G.

But in a carefully crafted move designed to help Chinese-based companies, China is building a homegrown 3G network (known as TD-SCDMA, which stands for Time Division–Synchronous Code Division Multiple Access) that initially is open to licensing solely by the country's own telecom operators. Only after the network is fully operational will China allow international competitors from the United States and Europe to compete for its 3G business. That means Chinese vendors are going to gain significant market share from the moment 3G rolls out.

From an investing perspective, the coming of 3G is enticing because investors can profit by playing both sides of the fence. On one side, during 3G's early rollout, there will not be any new killer applications available immediately. That being the case, I don't expect most cell phone users to upgrade right away—there's not yet a compelling reason to switch. This supposition is supported by an exclusive survey my group conducted in 2006 wherein only 10 percent of Chinese respondents told us they planned to upgrade to 3G in the first year of its availability.

The dearth of immediate upgrades will actually benefit China Mobile's existing business. The company will continue to grow by adding new customers in the rural areas of China who are going to continue to fuel demand for the cheaper, existing 2G technology for quite some time. China Mobile has already taken advantage of this disparity between technology adopters: It added nearly 48 million new users in 2006 alone by expanding into rural areas.

Here's the other side of this investment play: Regardless of how many customers upgrade initially to 3G, upgrades will inevitably continue for years to come. After all, China is the world's largest mobile phone market now, and market demand will eventually make China's 3G networks the largest in the world as well. As that happens, Chinese people will need new handsets that are compatible with 3G networks, presenting a new market opportunity similar to the one Microsoft enjoys every time it releases a new operating system. It's classic technology evolution: Out with the old and in with the new.

China-based Comtech Group (NASDAQ: COGO) is also poised to benefit from this changeover. Based in Shenzhen, the company designs technical components such as memory chips, circuit boards, LCD screens, keypads, and camera phones—all the components that make new cell phones smaller in size and yet offering more functionality. Comtech is already an established company with an impressive history.

Telecom and handset sales currently make up more than 70 percent of Comtech's revenues. The company counts some of China's largest cell phone and consumer electronic firms among its customers, such as TCL Corporation, Ningbo Bird Company (Shanghai: 600130.SS), Lenovo (Hong Kong: 0992.HK), and UTStarcom (NASDAQ: UTSI). In addition, Comtech works closely with over 30 suppliers of technology components, including multinational companies such as Broadcom (NASDAQ: BRCM), JDS Uniphase (NASDAQ: JDSU), and Matsushita (NYSE: MC). The 12-year-old company has grown up with the biggest telecom manufacturers in China, making its Chinese connections difficult to match. New competitors will have a tough time breaking into this club.

Comtech has also made significant headway into the digital consumer market, which has massive potential in China. It has expanded into broadband and digital home entertainment products by introducing Internet protocol (IP) television modules known as set-top boxes. If you have a box for your cable TV, then you have a set-top box. These boxes enable users to stream data, audio, and video transmissions on their TVs at bandwidths that were never before possible, and they pave the way for China's switch from regular to digital cable. At the close of 2006, the number of digital cable subscribers in China was just three million. By the end of 2008, it should reach at least 60 million. That's a lot of boxes.

Comtech and China Mobile are just two of the communications companies poised to take long-term advantage of the China Miracle.

But like all companies that I look at, they need to be continually vigilant about staying ahead of the competition and making sure that they give the Chinese people what they want. Their momentum has to be ongoing.

A Must-Have Strategy

Even in the short time that China has been investable, there are already examples of leading players not staying ahead of the game and losing their commanding lead in the marketplace. Motorola (NYSE: MOT) is one such company. At one time, Motorola was a premier player in the cell phone market. As the largest foreign corporate investor in China, with over $4 billion in direct investments, Motorola was wildly successful in selling products in China as well as making them there.

In the mid-2000s, Motorola derived nearly 15 percent of its profits from the greater China region of Mainland China, Hong Kong, and Taiwan and made more money directly from the China Miracle than any other American company. Its stylized, feature-laden RAZR cell phones were wildly popular there, and Chinese were willing to spend $300 or more to buy the RAZR.

But while Motorola took market share from other handset makers, most notably Nokia, it did so by selling its RAZR and follow-on KRZR phones at deep discounts. The RAZR floated in the market long enough that it started to lose its appeal, and the KRZR was not the big, exciting breakthrough Motorola needed. The company stumbled, and competition from more aggressive competitors ate into its China profits.

As the handset market becomes increasingly mature in China and around the world, manufacturers like Motorola need to come up with hot new products to get buyers to upgrade. Even though the Chinese love new gadgets, it now takes a truly special product to get them to buy yet another handset. Offering 3G models is going to help those companies already well positioned in the minds of China's consumers.

China Mobile, Comtech Group, and Motorola offer investors important lessons for investing in China. For a company to truly succeed, it must know its market and provide goods and services that not only will appeal to individuals, but also will become a must-have item. This is true of any company in any country, but unless the company has a solid sense of what will catch on with Chinese consumers, it is destined to fail.

Hitting the Road

The Chinese people are not just staying connected with each other via cell phones and the Internet; they are actually getting on the road and taking vacations all over the country. There is a great deal to see in China, from the Great Wall in the north to Hong Kong in the south. Whether they are flying across the country or taking a high-speed train to a local city, the Chinese people are finally enjoying the kind of travel that Americans and Europeans have enjoyed for decades.

One of the most popular destinations for domestic travelers is Xi'an. For over a thousand years, Xi'an was arguably the richest and largest city in the world. Its position as an anchor city on the Silk Road ensured that a huge flow of travelers and wealth passed through its city walls every day.

The emperor Qin Shi Huang, who unified China some 2,200 years ago and built the Great Wall, was buried near Xi'an in a massive underground complex. Qin Shi Huang had an army of life-size terra-cotta statues created and buried near his grave in the belief that they would protect him after his death. Centuries later, Xi'an fell into a long decline and eventually became a heavily polluted provincial capital.

In 1974, three local farmers accidentally found these terra-cotta warriors while sinking a well for irrigation. A total of 8,099 unique, life-size clay statues—foot soldiers, horsemen, chariots, horses, generals—were uncovered. The terra-cotta army museum became a famous attraction, and Xi'an found a new lease on life as a tourist destination.

My first visit to Xi'an was eight years ago, when my wife, Yvonne, and I took a private tour to the fabled museum. Back then, most of the visitors were either foreigners or overseas Chinese like us. The terra-cotta army was truly a world-class destination that attracted visitors from across the globe, but there were more visitors from abroad than from other parts of China.

We visited the terra-cotta museum again last year. This time, however, Chinese tour groups in colorful caps far outnumbered foreign tourist groups. Local tourists were visiting the museum in droves, coming from all over the country. The change was tremendous. I saw up close and personal how China's tourism industry is booming as part of the China Miracle. The numbers back this up. Overall, tourism is expected to grow more than 15 percent a year, thanks to rising affluence. China's National Bureau of Statistics reports that in 2005 Chinese individuals made 1.21 billion trips within the country, up 62 percent from 2000. That number is bound to keep rising as economic growth (and interestingly, the availability of credit cards) gives Chinese consumers more spending power.

Up until the past couple of years, most Chinese tourists preferred to travel in groups. However, most of the younger, more affluent Chinese urban professionals—whom I have dubbed Chuppies—are confident and too sophisticated to travel in large groups. They prefer to travel much like Americans and Europeans do—by themselves. An overwhelming 97 percent of the Chuppies my company surveyed prefer to travel independently instead of joining a large tour group. As a result, huge numbers of them are turning to the online travel service industry to help make their independent traveling easier and more tailored to their personal preferences.

Online travel services are just starting to take off in China. According to a 2005 survey by the China Internet Network Information Center, only 6.9 percent of Internet users selected travel as one of their most requested topics online. In addition, less than 1 percent of all trips taken in China are currently booked online. But my survey showed that this is changing. Online travel in China clearly has tremendous room for growth.

A company called Ctrip (NASDAQ: CTRP) caters to China's new generation of travelers. As China's homegrown version of Travelocity (NASDAQ: TVLY) or Expedia (NASDAQ: EXPE), it is China's largest online provider of hotel rooms and airline tickets. Hotel reservations account for 60 percent of revenue, and the remaining 40 percent comes from airline ticket commissions. An impressive 46 percent of the Chinese professionals we polled prefer using Ctrip to make airline and hotel bookings when they travel, more than all other travel agencies combined.

Established in 1999, Ctrip.com is growing more than 40 percent a year. Like many successful Chinese companies, Ctrip is managed by young Chinese entrepreneurs educated and trained in the United States. Its primary founder is James Liang, a 37-year-old Georgia Tech grad who learned the software business at Oracle, and then turned a $250,000 investment into a $3.7 billion online travel powerhouse in less than seven years. He is now personally worth over $200 million.

Liang and his team built Ctrip into one of China's best-known travel brands, which generates nearly 4 percent of the entire country's hotel room reservations. In a country as big as China, that is a jaw-dropping number of rooms.

Ctrip is a play on three key trends associated with the rise of Chuppies: increase in tourism, growth of the Internet and travel information databases, and popularity of independent travel. Online use is growing over 20 percent a year and now stands at about 120 million, making China the world's second-largest market behind the United States. And yet the penetration rate is still only 9 percent.

Online travel is just starting to take off, with only 10 percent of all trips booked online. Ctrip has already tapped deep into this market, and continues to grow by providing online features that travelers look for. The company has pioneered a unique hybrid online/offline airline ticketing business model that enables users to check schedules online, book through call centers, and then pay cash upon delivery of tickets. This strategy has been enormously successful: Ctrip handles over 20,000 hotel room bookings and air ticket sales daily, and nearly 80 percent of its business comes from repeat customers.

With its top-notch service and nationwide coverage, Ctrip will continue to win market share from competitors. Its main competitor is eLong (NASDAQ: LONG), a China spin-off of Barry Diller's Expedia. eLong has poured nearly $200 million into China during the past several years to catch up with Ctrip, but has consistently fared poorly in China and has not been able to gain much traction. In comparison, Ctrip has more than 60 percent of China's travel market, is three times larger than eLong, and sells two times more hotel rooms and six times more air tickets. It has a substantially higher operating margin and has reported impressive earnings every single quarter.

Ctrip has an overwhelmingly dominant position in the industry. Most of its other competitors are either SOEs, which are generally less efficient in customer service, or smaller mom-and-pop shops, which lack the capacity for large-scale customer services. In my opinion, high barriers to entry, like a highly fragmented travel industry with no central reservations database, along with its first-in-the-market advantage, will protect Ctrip from competitors for years to come.

Because of the increase in domestic travel and tourism, one area I've been paying attention to is lodging. Many of the well-known international brands like Hyatt and Intercontinental are already entrenched in big cities and have staked out prime real estate. I think, however, the smart investment play will involve China's second-tier cities like Chongqing, Hangzhou, Nanjing, Qingdao, Shenzhen, Tianjin, Wuhan, Xi'an, and Zhuhai. For travelers and businesspeople visiting these rapidly growing cities and business centers, finding affordable and comfortable accommodations can be a big problem. There may be one or two luxurious five-star hotels for foreign visitors, but most budget hotels in these cities are technologically outdated and garishly decorated, and have poorly trained staffs.

Modern travelers—especially tech-savvy Chuppies—are demanding more for their money than second-tier accommodations in the second-tier cities. There are several companies that are catering to this market, including Home Inns & Hotels Management (NASDAQ: HMIN). They are creating budget hotels all over China, and are certainly addressing a huge need. While I liked Home Inns after its initial public offering (IPO) in 2006—the company was started in 2002 as a joint venture between Ctrip and the Beijing Tourism Group—I haven't seen it yet return the kinds of profits that I would have expected from a major player in this segment. In a word, it hasn't gained enough momentum.

Still, the entire lodging industry bears watching as more Chinese travel within their own national borders. Investors should look for companies that can do what Holiday Inn did in the 1960s in the United States and Marriott Courtyard did in the 1980s. Like Americans in those decades, value-conscious Chinese will be demanding modern amenities and well-managed hotels across Mainland China. Leisure travelers as well as business travelers, especially those who own or work for small and medium-sized companies, will drive the growth of this industry.

Sure Bets in a Risky Business

Another factor that will affect tourism is gambling. In fact, gambling is an industry that's on the rise in its own right. The growth of Asia's casino industry is outpacing the rest of the world, and annual gaming revenue from Asia is expected to double to $23 billion by 2010. But gambling in China is permitted legally only in the Chinese city of Macau, and Mainland Chinese have been making Macau every bit the vacation destination that Las Vegas and Atlantic City are in the United States.

I only like to play games of chance where the odds are in my favor, so I rarely indulge in casino gambling. But many Chinese gamble heavily. One of my money management clients, a gaming industry expert and Las Vegas property mogul, once told me that the average Chinese gambler loses five times as much money as the average non-Chinese gambler.

I believe it. I have many Chinese friends who take gambling seriously and play big. For instance, my buddy Simon, a professional stocks and futures speculator from Taipei, once lost $2 million in one night playing baccarat at the Mirage in Las Vegas. According to my casino industry sources, over half of all so-called whales—those high rollers like Simon who routinely drop over $100,000 a night—are ethnic Chinese.

As with any industry in China, you must understand not only how the whales behave, but also how the culture and the masses will embrace the products and services available to them. The scene in Macau is frankly astonishing. There's very little of Las Vegas' smoothness; indeed, there is little in the way of creature comforts. You quickly realize that what the Chinese are there for—in great throngs—is the opportunity to match skills against the house.

American casino operators have been quietly watching Macau's growth, circling like hungry lions. But they've made the usual American mistake: The local home-field advantage is very strong, and a mini-Las Vegas simply won't work in Macau. You see, casinos in Vegas make money by catering to conventions and couples, offering entertainers like Celine Dion nightly and parading scantily clad waitresses around the tables with martinis. In China—once again—the situation is a bit different.

In Macau, gambling is taken so seriously that no one drinks cocktails while playing. Fine dining is considered a waste of money—and a waste of precious gambling time. Slot machines are largely ignored, and glamorous boutiques are mostly empty. But the gaming tables—baccarat and local dice games such as chicken, crab, and fish—are packed six deep.

Though Chinese gambling preferences may be different from what we're used to, the Chinese propensity for gambling—and Macau's unique position as the only legalized gambling city in the Chinese-speaking world—makes Macau a major beneficiary of China's economic emergence. Formerly a small Portuguese colony known exclusively for its legal gambling monopoly, Macau reverted to Chinese control in 1999. Barely the size of a dozen city blocks, Macau is Asia's sin city and it makes Las Vegas look like Disneyland. It is only 45 minutes from Hong Kong by jetfoil, making it attractive to Chinese Mainlanders both for day trips and for extended-stay vacations.

Macau now is a special administrative region, a status it shares with Hong Kong. Prior to the colony's handover, Macau's casino monopoly was controlled by Stanley Ho, the suave 85-year-old Hong Kong multibillionaire internationally famous for his ballroom dancing skill and stylish attire. However, the new government, in the spirit of free enterprise, opened up gambling competition in 2000 by issuing two new casino licenses to international bidders. The winners were Las Vegas Sands (NYSE: LVS), holding company of the Venetian resort in Nevada, and Wynn Resorts, Limited (NASDAQ: WYNN), the namesake company of casino industry legend Steve Wynn. Las Vegas Sands and Wynn now have the rights to sublicense to other casino operators for a piece of Macau's supercharged gambling action.

When Las Vegas Sands opened its Sands Casino in 2004, Macau experienced an unprecedented boom. Gross domestic product (GDP) grew roughly 24 percent in that year alone. The hotel recouped its entire investment in less than a year. In short order, huge high-end casino complexes entered the Macau casino market: the $1.2 billion Wynn Macau, Galaxy's StarWorld, Stanley Ho's 52-story luxury casino resort Grand Lisboa, Melco PBL's Crown casino complex, the MGM Grand Macau, and Las Vegas Sands' new entry, the Venetian Macau on Cotai Strip.

You might wonder if there will be overcapacity with so many new casinos in Macau. Personally, I don't think Macau will reach that point for a long time because of the increasing affluence in China and the Chinese penchant for gambling. People talked about overcapacity in Las Vegas back in the 1990s, and today it is still expanding profitably.

The key, of course, is to sort through the gambling companies to see which ones are operating the most profitable establishments. Las Vegas Sands profited mightily from being the first new player in the market, but has since been hit by high employee retention and construction costs. The competition has heated up, because operators know there is a lot of money to be made.

Case Study: Las Vegas Sands

Las Vegas Sands (NYSE: LVS) was a great play as it expanded its gambling business into China. As I mentioned, I'm not a big gambler, and to me this stock was no gamble at all. As competition in Macau opened up, LVS was poised to profit. And it did. The Sands Macau went from drawing board to completion in an amazing two years, and then recouped its entire investment the following year. At the outset, its only competition was the Wynn casino organization, and it capitalized on its preeminent status as the preeminent player during Macau's rapid casino expansion.

I recommended the stock right after we launched the *China Strategy* newsletter. By that time, the Sands Macau had paid for itself, and LVS was ready to enjoy the benefits of owning and operating one of the most profitable casinos of all time. The momentum on this stock was astounding, and we saw the stock double in less than a year. You can see this rocket ride in Figure 8.1.

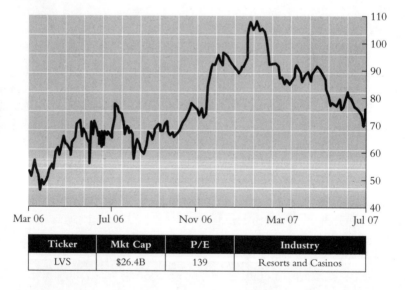

Ticker	Mkt Cap	P/E	Industry
LVS	$26.4B	139	Resorts and Casinos

Figure 8.1   Las Vegas Sands (One month before buy to one month after sell)
SOURCE: InvestorPlace Media, LLC.

However, the stock eventually started pulling back over intensified competition in Macau. Seeing the success of the Sands, a number of other high-profile casinos quickly entered the space. Las Vegas Sands' growth in Macau was still in double digits, but it lagged the pace of the gaming industry as a whole. Though the gambling pie was getting bigger, so to speak, Las Vegas Sands was getting a smaller slice by losing market share to new entrants. In addition, LVS was seeing its overall costs rise considerably around the world. Not only was it paying top dollar to keep employees from going to newer casinos, but it was paying a premium to expand its operations in both Macau (with another casino) and Singapore. Everything from interest payments to the cost of land was eating into its momentum.

That's when I decided to sell. I really liked this stock and still view it as the best play in the only city in the Chinese-speaking world that allows legalized gambling. But when the momentum is gone, you can't be emotional about it. It's time to move on. And we did, taking a 51 percent profit.

Smart investors need to compare the Macau performance of these gambling giants with each other in order to determine which ones are best serving the market. Once individual companies have established a level of dominance—as well as brand loyalty and popularity among gamblers—the best opportunities are certain to provide long-term gains for investors. Gambling is going to continue to thrive in Macau; there will be no stopping it.

The Richest Teacher in China

As Chinese people travel more and connect more with the outside world, they are increasingly exposed to unfamiliar aspects of life that they now desire for themselves. One area that has benefited significantly from this desire for a better life is education.

China's education sector is growing even faster than its economy as a whole. It is estimated that a typical Chinese household with a child spends more money on education than on housing and health care. An entirely new market for educational and test preparation services has grown up in just a few short years. Though private schooling has been part of Chinese culture for more than 2,500 years, Mao's regime limited the practice until the 1980s. Since then, a number of private schools have sprouted up, mainly in the largest cities. While public education is still the dominant form of schooling, there are now more than 70,000 private schools in China that serve over 14 million students. Many of these schools are funded by Western investors and institutions like the World Bank.

The demand for English-language education is particularly strong in China right now, and people are willing to pay a lot of money for training that will enable them to communicate and conduct business globally. Seeing the rise in education needs, I sought out companies that were capitalizing on this trend. One that stood out was New Oriental Education & Technology Group (NYSE: EDU), China's largest private education services company. In terms of size and impact, New Oriental has no peer.

New Oriental was founded in 1993 by Michael Yu, a graduate of Peking University. If Tsinghua University is known as the MIT of China, then Peking University is China's Harvard. Yu went on to teach English at his alma mater from 1985 to 1991, making $12 a month, which was considered a good salary at the time.

But Yu wanted more. Despite his wife lambasting him for leaving his post at such a prestigious university, Yu decided that he wanted to move to the United States. His student visa application was rejected, however, so he was forced to come up with an alternative plan. Yu made the most of the situation and started a test preparation school to help other Chinese students gain their own admission into U.S. graduate schools. Today Michael Yu is the wealthiest teacher in China's history, with an estimated net worth of $600 million.

From its first class of only 30 students, New Oriental has grown over the past 15 years to become China's largest private education service provider in terms of program offerings, enrollment, and geographic presence. It has a network of 37 schools and 149 learning centers in 35 cities, as well as an online network with 3 million registered users. Since its inception in 1993, more than 4.5 million students have taken a course at New Oriental. It enrolled more than a million students in 2006 alone.

The company has helped hundreds of thousands of Chinese students gain admission to U.S. universities by providing preparatory courses on the Test of English as a Foreign Language (TOEFL), which measures English proficiency, and Graduate Record Examination (GRE) standardized tests, which are required by U.S. universities.

Preparation for international secondary education is a huge and growing market. During the past decade, China sent more students abroad than did any other nation, and Chinese students now make up 14 percent of all foreign students worldwide. The total number of Chinese studying abroad increased fivefold between 1999 and 2002. More than 60,000 Chinese students are currently studying in the United States, and every single one of those students had to pass the TOEFL test, a fact that illustrates why New Oriental's preparatory classes are not only popular, but essential.

Most of the graduate students in the United States who are from Beijing and other major Chinese cities are familiar with Yu and his school. In fact, my research assistant, Fei He—who has a PhD in biochemistry from UCLA—once attended New Oriental's classes in Beijing to prepare for his standardized tests. Some 20 percent of Fei's former classmates at Tsinghua University came to the United States for graduate school, and those numbers are increasing.

Getting into top U.S. graduate programs is not the only reason Chinese students take classes at New Oriental. Although there are many Chinese college graduates seeking jobs, many of them have not been properly trained by China's outdated university system to thrive in a fiercely competitive business world. New Oriental's courses help them become more attractive career candidates in their business lives.

This push into higher education is driven by China's increasing prominence in the business world. As China becomes a major player in the global economy, demand for English-speaking workers is rising dramatically. Numerous multinational firms operating in China, from Motorola to General Motors, have complained about the lack of qualified local managerial talent. They regularly cite poor English skills as the single biggest problem they encounter. Thus, recent college graduates are attending New Oriental's classes to improve their English and technical skills in order to get promoted or find higher-paying jobs. To achieve this, according to a recent survey conducted in Shanghai, more than 15 percent of graduates are willing to spend upwards of 10 percent of their monthly disposable income on training courses.

In addition, the Chinese government recently made English language education mandatory for all high school graduates, making services such as those offered by New Oriental even more attractive. To my mind, New Oriental could be an educational vanguard for the next generation of Chinese workers by helping them with the training they need to participate in the global economy.

The company is currently going through an aggressive expansion phase, building numerous schools in fast-growing second-tier cities throughout China. As new schools open for business, earnings growth will accelerate. I look at New Oriental as being a singularly remarkable pure-play stock in a fast-growing sector of the world's fastest-growing economy.

Tapping into China's Desires

All of the businesses and industries I've discussed here are thriving because of increasing affluence among China's consumers. None of them are critical to, say, the country's production capabilities or export levels. But because of the sheer size of China's population and its relatively unfettered access to goods and services, businesses that tap into the unique desires of Chinese consumers have the potential to generate huge profits for themselves and investors.

It is essential that investors pay attention to lifestyle trends among consumers to ascertain what is appealing to the mass market. For example, cars are not going to rank among the primary purchases Chinese people will make—a markedly different consumer characteristic than we find in the United States. Cars are still incredibly expensive given income levels in China, and little exists in the way of servicing and maintaining them. The same applies to international travel, high-end home furnishings, and luxury items; they are simply out of reach of most Chinese and are thus not likely to generate huge revenues in the near future from even the most successful merchants.

However, personal items and personal enrichment opportunities are affordable to the vast majority of the population. Keep in mind that what China desires is also inextricably linked to what it can afford.

Desire is a huge motivator, and a huge driver of profits. No one needs an iPod, but Apple has sold more of its MP3 players than all of its competitors combined. No one needs a Nintendo Wii, but try finding one at your local store. The point of this chapter is that there are millions of people in China who can finally buy things they want—above and beyond buying the things they need. This is an important distinction.

The Chinese desire better lives for themselves in an era of prosperity. Better education, better vacations, better gadgets—these are the things we want for ourselves in the United States, and the Chinese are finding it to be true for themselves now that they've been exposed to it. Look at schools; look at tourism (from trip planners to airlines to hotels); look at popular device makers; look at entertainment (movies, theme parks, TV); and determine which companies have risen above the pack.

My belief is that those companies that have made inroads into China thus far have been successful, and they've got millions of new customers waiting in the wings.

China's Urbanization

There is one other area of what China desires that I think will be a long-term play for investors. It's a universal investing vehicle, but one of the few places in the world where it's not under siege is in Mainland China. I'm talking about real estate.

We all understand the value of a good real estate investment, but China's unique real estate environment requires a little background because of the way it is able to charge ahead while much of the rest of the world is experiencing severe real estate setbacks. Real estate in China is truly in a league of its own right now.

Having worked at the top firm in two of the highest-paying industries around—hedge fund management and investment banking—I've seen countless fortunes created almost overnight. It's mind-boggling how quickly wealth is being built by investors all over the world. But I've never seen so many people get rich as fast as I'm seeing it in China today. While millions of Chinese investors have made triple-digit returns in the past year, even more Chinese property owners saw the value of their real estate holdings double or triple in the past three years.

I've been interested in investing in Chinese real estate for many years, but I've never pulled the trigger. Up until recently, China's real estate market was a very difficult landscape to navigate, even for experienced investors like me. While visiting Beijing in 2000, I almost bought a traditional courtyard house in a good location in the western part of the city. The courtyard house was old and needed a lot of work, but it sat on a generous-sized lot and was available for only $300,000.

Similar lots in other major Asian cities—such as Taipei, Singapore, and Hong Kong—sold for well over $1 million at the time. By comparison, the Beijing house seemed like a good value. I ultimately decided to pass on the deal because the property needed extensive hands-on renovation.

In addition, there was another reason that I was hesitant to buy. At the time, there were complex restrictions on foreign ownership of real estate in China. I didn't want to deal with all of the red tape involved. But the property's value did go up sharply, and today that property is worth over $1 million—now that another buyer has fixed it up.

A year after I passed on the Beijing house, the Chinese government eased restrictions that limited foreigners from purchasing real estate. As a result, property prices started to move up. Prices in booming coastal cities like Shanghai were the first to increase.

Interestingly, up-and-coming second-tier cities in China like Suzhou and Hangzhou actually experienced greater price appreciation than the first-tier cities favored by Western investors. For example, between 2001 and 2005, average property prices in both Suzhou and Hangzhou went up between 90 percent and 110 percent, whereas nearby Shanghai experienced a more modest run-up of 80 percent. Property prices in China's other two top cities—Shenzhen and Beijing—climbed only 30 percent in the same time period.

Residential real estate prices increased less in top-tier cities because a larger supply of new homes came on the market in these growing metropolises. Most leading real estate developers, many of them from overseas, focused on building in first-tier cities and flooded these markets with new condominiums. The excess supply also depressed rent and lowered yield for investors. As a result, both real estate returns on capital and price appreciation were higher in many second-tier cities than in China's top three urban centers.

In the summer of 2005, the Chinese central bank started to allow the yuan to appreciate against other major currencies. This set off a wave of foreign investors clamoring for yuan-denominated assets. Money started to pour into China, and the central bank accumulated vast foreign reserves rapidly. Since then, the Chinese yuan has rallied 8 percent, and real estate prices also rose rapidly. Not coincidentally, the Mainland Chinese stock market also bottomed at the same time, then increased an astounding 400 percent over the next two years.

We saw similar situations in both Taiwan and Japan during the late 1980s. When a currency revalues higher, the stock market follows, and then real estate prices follow the stock market. The currency gain combined with stock appreciation followed by huge rallies in property prices created huge fortunes in both Taiwan and Japan. In 1989, the top three richest men in the world were all Japanese real estate tycoons, and number six was a Taiwanese insurance industry billionaire who invested his company's funds in office buildings.

China is now following this same pattern, and property prices have skyrocketed. As you can imagine, this worries the government in Beijing. Because high property prices made housing unaffordable for the masses, the Chinese government decided to curb property speculation at the end of 2005.

To limit property speculation, banks raised the down payment requirement for buyers. For instance, in Shanghai, the required down payment for most residential properties increased from 20 percent to 40 percent. Yet most overseas Chinese investors didn't need mortgage financing and continued to buy. Then the government changed the rules again and limited foreigners from buying more than one piece of property per person. But despite Beijing's best efforts, property prices have continued to move up in most parts of China.

In 2005, Shanghai's property market was soft. A typical condominium sold to middle-class Chuppies could be bought for about $130 per square foot. Today, the same condominium costs $200 per square foot.

As China's stock market boom picked up steam in 2007, property prices in Shanghai and Shenzhen started to rise furiously. Because Shanghai and Shenzhen are the country's two main financial centers, residents of these cities have made more profits from the Chinese stock market boom than Chinese in any other city. Stock investors and securities industry workers have been using their profits to buy local real estate. Property prices in both these cities jumped more than 50 percent in 2007. This amazing rise in housing prices accelerated after the huge rally in the Chinese stock market.

The Basis of a Boom

If China's economy is hot, then its real estate market is superheated. Of course, that wasn't always the case. As recently as 10 years ago, Chinese who had stable jobs with SOEs or the government could get apartments (the size depended on their years of service) at subsidized rates as part of their job benefits. That's no longer true today.

China's real estate industry has expanded rapidly in recent years due to several factors: the growth of the Chinese economy, an accelerating trend toward urbanization, an increasingly affluent urban population, and governmental reforms in the real estate sector.

I know I've used this figure before, but it's worth repeating: China now has more than two dozen cities larger than Chicago, the third-largest city in the United States. And millions of migrant workers are flocking into Chinese cities, which means that this number of urban hubs could double in the next decade. China's urbanization and its overall increase in prosperity have created a demand for higher-quality housing.

To top things off, overseas Chinese have invested heavily in Mainland China's property market to acquire yuan-denominated assets. This has also contributed to the greater demand throughout China for condominiums and houses.

In fact, during the five-year period from 2001 to 2005, the total gross floor area of primary properties sold in China grew at a compound annual growth rate of 25 percent. Thanks to property price increases, primary property sales revenue also climbed nearly 40 percent a year during the same period.

I expect this kind of growth in China's real estate sector to continue. Recent data shows that property prices are still soaring substantially in major first-tier and second-tier cities, up an average of 8.2 percent in August 2007 and 7.5 percent in July from one year earlier. Property prices in booming cities like Shenzhen skyrocketed 17.6 percent and

19.4 percent respectively in the past two months, while prices in the capital city of Beijing increased 13.5 percent and 10 percent respectively.

As China's real estate industry has grown in size and complexity, it has become increasingly specialized. Professional real estate services companies have emerged in response to these changes.

These real estate companies offer marketing and brokerage services, and they have grown considerably in the past several years. According to the China Real Estate Top 10 Committee, revenues and total floor area of the properties sold by the real estate services industry increased from $64 billion and 900 million square feet in 2004 to $128 billion and 1.62 billion square feet in 2006. That's a 100 percent increase in just two years.

With all of this appreciation in China's real estate market, investors are wondering how to get a piece of the profits. But as I've mentioned, investing in Chinese real estate is complicated. It's too difficult for you and me as foreign investors to go to China and buy property directly.

But we can take our cue from Chinese citizens. Many Chinese investors on the Mainland and in Hong Kong have found a way around buying property. Instead, they often buy property company stocks in place of actual real estate to benefit from the country's property boom. Yet up until recently, all of the major Chinese real estate development companies were listed only in Hong Kong and Mainland China. Finally, one of China's top real estate marketing and brokerage companies got listed on the New York Stock Exchange in July 2007. I've been watching this company since its IPO, and found it an exceptional way to take advantage of China's explosive real estate sector.

The name of the company is E-House (NYSE: EJ). Founded in 2000, E-House is one of China's leading real estate service companies. It has a large scope of services, good brand recognition, and a strong geographic presence. The company provides primary real estate agency services, secondary real estate brokerage services, as well as real estate consulting and information services.

As an early mover in China's real estate services sector, the company has experienced significant growth since its inception. It has rapidly become a leader in Shanghai's real estate services market within the past two years. Now the company has over 2,000 real estate sales professionals in 29 cities throughout China.

In my discussions with the company's billionaire founder and CEO, Xin Zhou, it has been abundantly clear that the E-House management team has a deep understanding of China's booming real estate business. Unlike property developers, the company positions itself as an asset-light real estate services firm that helps real estate developers sell properties.

Zhou has a clear vision for the future of his company. Unlike in the United States, new home sales still dominate the Chinese real estate industry with an 85 percent share of total sales, while the secondary home market makes up the remaining 15 percent of property transactions. As a result, E-House puts a strong emphasis on selling new homes for developers. New home sales are the company's biggest revenue source, generating more than 80 percent of its revenue. A recent Merrill Lynch research report pointed out that the Chinese real estate market will likely maintain its fast growth over the next several years thanks to strong demand.

One of the factors contributing to E-House's success is its proprietary real estate information database, the China Real Estate Information Circle (CRIC) system, the biggest and most comprehensive real estate database in the entire country. The database contains real estate sales data and information on land, residential, office, and commercial spaces, as well as real estate–related advertisements in 24 different Chinese cities.

E-House has more than 2,000 subscribers to its CRIC system, mainly domestic and international real estate developers. The powerful CRIC information database is a tremendous competitive advantage to E-House in China's highly fragmented real estate brokerage industry, because E-House is the only brokerage company in China that owns this nationwide comprehensive database. This allows the firm to access information that's not available to competitors.

Its expertise and singular database have propelled it to the top echelon of China's real estate market. The China Real Estate Top 10 Committee named E-House the largest real estate agency and consulting services company in China for three consecutive years from 2004 to 2006. E-House sold a total of 54 million square feet of primary properties with a transaction value of $5.4 billion in the past five years. And in 2006, the company sold nearly 22 million square feet of development property totaling more than $2 billion, with an average commission rate of 2.5 percent to 3 percent.

Primary real estate agency services—providing comprehensive marketing and sales services of new properties for real estate developers—represent the company's biggest revenue source. According to the company's third-quarter 2007 earnings announcement, "For the first nine months of 2007, revenues from primary real estate agency services were $59.0 million, an increase of 317 percent from $14.2 million for the same period in 2006." Nearly half of its revenues came from the richer eastern coastal provinces, like Shanghai, Jiangsu, and Zhejiang.

E-House has successfully maintained and enhanced its brand name and has also built strong business relationships with over 150 property developers, including leading domestic developers in China like Vanke, Neo-China Group, and Citic Pacific. It also has maintained an impressive profit margin, which is one of my favorite indicators of a company's operating performance. Margins came in at 44 percent in 2006.

E-House had had a fairly recent IPO when I first started examining it—and an oversubscribed one at that. IPOs have a way of distorting the underlying fundamentals of a company, as investors get excited about the IPO itself and not the company. So, one of the things I look for when investing in newly listed Chinese IPOs is the quality of the financial backers. Legendary Silicon Valley venture capital firm Sequoia Capital, which made its fame and fortune by backing Cisco Systems (NASDAQ: CSCO), Oracle (NASDAQ: ORCL), and Apple (NASDAQ: AAPL), is the primary backer of E-House. Sequoia partner Neil Shen, the cofounder of Ctrip, also invested in E-House back in 2004. He currently owns 10 percent of the company. Together, these investors gave substantial support and credence to E-House's bright future.

The Chinese real estate market, even more than the Chinese economy, shows no signs of cooling off anytime soon. As more citizens want to own their own homes—especially after moving away from rural and farming areas—there is no doubt that real estate will be one of the primary wants on the agenda of people who are making more money than ever before. I think that E-House, and eventually other real estate services companies, will give forward-thinking American investors yet another way in which to profit from the China Miracle.

Chapter 9

Buying What China Makes

In 2006, China became the world's largest exporter of manufactured goods. Almost any consumer item you can think of that costs less than $2,000—refrigerators, stereos, toothbrushes, T-shirts, computers, cameras, and on and on—is being manufactured in China and shipped to the rest of the world. No other country comes close to making so many different products and exporting as many of them as China.

Now consider this: As recently as 2000, China's exports were less than half of what the United States exported. In less than six years, China's rate of production and export grew so fast that it has now left the United States far behind.

Most of the goods China makes are shipped around the world in cargo containers, the 20-foot-long large metal boxes that are loaded onto ships, trains, and trucks for distribution all over the globe. I've seen reports that claim the ports of Shenzhen and Hong Kong in south China ship approximately 40 million cargo containers every year. This means that Shenzhen and Hong Kong alone are moving an average of one container per second every minute, day, week, and month of the year. One per second—that's a mind-boggling number, but even more amazing is that those 40 million containers represent less than half of China's total exported cargo shipments.

Exports are so vital to the Chinese economy that the government is spending as much as $50 billion to build more ports to ship more toys, furniture, electronics, appliances, and garments to the rest of the world.

A third of that port investment will go to Shanghai, which is currently the busiest port in Mainland China and the third-busiest in the world—after Hong Kong and Singapore. I expect that Shanghai will overtake Hong Kong within the next five years thanks to the creation of the Yangshan port, located on a reclaimed and partially man-made island 20 miles offshore from Shanghai. This new $16 billion port will double Shanghai's cargo capacity to 30 million boxes by 2010.

The Reality of China's Exports

There is no denying that China makes a substantial amount of the world's goods—the value of its exports will soon reach the $1 trillion mark. However, there is one fact underlying all of this manufacturing that will serve you quite well as an investor: The vast majority of China's production for export is done under contract for big companies that are based in other countries. The products in those containers are stamped not with local Chinese names, but with logos familiar around the world.

Here is why this information is important. China, like South Korea and Japan in decades past, is benefiting from overseas companies setting up *production* facilities within the country to take advantage of low-cost labor, quick and flexible manufacturing capabilities, and the ability to produce goods in huge quantities. Very little of what comes from China was *designed* there. Outside of some homegrown successes like medical equipment maker Mindray Medical (NYSE: MR), which has become very competitive in the global market, Chinese products are predominantly conceived, designed, engineered, and sold by companies headquartered in the United States, Japan, and Europe.

Think of it in this light: Apple (NASDAQ: AAPL) products have a uniquely American cachet, Sony (NYSE: SNE) products are uniquely

Japanese, and Braun Corporation (NYSE: PG) appliances are considered fine European products. But each of these companies does much, if not most, of its manufacturing in China. And when they sell their instantly recognized products, the bulk of a product's retail price goes to the brand owner, not the factories.

In general, only about one-fifth of the price (and often less) of any brand-name product is paid back to China. Thus, it is the companies using China as their manufacturing base that are making the incredible profits off the low cost of producing goods in the Chinese Mainland— not the companies doing the actual manufacturing. This underscores an important point that Wall Street ignores when looking at China: The development money that is flowing into the country from international corporations is one of the essential fuels that keeps the China Miracle running.

Many investors will get severely burned by not understanding this point. You do not want to invest in Chinese manufacturing firms that are, at the end of the day, contractors to other companies. You also don't want to invest in companies that are manufacturing goods for sale primarily into the domestic China market. The only worthwhile China play in manufacturing is buying stocks of well-positioned and strongly branded companies that keep their own production costs down thanks to manufacturing in China.

This might seem counterintuitive at first. After all, with such a huge and successful manufacturing industry, how can you lose by investing in the manufacturers? Many advisers will surely tell you that Chinese companies are churning out millions of goods every year for thousands of global customers. These factory companies are the engines of the economy, the Wall Streeters claim; they are the companies at the heart of China's nonstop production machine. How better to get in on the China Miracle than to invest in a part of the machine?

I'll say it again: Stay away from Chinese-based contract manufacturers for the next few years. That means car companies, electronics manufacturers, apparel makers, and every other company that currently has a low-cost assembly line or factory. These companies all require at least one of three elements to make them valuable, and they typically have none of them. I'll explain what this means in a moment, but first I'm going to tell you why everyone else is falling for manufacturing as a China play.

China's manufacturing capabilities are tremendous by any measure. The speed, the volume, and the low-cost operations are unrivaled anywhere in the world right now. Fans of China's manufacturing often point to the famed Foxconn (Taiwan: 2354.TW) facility in Shenzhen as a model for production that the rest of the world should envy. Foxconn is the trade name for Hon Hai Precision Industry Company, currently the world's biggest manufacturer of electronics. Like many successful companies in Mainland China, though, Foxconn is actually a Taiwanese company. Its founder, Terry Gou, has transferred so much of his company's manufacturing from Taiwan to the Chinese Mainland that Foxconn is now the largest exporter in Mainland China.

Foxconn's Shenzhen facility is a massive place, essentially a city-sized factory. It employs an estimated 250,000 people, most of whom live in dormitories situated on the Foxconn property. During peak production periods, as many as 3,000 new employees are hired every day. The company not only houses most of its employees, it also provides food for them, requiring 10 tons of rice and thousands of pigs and chickens for meals each and every day. The facility is almost like a self-contained city, and the goal of everyone in the city is to produce goods as quickly as possible for international clients who look to save money by working with Foxconn. These clients and their products include the Apple iPod, the Nintendo Wii, Motorola and Nokia (NYSE: NOK) cell phones, and parts for Dell (NASDAQ: DELL) laptops and Sony PlayStations.

The sheer scale of Foxconn's operations coupled with a cheap labor force help keep its costs down, making it attractive to international partners. Low-cost manufacturing is one of China's biggest competitive advantages and a key driver of its economic explosion. It is also one of the reasons that prices of many U.S. goods have declined by as much as 90 percent over the past eight years. Remember the introduction of the DVD player? It used to cost $800 to buy one just eight years ago—until Chinese companies started making them. Then the price plunged to $150 almost overnight, and everybody bought one. Now you can buy one for as little as $35. A five-megapixel digital camera that cost $700 three years ago now goes for less than $300. The average notebook computer had a hefty price tag of $1,800 in 1998; now you can buy one that's eight times as powerful for half that price.

Balancing Price and Production

Cheaper prices, driven by lower manufacturing costs in China, are fueling worldwide demand for goods from electronics to clothes. When you consider the steep price rise in oil and commodities, inflation would be significantly higher if it weren't for these inexpensive Chinese exports. In addition, the huge earnings growth experienced by corporate America during the past three years is due in large part to savings achieved by outsourcing manufacturing operations to China. The low cost of China's production has offset significant financial pressures from other areas.

Outsourcing production to China has actually been going on for 15 years. Some companies have relocated their own in-house manufacturing facilities to China, while others have outsourced their entire manufacturing process to Chinese firms. In neither case, as I've mentioned, do a significant amount of the profits from these operations stay in China; most of the money makes its way back to U.S. and multinational headquarters.

This gets to the heart of why China-based manufacturers are not good investments. It is the client—Apple, Nike (NYSE: NKE), Sony, Dell, and so on—that gets the lion's share of the profits, while Chinese factories get by on razor-thin margins. This is true even for well-run non-Chinese-based companies like Foxconn. Here's a perfect example: According to a study from UBS AG, China earns only $0.35 each on Barbie dolls that retail for $20 in the United States. For Chinese manufacturers to make any money, their production volume must be measured in the hundreds of thousands or millions.

Putting the burden of production on their Chinese partners allows American companies to spend their time designing products. Having lowered production costs, American companies can focus their attention on marketing and product innovation, which are the primary drivers of demand in our highly developed consumer society. Product marketing has been so successful in the United States that most consumers will not settle for generic goods anymore. I remember when pure generics were all the rage in the late 1980s and early 1990s. Products from cans of creamed corn and corn flakes to paper towels were wrapped in bright yellow generic labels and touted as money-saving items.

You don't see those products much anymore. Even Wal-Mart (NYSE: WMT), Costco (NASDAQ: COST), and Target (NYSE: TGT) brand their in-house products as "private label" with names like Kirkland and Archer Farms. Brands matter. I can tell you from firsthand experience that little girls, like my daughter, definitely want a Barbie doll or an American Girl doll, not just any generic doll.

Sneakers are another example. Kids and adults want Nikes and are willing to pay more for what the swoosh logo means than for the shoe itself. Take off the swoosh, and the shoe loses a huge amount of its value to the consumer. The design and underlying marketing messages are more valuable than the shoe, which—when you think about it—is just another cheap commodity. Add the branding and advertising, and it's an entirely different scenario. As a result, Nike shareholders, executives, and celebrity endorsers reap huge benefits from the shoes while Chinese contract manufacturers squeeze out substantially less robust profit margins. The brand and its promoters are rewarded at a higher level because it is much harder to build a world-class brand than to make shoes.

Let me repeat that, because you should keep it in mind when you invest in retail products: It is much harder to build a world-class brand than to make things. The world-class brand trumps the generic version, and delivers higher returns to its owner—and its shareholders.

Not surprisingly, branding also matters when selling into China, no matter where the goods are made. Those companies that can be the first to market with a significant brand are in an enviable position. Brands matter to Chinese at all levels—not just in the Chuppie or upscale markets—because the Chinese people are fed up with using substandard products and knockoffs of poor quality. And, just like in the United States, branding ultimately is a means of creating a sustainable competitive advantage in the marketplace. In China, this is especially true of high-priority goods and services such as education and health care—businesses that relate to the Chinese tradition of concern for family.

Brands and manufacturing are ultimately at opposite ends of the business spectrum. Manufacturing requires many resources and is physically labor intensive, thus expensive, whereas innovation and brand creation is not. Making things is a low-profit business, while high profits come from design, distribution, and marketing. It is in these latter businesses where you find the really big money.

Not only do the creators of brands and market-leading products benefit from low-cost Chinese manufacturing, so do American consumers. According to Morgan Stanley, we've saved over $800 billion during the past decade because of products manufactured in China. That's an average of $2,600 for every American. Plunging prices in everything from flat-panel monitors to children's pajamas have been made possible by China's low-cost manufacturing capabilities, and, as I mentioned earlier, low-priced Chinese exports have been a significant force in countering inflationary pressures in the United States.

Export is a key word here. International firms are having their products made in China for export back to the United States, Europe, and other markets. They are now just starting to sell those products to Chinese consumers. Manufacturing for export is the key to profits. Those companies manufacturing in China with the intent to sell to the domestic Chinese market are not likely to be big winners for many years to come. Not every Chinese citizen wants, or can afford, to drink several Cokes a day, or buy things like American-branded bicycles. And because of the valuation of the yuan, such products still have very low profit margins for domestic manufacturers.

Adding to the difficulty of manufacturing for the domestic markets is the pervasive problem of copycatting. Piracy has been a serious problem in China for a long time. Knockoffs of popular brands—even products with similar-sounding names and features—are developed almost overnight by unscrupulous businesses. Once they flood the market, these pirated products eat into the profits and market share of the original brands, potentially ruining the business of the market leader.

Only a handful of companies have managed to rise above these problems, notably Motorola (NYSE: MOT) and Procter & Gamble (NYSE: PG). They are both manufacturing in China for sale into the Chinese market, and have both had varying degrees of success over time. The reason for this success is that they both have at least one of the three elements I alluded to earlier that are required for success in manufacturing in China—as well as selling into China.

In fact, these elements are also at the core of every good investment in China. And they're really quite basic. A company must have at least one of the following three traits in order to be a worthwhile candidate for your investment dollars:

1. It must have shown sustainable growth in a growing industry.
2. It must have a product that cannot be easily duplicated. Procter & Gamble is an example of a company whose operations are so large

they cannot be easily taken down by copycats, while Apple is a good example of a company whose intellectual property (especially the iPod and iPhone) cannot be easily knocked off or pirated.

3. It must operate in a heavily regulated or controlled industry in which it has a strong advantage, usually in the form of protection offered by the government. A few strong SOEs fall into this category.

The Manufacturing Myth

One of the problems in trying to isolate a manufacturing play in China is that it is based solely on the availability of cheap labor. Right now, China provides the most extensive low-cost manufacturing services—although not necessarily the highest-quality services—in the world. While companies like Apple and Taiwan Semiconductor (NYSE: TSM), which I'll talk about in a moment, both derive huge economies of scale that ultimately translate to nice profits from manufacturing in China, they are not bound to China as the only place to get those cost savings. Ultimately, they could go to Mexico, Vietnam, India, or other countries to manufacture their products. They can, in effect, take their brands anywhere to be made, because the location of the factory matters not one bit to the end user.

Let me walk you through one of my favorite examples of how Wall Street tends to misrepresent the investment potential of manufacturing in China. From everything I've already discussed, it is probably obvious that of the vast array of goods coming out of China, many are electronics. At the heart of these electronics are semiconductors, the tiny silicon chips that control computers, TVs, phones, talking dolls, DVDs, modern appliances, and pretty much anything else that you plug into the wall or that runs on batteries.

The scope and scale of its electronics production now make China the world's fastest-growing semiconductor market. According to PricewaterhouseCoopers, products made in China accounted for 90 percent of the growth in semiconductor consumption in 2005 (the most recent year for which total numbers are available). That means that the market for semiconductors in China was bigger than the United States, Europe, and Japan. Yet, more than two-thirds of those semiconductors ended up in products that were then exported out of China. They did not go into products that were sold to the domestic Chinese market.

Even more telling is that China buys its semiconductors from multinational companies, not its own homegrown developers. While the top suppliers to China are all multibillion-dollar international enterprises, the largest semiconductor firm headquartered in China had not even cracked the $200 million mark in 2005. (On a related note, this is another indication that China has not yet been able to move into the top tier of electronics developers and designers, and is relying primarily on its manufacturing skills in serving its electronics partners.)

The fact that China buys the bulk of its semiconductors from foreign firms—many of which have their manufacturing inside China—is very rarely reported. Unsuspecting investors listening to the so-called experts on Wall Street might be tempted to put money in Mainland Chinese semiconductor companies like Semiconductor Manufacturing International Corporation (NYSE: SMI). As someone who has studied this market extensively, I can tell you that making such an investment would be just about the worst thing you could do. Mainland Chinese semiconductor companies are bad investments. Period. They have all fared poorly, despite the growth of their industry, because they focus on low-margin services like contract manufacturing. Plus, the competition is fierce, so profits are reduced even more.

As I've said, the real money is in higher-margin services—like chip design and product development. In those areas, U.S. and Taiwanese semiconductor companies outpace their competition by leaps and bounds. By outsourcing low-margin manufacturing to semiconductor factories in China, U.S. and Taiwanese corporations can concentrate on core strengths like research and development (R&D). Two of the most notable such firms are National Semiconductor (NYSE: NSM), which does roughly half its business in China, and Taiwan Semiconductor (NYSE: TSM). Both are industry giants, but over time, I've found more to like in Taiwan Semiconductor. The company is not just the global semiconductor industry leader, but the creator of the semiconductor foundry as we know it. Foundries are semiconductor wafer fabrication (aka "fab") plants that make integrated chips for other companies. Because of the high cost to set up new semiconductor manufacturing facilities (more than $3 billion) and a short product life cycle (about five years), semiconductor developers increasingly use foundries to manufacture their chips.

Taiwan Semiconductor is in an incredibly desirable position as a manufacturer to the semiconductor industry: It is supplying products to clients that are often in competition with each other. And that client list reads like a who's who of global semiconductor giants, including Intel (NASDAQ: INTC), Texas Instruments (NYSE: TXN), Nvidia (NASDAQ: NVDA), ATI Technologies (NASDAQ: ATYT), and many more. Those companies design, develop, and create the chips and pay Taiwan Semiconductor handsomely to manufacture them.

The company was founded by Morris Chang, a legend in Taiwan. Dr. Chang was born in Zhejiang province in China and moved to the United States in 1949 to attend college. He wanted to become a writer, but his father convinced him otherwise. He earned a PhD in electrical engineering from Stanford University, and then became a vice president at Texas Instruments. Chang left Texas Instruments in the early 1980s to become president and chief operating officer of General Instrument Corporation. After only a year there, he was recruited by the Taiwanese government to lead efforts to promote industrial and technological development in Taiwan.

Chang saw that there was a growing demand from businesses that were increasingly outsourcing their manufacturing processes to Asia. But there was a void in meeting demand for computer chips. He took the entrepreneurial route to filling that void and founded Taiwan Semiconductor. Today, almost 20 years later, it is one of the most successful companies to ever emerge from Taiwan. It is the world's leading semiconductor foundry and currently commands 50 percent market share. The company maintains a wide lead over competitors through superior technology, more efficient manufacturing processes, and developing strong partnerships with its customers.

Taiwan Semiconductor has benefited from two primary strengths. First, it offers a premium product, which differentiates it from most electronic contract manufacturing firms where cutthroat pricing is a big problem. It makes premium logic chips (which process data) for its customers instead of commodities like memory chips (which merely store data). Second, the company benefits greatly from economies of scale, so the more chips it makes, the lower the cost per chip and the higher the profit.

The company invests a substantial amount of money in new equipment, which allows it to manufacture the most advanced chips at the highest profit margins. The company's newest plant cost a reported $7.5 billion, and it has another advanced plant planned for Taiwan. It also recently increased the capacity of its factory in Shanghai. Its strong production capability has allowed it to ride successfully through the tech booms and busts of the past two decades, and it is currently way out in front of the current boom. As I write this, its capacity utilization is running at over 100 percent; this happens when a plant runs at stated full capacity and then implements production processes that help it exceed that utilization rate.

This semiconductor company is a perfect example of how a Chinese manufacturing play should look: It is getting its economies of scale by manufacturing in China even though it is headquartered elsewhere; it has established a dominant industry position and a huge operation that is not easily attacked by competition; and within its industry it is a well-respected brand. Other companies that have succeeded using some of these principles are Apple and Nike.

Another company I get asked about frequently because it has excelled due to China's manufacturing is Wal-Mart. The world's largest retailer is in an interesting position because it is able to keep its costs low by getting products directly from Chinese manufacturers—a rarity in American business. Wal-Mart has an estimated 6,000 suppliers based in China, and buys nearly $20 billion worth of goods from Chinese businesses. These suppliers make everything from tools and extension cords to holiday decorations. They are often no-name suppliers that make cheap goods American consumers will buy when brand doesn't matter. Remember, with the Barbie example brand matters, but do you know the brand name of the garden gloves or party decorations you buy? Probably not. The most inexpensive offerings will usually do just fine, primarily because such wares are either disposable or simply utilitarian.

Wal-Mart is able to be successful thanks to low-cost Chinese manufacturing, but that does not make it a bona fide China play. Its revenues are not dependent on selling to China nor is it beholden to China for all of its products. It has taken advantage of the China Miracle, yes, and has turned that to a global strategic advantage. However, it could—with little difficulty—find suppliers outside of China. And its growth comes from sales in the United States. The Chinese consumer is not yet its primary customer, although I'm sure Wal-Mart has its sights set on making that happen.

The Outsourcing Backlash

Every year, more and more companies are moving their manufacturing from U.S. factories to China in an effort to keep their bottom lines as low as possible. This process, known as outsourcing, has become a matter of concern for many Americans. Many investors have told me that they fear a backlash against China as more and more U.S. companies contract with Chinese-based firms to make their products. Their concern is that the United States is losing jobs to China, and that Americans might get angry enough to stop buying Chinese products.

This is a political hot button for many Americans, and I think it needs to be addressed. For managers and executives, outsourcing to China is a way to become more cost-competitive. But for American factory workers, outsourcing causes concerns about job security—concerns that are valid but may be misplaced.

The reality is that less than 10 percent of the U.S. workforce is in manufacturing, and manufacturing functions have been outsourced for decades. Long before China's economic emergence, American companies—especially high-tech manufacturers—were outsourcing their manufacturing to Mexico and smaller Asian countries, such as South Korea and Taiwan. This has been a fact of business life since the 1980s. Those manufacturing jobs that have remained in the United States tend to be ones that require higher levels of skill and can't be easily outsourced.

U.S. computer companies like Hewlett-Packard and Dell have long used low-cost outsourcing to increase market share at the expense of slower-growth companies like Toshiba. Their success has created a multitude of new American jobs in marketing and product design—jobs that are higher paying and part of higher-profit businesses rather than low-paying manufacturing jobs.

The economic reality is that workers in Chinese factories compete mostly with workers in factories located in Mexico, South Korea, and Taiwan—and China is winning that competition. In fact, much of the widely touted U.S. trade deficit with China increased at the expense of Taiwan and South Korea because the United States isn't getting as many products from those countries as it used to. And, as we saw earlier, Taiwanese and South Korean businesses have moved their own production facilities to China as they continue to manufacture goods for U.S. companies.

Look at how the production of computers has changed in the past decade. More than 40 percent of all notebook computers are manufactured by Taiwanese companies such as Quanta (Taiwan: 2382.TW) and Compal (Taiwan: 8078.TW), two companies most Americans have never heard of. Yet, there are no notebook computer factories in Taiwan today because Quanta, Compal, and the others shifted their production facilities to China. The world's notebook production capital is now in Kunshan, a small county located less than two hours away from Shanghai. As a result of Quanta and Compal outsourcing their production to Kunshan, thousands of Taiwanese workers lost their jobs to China.

This same shift in jobs has occurred in U.S. industries like furniture making and appliance manufacturing. These are important industries, yes, but not high-growth or even high-profit businesses in a society where intellectual capital—in the form of innovation, technology, and design—is the most valuable commodity in business.

But as factories in the United States have shut their doors, a rising tide of concern over the outsourcing of manufacturing jobs has led to an increasing percentage of Americans who are in favor of protectionist trade policies. Much of this concern is directed at China.

Such sentiment ignores one salient fact: Chinese companies are working for American companies; they're not competing against them. They are not producing cars to compete with General Motors (NYSE: GM) or computers to compete with Apple. Instead, they are working for Dell, for Intel, for Hewlett-Packard (NYSE: HPQ), for Wal-Mart, for Nike, and for many others. It is subcontracting, not competing. Working for U.S. companies means they are working for American management and American shareholders. And the reality is that if protectionists were to shut down every China factory today, the jobs that were sent there would never come back to the United States. They would just go to India or Vietnam or Mexico.

Compounding the sentiment against outsourcing has been the recall of toys and pet food manufactured by some of the less reputable firms in China. While these goods represent a mere fraction of China's exports, people are right to be concerned. Poor-quality and even dangerous products should never make it to our store shelves, regardless of where they are made.

Yet most people do not realize that quality problems with shoddy Chinese imports could be avoided if U.S. importers would be willing to spend just a bit more on quality inspection and control. Even if the cost of this control is added to the cost of goods, it would still be far less expensive for consumers than buying the same goods made in more developed countries. Now that we are used to low-priced goods from China, many American consumers no longer want to pay for more expensive goods made in Europe or elsewhere. But a slight surcharge that helped to improve quality would be a negligible price to pay.

A surcharge is fine, but arbitrarily slapping tariffs on China or making it difficult for the country to export to the United States would have a negative effect on both American consumers and shareholders. Protectionist measures against China would make it more expensive for American consumers to buy Chinese-made goods. Protectionists don't realize that this would harm profitable American businesses that design and distribute these goods. Corporate earnings and investors alike would be hurt as a result, and consumers would have to lower their standard of living—they simply couldn't afford to buy the number of things they wanted if prices rose substantially.

Political rhetoric aside, China's economic emergence has benefited most Americans. In an increasingly global economy, barriers are broken down as finished products require cooperative efforts from workers in different parts of the world. The old economic paradigm of one country versus another simply does not reflect today's global reality.

China, with the exception of the isolationist years before economic reforms, has always been one of the world's smartest and wealthiest global traders. And whether we're talking about today or 3,000 years ago, free trade has always produced wealth and a win-win situation for all parties involved. With improvements in communication, technology, and transportation, free trade and globalization in the modern era are creating unprecedented wealth and opportunities for investors like us. To miss out on the opportunities presented by doing business with China is to miss out on the greatest investment opportunity we will ever get.

Now that you have a clear sense of what criteria manufacturers must have in order to be viable investment opportunities, I want to tell you about who will be buying those products. There has been an explosion of China's middle class, and for the first time they have access to some of life's modern conveniences. In the next chapter we'll investigate what's creating new members of this middle class and what their consumer profile looks like.

Chapter 10

The Wealth of Chuppies

For half of the twentieth century, China's isolation and its inefficient planned economy practices ensured that its population
would be relegated to third world status and all that that entails.
Poverty and limited access to basic goods and services were the norm
across the country.

Since reforms began in earnest, market forces have significantly
changed the quality of life in China. Free enterprise has lifted a third
of the population out of poverty in the past two decades, and China
is hurriedly creating a modern infrastructure that will provide its people with a standard of living and modern convenience that compares
favorably to the West.

This is a significant cultural and economic shift for China. When
several hundred million people suddenly have the monetary means
to become full-fledged consumers and participate in the economy, the
entire national dynamic changes. Nowhere is this more evident than
in the rise of the Chinese middle class. As consumers, they are similar in
many ways to America's yuppies: young, upwardly mobile professionals

with a penchant for buying the finer things in life. I think of them as Chinese yuppies, and coined the term *Chuppies* to identify them.

The Chuppies are in an enviable position. They are the people acquiring wealth and driving the Chinese economy continually upward. And in the near future, they will begin replacing American consumers as drivers of the global economy. Today, American consumers, along with the help of Chinese producers, account for approximately 40 percent of the world's gross domestic product (GDP), and are responsible for as much as 60 percent of total global economic growth. However, many of the affluent urban baby boomers, who have kept the U.S. economy strong, are set to retire in the coming decade. Western Europe does not have the population demographics to pick up the slack. Thus, global consumerism will inevitably be driven by the more than 50 million Chuppies and their families who make between $15,000 and $125,000 a year (see Figure 10.1).

This income may not be much by our standards, but it is a generous amount of money in China. The average wage in China is now over $2,000 a year, another number that is low compared to the West,

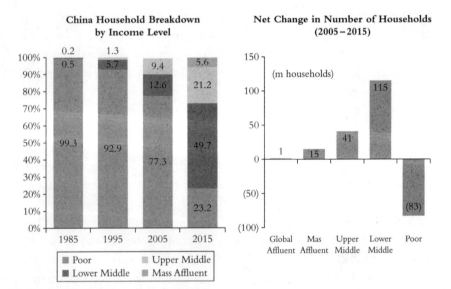

Figure 10.1   An Emerging Middle Class
SOURCE: InvestorPlace Media, LLC.

but is extremely significant in a country with a very low cost of living and where wages barely exceeded $100 a year two decades ago. This current per capita figure factors in the hundreds of millions of people who are just now emerging from poverty and working in low-paying jobs. Regardless, Chuppies are making the kind of money that allows them to buy homes and cars, and to indulge in leisure activities like travel, gambling, surfing the Internet, and playing video games.

This fast-growing segment of the population embraces American-style consumer ideals (another Yuppie-esque trait), and their purchasing power will become increasingly influential in shaping China's future growth. Not only will the things they buy have an effect on retail trends throughout China, but those purchases will also be instrumental in determining which companies achieve success in the consumer marketplace.

I first experienced the impact of Chuppies when dining out on my trips to China. I take a great deal of pleasure in enjoying a good meal at a nice restaurant, and seek out such experiences whenever I visit the Mainland. Given the popularity of Chinese restaurants in the United States, you'd probably think that it wouldn't be a problem to find great Chinese restaurants in China itself. Up until recently, however, it was a huge problem. Understanding why things have improved of late will help you realize the dramatic transformation taking place there and the magnitude of the opportunities that await you.

During my most recent visit to Shanghai, I actually had three very good meals. All three restaurants were packed with hungry patrons, and judging by the number of Shanghainese speakers, locals outnumbered visitors. There are now plenty of great restaurant options in Shanghai, even at 3 A.M., with a broad offering of fantastic Asian food, including Chinese, Japanese, Korean, and Thai. But things weren't always this way in Shanghai. As recently as 2000, my family and I had a tough time finding good meals outside of our hotel after 8 P.M. Several of Shanghai's most famous restaurants back then were poorly run state-owned enterprises (SOEs) such as Meilongzhen and Lu Bo Lang. They often ran out of their best dishes after 7 P.M. The food was mediocre, though the settings were admittedly impressive. Pictures of famous customers dining at these establishments, including Bill Clinton and Queen Elizabeth, only made the experience more disappointing when they didn't live up to expectations.

More important, the people eating at these famous restaurants back then were expats—Chinese visitors from overseas—and tourists. There were few, if any, locals to be found, because they couldn't afford to eat there.

By 2002, privately owned, cavernous Chinese restaurants that served tasty food for low prices were quite popular. A family of five could eat quite well at these establishments for under $20. I noticed that these restaurants were always packed and drew people from all walks of life. Laborers and professionals dined together in the same huge hall, and most of the customers at these restaurants were emerging middle-class local Chinese.

Two years later, in 2004, it was even clearer that the development of Shanghai's restaurant scene reflected the rising affluence of young Chinese urban professionals. As the Chuppie segment emerged from the middle class, they developed a preference for dining out at more refined restaurants away from the masses. They were willing to pay more to dine in a sophisticated setting. As a result, the big and cheap restaurants that once dominated Shanghai's dining scene went into decline. Today, thanks to Chuppies' increasingly discriminating taste, I can now find some of the best Chinese food anywhere in the world in Shanghai.

The way in which restaurants cater to the affluent segment of the middle class is indicative of the importance and influence of this segment. Combine their rapidly growing demographic with discriminating taste and increasing income, and you have the Chuppies. As far as I'm concerned, they are destined to become the world's most important consumer group over the next 15 years.

Consumers in both the United States and Europe have long been drivers of the global economy. Most of these consumers are baby boomers born before 1965. They have acquired wealth and affluence over the past three decades and tend to spend a lot of money on nearly every product you can imagine. The stark reality, however, is that the boomers are aging. The oldest of the boomers are now over 60. Many of the people in this key demographic will soon be retiring from the labor market. The result is that their income and spending power will gradually decline in the coming decade as more and more of them exit the workforce.

This has already had a significant effect in many European and some Asian countries, where older people have retired and there simply are not enough members of subsequent generations to fill all the newly vacant job slots. Germany and Japan, for instance, have the second- and third-largest economies in the world, yet are among the nations with the lowest birth rates and highest percentages of seniors. And there is concern that there may not be enough younger people to provide services—especially health care—to boomers who are expected to live well into their eighties and nineties in those countries.

The United States has not yet faced this dearth of workers because of a higher population of young people. But the fact remains that there are proportionately fewer younger people in the workforce than there were during the boomers' peak years, and they will not have the breadth of buying power that boomers have had and will continue to have for just a few more years.

This raises a trillion-dollar question: When the boomers retire in the coming decade, who will pick up the slack in global consumer spending?

The answer is China, the world's fourth-largest economy with a fast-growing middle class numbering over 150 million. China's emerging middle class went from living at subsistence levels to having the means to dine out at least once a week at a midpriced restaurant in less than 15 years. Figure 10.2 shows just how much progress they've made in the past 20 years.

Number per 100 Urban Households					
	Refrigerators	Color TVs	Automobiles	Computers	Cellular Phones
1985	6.6	17.2	–	–	–
1990	42.3	59.0	–	–	–
1995	66.2	89.6	–	–	–
1999	77.7	111.6	0.3	5.9	7.1
2000	80.5	116.7	0.6	9.4	18.3
2001	82.2	119.9	0.8	12.5	30.6
2002	87.4	126.4	0.9	20.6	62.9
2003	88.7	130.5	1.4	27.8	90.1
2004	90.2	133.4	2.2	33.1	111.4

Figure 10.2 Rise of a New Global Consumer Class
SOURCE: InvestorPlace Media, LLC.

The demographics of China's population skew much younger than in other developed countries, with 71 percent of the population between 15 and 64 years old. While the Chuppies are a relatively small slice of the Chinese demographic pie at the moment, the number of Chuppies and their dependents is nonetheless staggering. They comprise at least 50 million consumers, and their ranks continue to grow at over 10 percent a year.

Chinese citizens under 45 are called "the lucky generation" by the media because they escaped the ravages of the Cultural Revolution—the disastrous radical movement that lasted from 1966 to 1976. During that period, almost all Chinese students were forced to give up their education and move to labor camps in rural farms to work alongside peasants. The movement prevented most Chinese born between 1950 and 1960 from receiving a higher education and caused tremendous suffering. Today, a large percentage of this unlucky generation continues to live in dire poverty because of their lack of education.

For the most part, those who were born after 1960 were too young to work in the countryside and came of age when China was starting on its path to economic reform in the 1980s. Today, they are well educated, savvy, and confident. They are also more concerned with their health. Because of better nutrition and a higher standard of living, Chinese younger than 40 often look different from members of the older generation. It's not just more hair and fewer wrinkles. The hardships suffered by many older Mainland Chinese have had a lasting effect on their physical appearance, whereas it is difficult to distinguish Chuppies younger than 30 from young ethnic Chinese professionals from other parts of the world.

Determined to Make Their Mark

No longer hindered by radical ideology, the Chuppies grew in prosperity as the China Miracle unfolded. Many Chuppies are proficient in English, and as globalization accelerated after the 1990s, a lot of them worked for and with foreign firms. They embraced globalization and talk often about the importance of getting China to "connect with the rest of the world." An overwhelming majority of Chuppies actually prefer to work with foreign companies rather than the old guard of Chinese SOEs and government entities. As you saw in Chapter 5 on SOEs, a significant majority of the successful entrepreneurs, professionals, and business leaders in China are in this age group.

Significantly, more than any other demographic group in China, Chuppies embrace American-style consumerism. They love stylish gadgets that set them apart from their less well-off countrymen. Their spending habits and rising income are defining them as a significant consumer force. I really believe that Chuppies will succeed the Yuppies as the driving force of global economic growth.

And yet Wall Street analysts, who usually visit only the Western establishments in China—if they even bother to go there at all—are missing this. While many articles and studies have been written about China's emerging middle class, there have been almost no widely published studies outside of China that deal with this emerging economic force.

That doesn't mean that the whole world is completely oblivious to Chuppies. In fact, not long ago, former Intel Capital Vice President Claude Leglise had this to say about investments in China: "I am particularly keen on companies that are targeting Chinese domestic consumption. American companies that use China as a low-cost source of goods or services—that's a viable investment strategy. But the part that's really fascinating is domestic consumption."

Intent on finding what really lies at the heart of consumerism in China, my company conducted the very first Chuppie consumer survey to be published in the United States. As part of my investment strategy, it was crucial to determine the investment opportunities presented by this influential demographic. Nobody had been following this group closely; certainly nobody on Wall Street. The Street talks about China's middle class as a whole, but the focus should be on the Chuppies in particular. I believe that understanding and following this particular group of consumers will keep you several steps ahead of Wall Street and other investors in the coming years.

To that end, my team in China surveyed 138 Chinese professionals under 45 years old who are making $10,000 to $80,000 a year. To put that in perspective, $10,000 in China is roughly equivalent to $40,000 in the United States in terms of purchasing power. A household making $10,000 a year in China is in the top 10 percent of all households in the country.

Our survey was designed to help my company better understand consumption habits in China in order to make the best investment decisions. And the results certainly provided a better insight as to where those investment opportunities lie. Here's what we found.

Housing

A full 67 percent of all Chuppies surveyed own their homes, while 14 percent rent and another 19 percent live at home with their parents. In an era of rising home prices, most Chuppies have already taken action and bought places of their own.

Seventy-eight percent of the homes were purchased by Chuppies for under 1 million yuan ($140,000). The rest were purchased for between 1 million to 3 million yuan ($420,000). Many of those homes are worth quite a bit more now. Many Taiwanese investors I know bought homes in Shanghai in the 3 million to 5 million yuan ($700,000) range. For $600,000, one can buy a new 2,000-square-foot condominium in a nice Shanghai neighborhood.

Even with the recent 15 percent decline in the Shanghai residential property market, home ownership is still a high priority in urban China. Many young women in Shanghai will not marry a man unless he has his own place, so it is not surprising that 63 percent of those who don't already own a place are saving money to buy one.

Disposable Income

Unlike many of their countrymen, Chuppies have disposable income that allows them to make impulse purchases, indulge in fashion and entertainment, and buy luxury goods. In the area of fashion—a decidedly new consumer goods sector in China—Chuppies have a keen awareness of high-end designer goods and are buying them. A full 85 percent of our survey takers know the names of top European designers. Unlike in Europe and the United States, most buyers of luxury designer goods in Asia are young people under 35 years old.

A quarter of our respondents said that they would be willing to buy a new Louis Vuitton purse worth 10,000 yuan ($1,400). The reason this is important when considering Chuppies is that 10,000 yuan is a lot of money to someone who makes only 20,000 yuan a month. Many young women say they would save money on food and rent to buy an expensive purse. The results clearly point to disposable income and a willingness to spend it. For example, it is not uncommon for a Chuppie to cut back on his or her food budget from, say, $10 a day to $3 a day so that in six months he can get that shirt from Prada or she can splurge on a Gucci handbag.

In addition to buying goods, Chuppies are traveling with their extra cash. A full 71 percent of our respondents have traveled outside of China, and another 14 percent have been to Hong Kong or Macau. Unlike many older Chinese, Chuppies are also more interested in traveling alone than being a part of a large tour group.

Personal Finance

An overwhelming majority (80 percent) of the Chuppies we surveyed have at least one credit card, which is 15 times that of the national average. Most of these credit cards (84 percent) were issued by a Chinese bank.

This finding ended up being one of the real jewels of the survey, as it is generally thought that most Chinese do not have credit cards. Clearly, we've uncovered the very beginning of an important new trend.

At the moment, Chuppies tend to be more disciplined in paying off their credit cards and avoiding debt than their American counterparts are. In fact, Chinese consumers across the board are less likely to go into debt—so far. Part of the reason is that across all demographics, only 45 million credit cards have been issued in China, which amounts to four cards per 100 adults. That number, however, is skewed by the huge numbers of non-Chuppies without cards. Chuppies in large cities typically have at least one card.

That may also change as advertising experts, like Jason Jiang (the founder of Focus Media whom I mentioned in Chapter 5 as part of the new generation of rich entrepreneurs), increasingly convince consumers of the benefits of instant gratification and living large, which is so much easier when they have credit cards.

Plus, with international banks now allowed to compete in China, I expect consumer credit to be one of the businesses banks will focus on in urban areas. I also expect Chinese banks to follow suit to keep up with their international competitors, and the number of credit cards in China should skyrocket in the next two years.

Despite their credit cards and zeal for luxury goods, however, Chuppies follow their countrymen's lead and are exceptional savers. Almost half of those we surveyed manage to save at least half of their income at the end of the month. China's poor health care system and lack of good investment options force Chinese to save money aggressively and keep their money in reserve.

Case Study: Focus Media

In the 1990 comedy *Opportunity Knocks*, Dana Carvey played a con man who came up with the idea of installing electronic advertising screens in toilet stalls to boost sales. Fifteen years later, Jason Jiang—a 32-year-old advertising entrepreneur in Shanghai—used a similar idea to build a multibillion-dollar company from scratch in less than three years. Instead of installing screens in public bathrooms, though, Focus Media (NASDAQ: FMCN) installs them in elevators of office buildings.

I first heard of Focus Media a couple of months before its initial public offering (IPO) because my former employer, Goldman Sachs, had invested more than $10 million of its own money in Focus Media. From my experience at Goldman, I know that any time the firm puts its own money on the line, it tends to make serious profits.

FMCN went public in July 2005 and raised $172 million for expansion and acquisition. After the IPO, FMCN grew rapidly by installing advertising screens in buildings, shopping malls, and supermarkets across China, targeting specific demographics to further suit the advertiser's requirements.

I got to see the results of Focus Media's efforts firsthand on several of my trips to China. It was fascinating to observe the 17-inch advertising screens, especially in skyscrapers, and how people reacted to them. Riding up an elevator in a 50-story office building, several of my American friends from Los Angeles were mesmerized by the Hennessy cognac commercial playing on the screen. I have to admit that I was impressed as well.

By placing these ad-playing television screens in fancy high-rent office buildings, advertisers can reach the crème de la crème of China's urban consumers—foreign expatriates, successful entrepreneurs, senior executives of SOEs, high-ranking government officials, and, of course, Chuppies. At that moment, I developed a greater appreciation for Jason Jiang's genius. His instincts have made him a billionaire, and rightly so. He is the embodiment of a smart entrepreneur who identified a potential market and then capitalized on it with a singular focus.

With increasing affluence in China, the advertising market is growing quickly. Focus Media continued to leverage that growth by expanding through acquisitions to run ads in elevators, cinemas, and stores, and on outdoor electronic billboards as well as tens of millions of cell phones. All in all, FMCN was the kind of stock I love: innovative, entrepreneurial, and dominant in a fast-growing market.

So as Focus Media was getting ready to report earnings in February 2006, I actually had to make a difficult choice (see Figure 10.3). I had seen a pattern emerge in strong Chinese companies like Focus Media where the stocks rallied ahead of their earnings reports and then sold off after earnings were announced. It's actually a fairly typical pattern with strong growth companies, and I believed the same thing was possible with Focus Media. Why? For one thing, the stock had done exceptionally well in the preceding months, and earnings expectations were very high.

I had also heard from some of my sources in Shanghai that the company's forward guidance could come in below Wall Street's expectations. There weren't any serious long-term concerns here, as any possible slowdown would be due to winter seasonality in Focus Media's advertising business, and the fact that

(Continued)

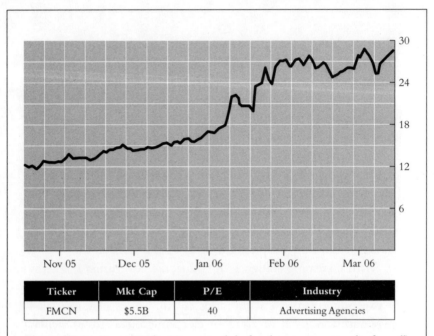

Ticker	Mkt Cap	P/E	Industry
FMCN	$5.5B	40	Advertising Agencies

Figure 10.3   Focus Media (One month before buy to one month after sell)
Source: InvestorPlace Media, LLC.

the whole nation practically shuts down for a week for Chinese New Year.

However, any forward guidance that might come in below expectations could result in short-term selling of the stock. Even if Focus managed to beat Wall Street's earnings estimates and deliver in-line guidance, I still expected the stock to sell off because expectations were so high. Additionally, when a stock runs as far and as fast as FMCN had, there was the risk of it getting overextended and becoming susceptible to selling pressure.

Because of the rally and the potential for a sell-off, I took the opportunity to lock in my profits. After holding FMCN for three months, it was up 83 percent, and that was a fantastic return by any measure.

It's worth noting that I still think Focus Media is a great company and a good long-term investment. But since my goal is to capitalize on near-term profits, the possibility of the stock's short-term momentum breaking down necessitated the sell.

I told my clients that if they had not gotten the chance to buy FMCN, they should be patient. When the stock pulls back and some of the shorter-term risk is out of it, it is quite likely that the stock will experience new momentum. And any stock that exhibits momentum driven by the China Miracle is worth jumping into.

Dining

As I mentioned, Chuppies like to dine out. Nearly half eat out for dinner at least three times a week. Roughly half of our respondents also eat at a Western-style restaurant at least once a week. And a full 57 percent of those surveyed ate at Pizza Hut at least once during the past three months. That's an interesting statistic for a single brand name. Pizza Hut is a popular midpriced restaurant of choice for Chinese interested in Western food and celebrating Western holidays. Along with Kentucky Fried Chicken, it is the reason I think restaurant purveyor Yum! Brands (NYSE: YUM) does well in China. Yum! is one of the few real American "China plays" for investors.

Cell Phones

Every Chuppie we surveyed owned at least one mobile phone. Nokia (NYSE: NOK) is the most popular brand, with Motorola (NYSE: MOT) a distant second. Interestingly, none of the Chuppies we surveyed owned a Chinese-made cell phone. Chinese-made cell phones are generally cheaper and less trendy than the phones made by Nokia and Motorola.

However, only 12 percent of the Chuppies surveyed plan to upgrade to third-generation (3G) services as they become available. I think this will change as enhanced services become available that are 3G-specific. The Chuppies love having the latest and greatest technology and gadgets, and I expect them to upgrade rapidly to 3G after unique features and appealing applications are introduced. Once 3G becomes something that China desires, it's only a matter of time until nimble companies capitalize on the trend.

Transportation

Most Chuppies do not own cars, because public transportation is cheap and efficient in major Chinese cities. Car ownership is expensive in Shanghai, where new owners must pay thousands in additional taxes and fees to register their vehicles. This is comparable to American cities like Manhattan, where I once had to pay $600 a month just for garage space. It's not surprising that most people in New York City and Shanghai do not own cars.

Most of the cars Chuppies have purchased cost them between 80,000 and 200,000 yuan ($10,000 to $25,000). A smaller percentage paid between 200,000 and 400,000 yuan ($25,000 to $50,000) for a car. Most of them do not have plans to buy a car in the near future.

Even though Chuppie attitudes toward car ownership have more to do with where they live than anything else, China's auto industry is still not a good investment right now. Most local car companies are losing money despite rapid growth and recent partnerships with American automotive giants like Chrysler. Low-priced Chinese autos like the Cherry—which has gotten a lot of U.S. media coverage—also have a reputation for being poorly made and unattractive looking.

Big Picture

Chuppies believe that government corruption is the greatest internal crisis facing China today, with 41 percent of the votes. This is further confirmation that you need to avoid most state-owned enterprises. Concerns over health care costs and rural poverty were roughly equal, with slightly over 20 percent of the votes each. Environmental pollution is fourth with only 13 percent of the votes.

I was only mildly surprised to learn that Bill Gates surpassed Mao Zedong as the most admired figure among Chuppies, with 43 percent of the votes. The chairman of Microsoft beat out the founding chairman of the Chinese Communist Party as the man Chuppies most look up to.

It's amazing how times have changed: Lei Feng, a Communist worker who sacrificed his life to public service—once touted as a role model in elementary school textbooks—received only 3 percent of the votes.

While hard work is still extremely important and highly valued, so is the prospect of being rewarded for that work. This has given rise to the entrepreneurial class in China as well as the accumulation of personal wealth and savings. The ability to buy desirable items—in addition to the basic necessities—is becoming part of China's consumer DNA. The Chuppies are not spending just on high-end designer items, though. They are practical people and are also spending heavily on education and health care, two overlooked areas that I believe are strong sectors that will provide great opportunities to investors.

The fundamental concept to take away from the survey is that Chinese who are economically successful want to be part of the global community. The government isolated its citizens for much of the past 40 years, but the rising prosperity resulting from the China Miracle has opened up consumerism as a vehicle for many Chinese to feel like participants in the world around them. As consumer spending grows, more businesses and jobs will be created to meet that demand. In turn, greater prosperity follows for both the Chinese people and investors like you and me.

This consumerism is too often ignored by analysts even when examining cultural trends that should provide obvious indicators of consumer shifts. Take the release of the movie *The Da Vinci Code*. The Ron Howard–directed thriller starring Tom Hanks was one of the most anticipated movies of 2006 and actually set a new box office opening record in China.

On the face of it, this is surprising. After all, *The Da Vinci Code* is based on Dan Brown's best-selling novel, a controversial story dealing with Renaissance paintings, church conspiracy, secret societies, and other subject matters unique to Western civilization. Most Chinese do not know Christian religious history and have never visited the Louvre, where Leonardo da Vinci's painting, the Mona Lisa, is housed and where much of the movie takes place.

So why did so many people in China rush to see the movie? Because a growing number of Chinese, especially Chuppies, are trendy and eager to learn. They knew that the novel was an international best seller and went to see the movie based on its buzz. Most Chinese wouldn't be able to relate to the movie's basic history, but they went in order to learn about Western culture and be a part of the global *Da Vinci Code* phenomenon.

What's more, Chuppies and the up-and-coming middle class are paying $8 to see movies in an actual theater. This is also a significant cultural change. Many Chinese still resort to buying the $1 or $2 bootleg on the street, but Chuppies want the full experience.

So there is more going on here than just the fact that *The Da Vinci Code* did blockbuster business its opening weekend in China. It's an indicator of what consumers are looking for and where they're willing to spend their money. Digging beneath the surface of the box office numbers says a lot about what's going on in China today. It is similar to understanding the impact of how over the past 10 years, more than 200 million Chinese went from living on less than $2 a day to being able to eat out at a midpriced restaurant at least once a week. That's the kind of knowledge and understanding that is crucial to building investment wealth from the Chinese economy.

The existence of the Chuppies gives statistical credence to the impact of the vast wealth creation and social upward mobility in the country. The two-year 300 percent run-up in the Mainland Chinese stock market and the five-year 200 percent run-up in many urban property markets have created significant wealth for millions of Chinese in the relatively short period of time since reforms were implemented.

While it may seem like the Chuppies are just a number in a demographic segment, I'd like to give you insight into some of their personal stories to show you just how real the China Miracle is. I know several people who personify the kind of prosperity that's becoming more common on the Mainland. Their ambition and success are inspiring and show the various ways in which the shape of China's economy is changing. Their stories are not about the huge factories turning out clothes, computers, dolls, and TVs. Rather, their stories show why investing in China is about so much more than buying shares in another faceless SOE.

The Rise of the Chuppies: Frances

Through a combination of savings, hard work, and good investments, millions of Chuppies under 30 have already amassed assets of $100,000 on incomes of less than $2,000 a month. By contrast, many young

Americans make more than twice that amount but have a tough time building a financial nest egg.

Frances is a consultant for my *China Strategy* newsletter and fills my need for an in-China consumer trends analyst. She is a typical Chuppie living in Shanghai today. Like millions of others living in Shanghai, she originally came from another part of China. A native of Wuhan in central China, Frances moved to Shanghai after college several years ago and found a job in the city.

Her first job as an account representative at a state-owned dairy company paid only $3,000 a year. Eager to improve her situation, Frances found a new position working as an account executive at a public relations firm that handles promotional events for several prominent French luxury product lines, such as Chanel and Remy Martin. Her income doubled with the new job, and she gained exposure to both a high-end clientele in Shanghai and high-end luxury goods.

True to Chuppie form, instead of spending her money on luxury designer goods, Frances saved her money to buy a condominium. She bought a small condo three years ago for $40,000, and moved her mother from Wuhan to Shanghai to live with her. Today, her condo is worth more than $55,000.

After working in public relations for two years, Frances found a better-paying opportunity with the Texas-based cosmetics company Mary Kay International. Mary Kay has a sales force of 320,000 in China, and Frances worked at China's corporate headquarters as a communication executive for the company's sales reps. Today, she travels often to different provinces throughout China and communicates constantly with the pink army of Mary Kay sales reps. Frances is making more than $15,000 a year, which is in the top quartile of earners in Mainland China.

I met Frances two years ago in Shanghai and was very impressed by her knowledge of a variety of consumer trends. I hired her to contribute to my boots-on-the-ground team of researchers because of her constant contact with ambitious young Chinese men and women throughout the country. Frances helps us keep a pulse on what (and where) Chuppies are buying. In fact, her observations helped lead me to companies like travel facilitator Ctrip and online gamer The9, two companies that have become successful thanks to shifts in China's popular culture.

In addition to being a successful professional, Frances is also a successful investor. She characterizes herself as a conservative investor and says she is concerned about the high valuations in Shanghai's A-shares market. Nevertheless, she has a portion of her liquid net worth in Chinese domestic mutual funds, which have done well. She also dabbles in currency speculation and has made some nice gains in that area. As a result, at the young age of 29, Frances has managed to build a nest egg of approximately $100,000 on an annual income below $20,000.

Frances's story is a good example of a broader phenomenon: Many Chinese businesspeople who are successful often invest in securities and real estate.

Capitalizing on the Opportunities: Kou Men-Yuen

Stocks and real estate are two of the biggest wealth-creating opportunities for hundreds of millions of Chinese entrepreneurs. For instance, Zhu Jun, the dynamic founder and chairman of online gaming company The9 (NASDAQ: NCTY), is a significant player in Shanghai's real estate market. In fact, more Chinese centimillionaires and billionaires have made their fortunes from real estate than any other industry.

Recently, I visited my friend Kou Men-yuen, the chairman and founder of Gold Taiyuan Group, a wildly successful real estate development company. Kou's story shows how China's thriving real estate market has created vast fortunes.

With a personal net worth of more than $300 million, Kou is a leading real estate developer in the Pudong area of Shanghai. Pudong, officially known as Pudong New Area, is the newest section of the world's fastest-growing major city.

Once a rural stretch of farmland, Pudong sits across the Huangpu River from the older, established sections of Shanghai in Puxi. As recently as 15 years ago, Pudong was still mostly weeds and swampland. In the early 1990s, ex-Shanghai mayor Jiang Zhe-min became China's president and decided to restore Shanghai to its former pre–World War II glory.

In order to raise Shanghai's profile, Jiang set in motion a new policy that turned the Pudong area into a Special Economic Zone. The Chinese government worked hard to transform Pudong into China's version of Manhattan, and by the mid-1990s, nearly 30 percent of the world's construction cranes were located in Pudong, helping the boom-ing district build out its infrastructure.

The story of how my friend Kou became a centimillionaire mir-rors the emergence of Pudong. A native of Pudong when it was still rural farmland, Kou moved to Hong Kong during the early 1980s. At a time when Mainland China had a shortage of goods, Kou started his own import-export firm and made incredible profits in his business. By the late 1980s, he had amassed a small personal fortune and decided to enter the furniture manufacturing business in order to use China's cheap labor to good advantage.

When Jiang decided to make Pudong China's financial center, Kou was ready to invest heavily in his hometown. Because he knew the local officials and the geography of Pudong better than other devel-opers, Kou was able to buy large tracts of land at prime locations at a very nice price. His real estate empire grew right alongside Pudong's emergence.

In 2001, Kou made a very smart move: He built a residential complex called Xiang Mei Garden across the street from Shanghai's biggest park. The complex contains more than 2,200 high-rise condominiums with plenty of greenery and recreation space. The units sold well because of the complex's excellent location and design. Xiang Mei Garden's suc-cess catapulted my friend into the ranks of China's superrich.

Kou owes his success to two major factors. First, he had overseas connections that helped him get his Pudong projects off the ground. He used resources and initial capital from Hong Kong to start building in Pudong. Many other Chinese entrepreneurs I've discussed in these pages also had strong overseas connections when they started, including Zhu Jun of The9 and Shi Zhengrong of Suntech Power.

And second, in addition to his foreign connections, Kou also had local knowledge of Pudong. Many foreign investors who moved into Pudong during the 1990s went bust. But because Kou was originally from Pudong and had superior local connections and knowledge, he was able to thrive where others failed. The combination of foreign resources and local knowledge was crucial to his success.

Even though Kou is already very rich, it is a near certainty that he'll continue to be successful in new projects. That's because he is at the right place at the right time doing the right thing. He watches the trends in China and he takes advantage of them, looking at their potential for long-term returns.

That is exactly what investing in China is all about. You need to take a local perspective, mix it with a global strategy, and add in consumer trends. Kou exemplifies good business strategy, and you should look for these qualities when investing in any company that operates in China.

When you invest in China, look for the trends that provide an indication of how Chuppies are spending their money. Do it in the same way as you would when assessing the consumer sentiment in the United States. Are home sales rising, and where? Are luxury good manufacturers noting rising sales in the Mainland? To what degree are restaurant chains and vacation hotels expanding? Are U.S. filmmakers seeing a significant revenue uptick from their China releases? And what kinds of movies are the Chinese going to see? When you apply these types of questions to your China investments, as you would to similar investments in the United States, then you have a basis for informed investing in the movers of China's economy.

In all cases, the important question to ask is this one: Are these companies seeing their bottom lines positively affected by their positions in China?

Here is one last note about the importance of China's consumers to the global economy. Not long after I started talking about the rise of the Chinese middle class, *U.S. News & World Report* did a cover article on the Chuppie phenomenon. The magazine even appropriated my term.

That should give you an indication that understanding Chuppies will put you on the right track to profiting from China's economy.

Chapter 11

Serving the People

I've talked extensively about what it is that China's economy needs and desires, what is made in China, and how the increasingly afflu- ent Chuppies are fundamental to the country's growth.

One thing I haven't talked about is the population as a whole. With 1.3 billion people, China is home to more than one-fifth of all the people in the world. Regardless of their income level, they are each in some way contributing to the China Miracle—as producers and consumers, and oftentimes both.

Not every person in China is going to buy soft drinks or TVs, just as not every consumer is going to buy cattle or grain or farm tools or wheelbarrows. And very few of them, in relative numbers, are going to be buying things we consider to be staples of the U.S. economy, such as houses and cars.

However, as people they will all require food, water, shelter, medical services, and means for generating income. In this way, the people of China are like those of any other nation; there are certain facts of eco- nomic life that apply to all of us, no matter where we live. Yet China is in a unique position in regard to other countries. Its supercharged economy is creating a world power that resembles no other nation. For example, it is emerging from third world status so quickly that many of its cities now have a better infrastructure than icons like New York, London, and Tokyo. Unlike other countries long mired in poverty, China is moving millions of its people up from a subsistence level every single year. In the span of a decade its economy has leapfrogged the economies of all but three other nations.

The Need to Feed

With that growth has come the need to pay more attention to the physical needs of the Chinese populace.

As emerging countries develop, they require more resources to sustain their ever-growing populations. I've talked about commodities from iron to energy, but the most basic—and most important—resource of all is food. Nations with growing economies and rising populations need more food, plain and simple.

China's rising middle class is calling for both a greater quantity and a better quality of food. This is no easy task for any country. With industrialization and urban sprawl taking over, Chinese farmers are continually asked to produce more crops from shrinking amounts of land. They also have fewer farm workers. If you add environmental pressures to the mix, you've got a situation that's even more challenging.

One of the best ways to increase crop output without having to install expensive equipment is to use fertilizer. A couple of possible plays are two fertilizing companies that are the best of their breed.

It is estimated that one dollar out of every three dollars earned in China is spent on food. Why? Because the dietary habits of Chinese are changing. People are switching from starch-based diets (rich in grains and vegetables) to protein-rich diets (which contain more meat). This is a natural shift that many countries experience when moving through the various stages of economic development.

This shift is best illustrated by the rising meat consumption in China. Meat consumption there has tripled over the past two decades and continues to grow at 4 percent to 5 percent per year (still not enough to sustain the McDonald's hamburger franchise, but that's another story). As a result, farmers must produce increasing amounts of grain to feed livestock. In order to grow these grains, farmers can't rely on ground nutrients alone; they need fertilizer.

With 850 million farmers challenged to feed over 1.3 billion people, China consumes more fertilizer than any other country. Making things complicated is the fact that much of western China is unusable for crop production. The western part of the country is full of barren land that is too remote because of a lack of suitable transportation and infrastructure. As a result, southeastern China is the main home to much of the country's agriculture. Farmers in this region often double- and triple-crop their land in order to produce more rice, fruits, and vegetables—all of which depend on fertilizer to grow.

In addition, global demand is driving up the prices of many agricultural commodities, like rice, coffee, sugar, bananas, cocoa, and palm oil. These in-demand crops all need large amounts of fertilizer to grow.

Fertilizer isn't used just to grow food crops—it's also used to grow products for other industries. The push for developing eco-friendly biofuels in China is huge right now. Given that biofuels are mainly made from natural plant-based sources like corn, soybeans, and sugarcane, these plants require farmers to buy even more fertilizer.

Increasing demand for food, animal feed, and biofuels is providing a very positive outlook for the fertilizer industry. I expect China's fertilizer demand to grow by 15 percent to 20 percent per year over the next five years.

I know it doesn't get much less glamorous than fertilizer in a world of high-tech hype, but it also doesn't get more essential.

When considering the demand for fertilizer, I decided that the two primary players in this field were equally good bets to benefit from the China Miracle. I don't usually do this, as competitors in most markets typically have to cannibalize each other to increase their market share or their revenues. But in the case of the fertilizer market, the demand is so huge and the competitive landscape so small that the number one and two players in the industry have both been extremely successful without beating each other up. Contrast that with high-tech plays like Dell versus Gateway versus Hewlett-Packard, which is an ongoing competitive bloodbath.

In addition, I liked how these two companies were positioned, how they were expanding their businesses, and how they were building their China positions. I felt that since both companies were doing so well in a market that caters to what China needs—and needs desperately—there was very good reason to have positions in both.

The first of the two companies is Potash Corporation of Saskatchewan Inc. (NYSE: POT). Known simply as Potash Corp., it is the world's largest fertilizer producer. With 22 percent of the world's overall potash capacity and 75 percent of its excess capacity, Potash Corp. will play an essential role in global agriculture for years to come. The second is Mosaic Company (NYSE: MOS), the world's second-largest fertilizer producer, which gets nearly 10 percent of its business from China, a number that has plenty of room for growth given China's explosive demand.

Both Potash Corp. and Mosaic are world leaders in the production of the three major types of fertilizer: phosphate, potash, and nitrogen. Producing fertilizer is no easy feat, and it's a very expensive process. Let me explain why.

Phosphate fertilizer comes from phosphate rock, which is found in ore beds rich with the fossils of ancient marine life. The phosphate rock is crushed and combined with acids to produce phosphoric acid, which is used as a feedstock for fertilizers.

Fortunately, phosphate rock is plentiful and can be found in many regions around the world. However, high-quality phosphate rock is scarce. As a result, roughly a dozen countries generated a staggering 97 percent of the world's total production between 2006 and 2007. That means a large amount of phosphate—a full 45 percent—is traded across borders. Mosaic is the number-one phosphate fertilizer producer, with 15 percent of the world's capacity and 56 percent of U.S. production. The United States is the largest exporter, while China is the second-largest importer after India. Potash Corp. is the number-three phosphate fertilizer producer, with 2.4 million tons of output or 6 percent of the world's capacity.

The second kind of fertilizer is potash. Potash is mined from underground deposits left behind when giant bodies of water evaporated millions of years ago. Good potash deposits are rare, and although it is consumed in more than 150 countries, potash production is limited to only 12 countries. The world's largest deposits are in Saskatchewan, where Potash Corp. has all of its potash business. Almost 80 percent of the world's potash production is traded across borders. Canada is the largest potash-producing region, while China is the largest importing country. Potash Corp. is the number-one potash mining and processing company, with 13.2 million tons of output or 22 percent of the world's capacity. Mosaic is the number-two potash mining and processing company, with 13 percent of the world's capacity.

The high cost of building mines keeps would-be competitors out of the fertilizer market altogether. In fact, no new potash mines have been built since 1995! This is because the development of mines and new processing facilities carries a staggering level of capital costs: It costs about $2 billion to set up a two-million-ton potash project, or $1.3 billion for a plant with the capacity of one million tons of phosphate. This financial barrier to entry is a tremendous competitive advantage for strong fertilizer producers like Potash and Mosaic. The complex methods used to produce fertilizers are simply too expensive for new businesses to jump into the industry.

Nitrogen fertilizers, the third type, are made from organic waste material. It takes less work to produce them than mined fertilizers, and both companies have a significant presence in this sector as well.

Now here's the background on these companies and why I like them. I'll start with Potash Corp. Headquartered in Saskatoon, Canada, it went public on the Toronto and New York stock exchanges in 1989. The company produces all three major kinds of fertilizer in locations around the world: potash in Canada, phosphate and feed supplements in the United States and Brazil, and nitrogen in the United States and Trinidad. Each business segment contributes one-third to the company's total sales.

The company has maintained a dominant position in the market due to expanding and leveraging its existing capabilities. Yet, in addition to its internal growth strategies, Potash Corp. has used its strong cash flow to invest in areas that will further enhance its long-term value and international advantages in potash. Its investments include 32 percent in Sociedad Quimica y Minera de Chile S.A. in Chile, 28 percent of Arab Potash Company in Jordan, 10 percent of Israel Chemicals Ltd. in Israel, and 20 percent of Sinofert Holdings Limited, the largest importer and largest integrated distributor of fertilizer products in China.

These investments were important contributors to the company's success in 2006, and give it significant control over future supplies.

The company is aggressive, as well. In the first half of 2007, Potash Corp. reported that its sales jumped 40 percent to $2.5 billion while gross margin almost doubled. To me, these big numbers reflected strengthening price and volume performance in all three business segments. The company greatly benefited from a significant increase in potash volumes. Plus, potash supply is very tight now as global customers attempt to rebuild inventories in the face of extremely high consumption.

I'll turn now to Mosaic. Headquartered in Minneapolis, Minnesota, the company was founded in 2004 by combining two giants of the fertilizer industry: IMC Global and Cargill Crop Nutrition.

Mosaic produces all three major kinds of fertilizer. Phosphate accounts for 53 percent of the company's sales, potash makes up 21 percent of sales, and nitrogen contributes to 3 percent of sales. Mosaic's phosphate business segment includes fully integrated operations in Florida and Louisiana. In 2006, Mosaic produced 9.9 million tons of phosphate fertilizer, and 5 million of those tons were exported.

The company operates six potash mines in North America: four large-scale mines in Saskatchewan, Canada, and two mines in the United States. The company produced 10.3 million tons of potash last year, and 40 percent of it was exported abroad to nations like China, Brazil, India, Japan, and Malaysia.

In 2007, Mosaic's second-quarter earnings report showed that net sales increased 44 percent to $2.2 billion. Gross margin—something I place a lot of emphasis on—for the quarter was 28.4 percent! Earnings during the first three quarters of 2007 skyrocketed 265 percent. That's momentum. And in order to meet strong global demand for fertilizers, Mosaic expanded its Saskatchewan potash mines by adding 1.1 million tons to an annual capacity of 5.3 million tons.

With greater volumes, higher prices, and lower unit costs being factors in the strategies of both companies, Potash Corp. and Mosaic are well positioned to deliver record returns and increased value for shareholders. As I expect the strong agricultural market to last at least a few years, both these companies offer potentially strong return on momentum for some time to come. And should either of them lose momentum, the sheer size of the demand for fertilizer in China will continue to present a variety of opportunities well into the next decade.

China's upwardly mobile citizens will expect, naturally, that there will be enough food for them to buy. And with that upwardly mobile status, they will begin to buy a greater variety of food, some of it at a premium. For many, paying higher prices for better and more diverse food products will mark the first time they've experienced this phenomenon.

In fact, across the country, people will now have the opportunity— many for the first time—to spend money in ways that no one expected 20 years ago. Things as disparate as life insurance, better health care, and even American-branded fast food are among the options that Chinese are able to consider as their income levels increase. We take these things for granted; indeed, they are such a part of our daily lives that we rarely give them a second thought (although the cost of health care is now part of our ongoing political debates).

But for the people in Mainland China, these are businesses that offer new opportunities for them in their personal lives. And smart investors should keep track of how quickly the Chinese people adopt and embrace, and spend their money on, these previously off-limits goods and services.

A Plastic Plan

There are many businesses that have a huge potential to capitalize on the new lifestyle options available to the average Chinese citizen. One of them involves those little pieces of plastic that you and I carry around with us every single day: credit cards.

As I've mentioned, increasing wealth and rising income levels in China are leading to more spending by people in every region of the country, and that condition is only going to accelerate. The way the Chinese people manage that money is going to change substantially in the months and years to come as foreign banks are permitted to do business in China. I expect these banks to bring their credit card expertise to China, resulting in an explosion of new plastic that will unleash pent-up consumer demand.

As we've discussed briefly, China's credit card penetration rate is only 2 percent, compared with 100+ percent in the United States. That's a startling contrast, but several factors will lessen this gap in the near future. First off, China opened its doors to international banks only a few years ago. Prior to that, non-Chinese banks were prevented from doing business in Mainland China. Now that China is welcoming select banks to operate within its borders, financial institutions from around the globe have been lining up to enter the country. At the head of the pack is financial giant Citigroup (NYSE: C), which in 2006 led a consortium that acquired 85 percent of the Guangdong Development Bank (GDB). Citigroup expects to have not only operational control and significant influence on how the bank is run, but also access to GDB's 500 bank branches.

You and I both know that one thing U.S. banks are extremely good at is marketing credit cards, and I look for consumer lending to become one of the biggest growth sectors in China. It's a relatively new concept to most Chinese, who have not had access to credit and are traditionally risk-averse. This has led to the reputation the Chinese have as renowned savers. The savings rate in the country is 35 percent, another sharp contrast to America's financial state, where the savings rate is under 2 percent.

With more money in their hands—you'll recall that the annual income has increased from $100 to over $2,000 per annum over the past 20 years—I think the Chinese will appreciate the fact that more money buys more things, even when purchases are made on credit. This realization will be driven in part by aspirational consumption as well as marketing messages from financial institutions. It's very likely that the number of Chinese with credit cards will double next year and continue to grow rapidly for a long time.

Chinese banks are already trying to preempt credit card competition from the newly established foreign banks by issuing credit cards en masse, especially to the more affluent middle-class Chuppies. Based on what I've learned from my analysts in China, it's far easier to get credit cards today than it was just a year ago.

My consumer-trend analyst, Frances, is a great example. She's the woman I told you about in the previous chapter. Frances had one credit card for a little over a year. She had to fill out more than five applications in order to get that card, and it came with a credit limit of 10,000 yuan. Things have changed markedly in intervening months. Over the past year, she's received two new gold cards from different Chinese banks . . . without even applying for them!

Those cards came preapproved and with higher credit limits of 20,000 and 15,000 yuan, even though she didn't have to disclose any financial information. Her total credit line went from 10,000 yuan barely a year ago to 45,000 yuan today without any increase in her personal income.

Frances also told me that she is tempted to buy a new Louis Vuitton purse with her new credit cards. Therein lies a trend: I believe greater access to credit cards will unleash pent-up demand and lead to the greatest consumer explosion the world has ever seen. Chinese people will begin to use credit cards in the same way that industrialized nations do. And it won't be solely for luxury goods; household appliances, TVs, stereos, home furnishings, and clothing are all certain to be acquired in greater numbers thanks to the availability of credit cards. Most important, these goods are not solely the domain of Chuppies—every Chinese home can benefit from appliances such as microwaves and washing machines as well as television sets.

So how do you profit from the expected increase in credit card use? Here's something that might sound contradictory: You don't profit by investing in the banks—at least not yet. China's banking sector is still a mess and is undergoing tremendous chaos as international banks set up shop and compete for market share. The situation will ultimately get better, and the Chinese government is doing a good job at enforcing better practices within domestic banks; but I believe it will be some time before everything is cleaned up to the point where you want to invest in banks as a means to tap into the China Miracle.

Instead of looking to banks, the best way to profit from credit card growth will be by investing in the products Chinese consumers will spend their money on, as well as those companies that will benefit from encouraging the use of credit cards. The majority of your stocks should fit into those categories. As I've pointed out, these are industries and businesses like tourism, entertainment, wireless communication, consumer electronics, health care, education, and dining out. If the Chinese desire it and can now buy it with a credit card, then it's an investment that is already on the right track.

There's another industry that stands to benefit from credit cards simply because the cost of service is typically higher—and less subject to consumer trends—than that of services in other businesses. I'm talking about health care.

Keeping Healthy

Health care is a major issue in the United States right now—not necessarily the quality of health care (there are great doctors and hospitals), but its cost. As prices rise, more and more Americans are paying their medical bills or their co-pay plans with credit cards.

The importance of health care today cannot be overstated. This is true worldwide, but the United States is especially concerned with health care and medicine due to aging baby boomers. Boomers born between 1946 and 1964 make up the largest demographic group in the United States, accounting for more than a quarter of the total population and a much greater proportion of the economy. With all of us getting older and living longer, we're going to require more health care services as a nation than ever before. This is also true in Europe and Japan. The result is that health care costs around the world are likely to rise sharply.

In China, health care costs are already rising about 12 percent to 15 percent a year because of the shift from a government-controlled economy to a market economy. From 1978 to 2003, the Chinese central government's share of national health care spending fell by two-thirds, from 32 percent to 12 percent. Due to this shift, Chinese consumers bear more of the burden for their health care than they used to, and personal health care spending has increased a whopping 4,000 percent since 1978.

A country the size of China has the same health issues common to the rest of the world, but the diversity of its population creates some unique concerns. Much of the population still lives in the countryside and on farms, which are breeding grounds for various forms of the flu, and China's polluted air and water have been singled out by international health organizations as among the very worst in the world.

I remember well the outbreak of severe acute respiratory syndrome (SARS) that hit China in 2003. In my mind's eye, I can still see the images of people walking around the streets of China wearing surgical masks to avoid getting hit by the sometimes fatal virus. Travel in and out of the country was curtailed, and there were fears that the virus would spread around the world.

I was not in China at the time, but I did watch the news virtually every night as it was broadcast from China and other countries. The Chinese government came under severe criticism for trying to keep information about the outbreak quiet and not doing enough to protect its citizens. The tragic event made the Chinese government even more aware of the need to improve its health care system, and doing so has since become a top priority.

But China faces the same problem with rising medical costs that the rest of the world has been wrestling with. Costs will continue to escalate in the coming years as more people get older, and service providers will be forced to cut costs by using less expensive medical instruments and laboratory devices. This is a leverage point for investors: With costs rising around the world, companies that provide cheaper medical solutions will do extremely well in the health care arena.

China is all too aware of the need to contain costs. The move away from central government sponsorship of medicine and treatment to a general pay-for-service model (similar to what we have in the United States) has hit the Chinese people hard. As a result, China's health care costs are actually growing faster than its economy.

From 1978 to 2003, the Chinese central government's share of national health care spending fell by two-thirds, from 32 percent to 12 percent. During the same period, personal health care spending in the country increased dramatically by a factor of 40, rocketing up from $1.35 to $55 per person—a stunning 4,000 percent increase. Health care costs continue to grow 12 percent to 15 percent per year.

The government is trying to keep these costs in check. It has imposed price controls on routine services and standard surgeries at publicly owned hospitals. However, when you dig below the surface, you'll find a loophole in this policy: The government allows medical facilities to earn profits from high-technology diagnoses such as ultrasound imaging. In order to make a profit, Chinese hospitals routinely prescribe these premium diagnoses.

Diagnostic testing is generally viewed as an effective method of reducing costs and improving the quality of health care. Since the SARS outbreak, in-vitro diagnostics (IVD) of blood, urine, saliva or other bodily fluids, cells, and other substances from patients have been used more frequently to diagnose and analyze various diseases and disorders. China's IVD market is projected to grow 14 percent a year through 2010, making it the fastest-growing IVD market in the world and more than double the average of 6 percent.

Through the end of 2006, there were nearly 20,000 hospitals and over 40,000 health care clinics in China. The market penetration of medical equipment commonly used in the West in still very low in these health care facilities. Thus, there is plenty of room for growth as more and more hospitals purchase advanced technology to compete for patients and generate additional profits. As a result, China's medical device market is projected to grow 35 percent from $7.5 billion in 2004 to $10.1 billion in 2008.

There are many companies in China that are producing medical devices, just as there are many companies making computers and TVs. But medical devices are significantly different from other electronics devices: They must have an exceedingly low failure rate and a high performance level in order to succeed in overseas markets.

Sorting through the myriad of medical instrument companies, I came upon Mindray Medical (NYSE: MR). Of all the Chinese companies traded on the American exchanges, Mindray is ideally positioned to benefit from several of the most significant socioeconomic trends in the twenty-first century: (1) China's economic emergence and health care industry reform, (2) the graying of the population in developed countries, and (3) rising health care costs around the world.

In many ways, Mindray Medical is the Chinese company that epitomizes my entire investment philosophy. It is a private-sector company started by two Chinese scientists with advanced degrees; it is not a state-owned enterprise (SOE). The company's largest outside shareholder is one of the smartest global investors around: Goldman Sachs. And it is capitalizing on important trends occurring both within China and throughout the rest of the world.

Mindray is the number-one medical devices company in China, and is growing swiftly in the global medical device and laboratory instrument industry, which already rakes in $80 billion a year. The company manufactures and sells more than 40 medical devices in three business segments—patient monitoring devices, diagnostic laboratory instruments, and ultrasound imaging systems—and it is the leader in all of these segments in China.

The company was founded in 1991 by CEO Xu Hang, a graduate of the prestigious Tsinghua University in Beijing. Mindray obtained its ISO 9001 quality assurance certification in 1995, an important recognition of high-quality standards in the medical instrument industry, and most of its products are Food and Drug Administration (FDA)-approved for use in the United States or are CE marked for use in Europe.

In 2006, the stock was offered to investors on the New York Stock Exchange and proved itself as a China-based business that has all the qualities of a sound investment: great earnings growth, high profit margins, a large and rapidly growing user market, favorable government relations, fast-growing penetration into a giant global market, top-tier institutional sponsorship, reasonable valuation, tremendous international growth, and a dominant industry position within China itself.

Not only has Mindray dominated the business in China, but it is now the world's leading low-cost producer of high-quality medical devices. It has a tremendous competitive edge in that it sells its products 30 percent cheaper than its international competitors. In total, Mindray's products are sold in over 120 countries, and the company's international business has tripled since 2003. Currently, approximately 43 percent of sales come from outside of China, up significantly from only 26 percent two years ago.

The company's U.S. market grew from nothing three years ago to become its largest foreign market today. The United States is also the company's fastest-growing market; Mindray's North American sales shot up by 73 percent in 2006. Even with this impressive growth, its global market share is still only 0.3 percent, giving it nearly unlimited room for growth.

If the way it has scaled up in its homeland is any indication, Mindray has positioned itself well for global growth. Within China, the company has the largest sales and service network of any medical device manufacturer, with over 1,950 distributors and 500 direct sales and support personnel. This extensive network gives Mindray the advantage of being close to its customers, enabling it to be more responsive to local market demand than its competitors. As a result, sales and earnings have been soaring at over 50 percent per year. It's hard to find that kind of return from manufacturers who are selling almost exclusively in heavily developed regions like Europe and North America. A growth rate like this is one of the reasons I believe smart investors—with an eye toward wide-open markets—can profit from China's growth.

Another thing Mindray is poised to benefit from is Beijing's plan to increase health care spending. As part of Beijing's Social Harmony campaign, the budget allocated for health care in rural areas is expected to increase by 20 percent per year over the next several years. Since Mindray is the market leader in China for standard hospital and clinic equipment—with market share ranging from 25 percent to 32 percent for devices in this category—the company stands to be one of the biggest beneficiaries of the spending increase.

I also like the fact that Mindray spends heavily on research and development, which has resulted in a steady stream of new products. Ten percent of revenues are spent on R&D, and in the past three years the company developed more than 20 new products, which now comprise more than 35 percent of revenues.

Most important, Mindray is an entrepreneurial private-sector company with quality management. It's a company where management's interests are aligned with the interests of shareholders. The two top managers own 46 percent of the company, and Wall Street powerhouse Goldman Sachs (still the quintessential smart money institutional investor), owns an additional 6 percent of the shares.

Mindray is an exceptionally fine representation of how China-based manufacturers can succeed in serving the needs of both the Chinese people and the demands of the international marketplace. By focusing on seemingly disparate elements—low-cost equipment in an industry with a reputation for overpriced services—it has managed to succeed in a way that should make any investor, in any country, sit up and take notice.

As more and more Chinese companies gain expertise in the health care arena, they will find their way to the global market and then to global exchanges. Many of them are certain to be low-cost, low-reliability, low-function providers, offering little more than a cheap alternative to quality wares from competitors. But those that can marshal China's resources, such as low-cost manufacturing coupled with performance comparable to established providers, will gain substantial inroads into the health care market. Hospitals worldwide will continue to expand, and pricing pressure will force them to continue looking at ways to improve their bottom line. Assistance in achieving economies of scale will not come from India or Vietnam or even Europe and Japan; it will come from manufacturers based in China.

Health care is directly tied to the health of individuals within a nation. Though we don't like to think about it—and rarely do—we view health care as a necessity that goes hand in hand with getting older. I will bet that most of us rarely considered the importance of health plans when we were in our twenties. Such things matter more as we age, and when we have families to take care of. (I'd also bet that we think of investing in the same way.) It's when we get married and have children that we start giving serious thought to our physical and financial well-being. This leads us to consider our own mortality—and its financial repercussions. On the surface it may be grim to think about, but these concerns lie at the heart of the life insurance business. And this is a business that the Chinese are just now being exposed to.

Investing in Insurance

Many individual investors scoff at the thought of investing in insurers. It's such a staid business that we usually look to more dynamic industries. Whether it be offering coverage of automobiles and homes or providing life and casualty plans, insurance could hardly be less interesting to most investors. However, none other than Warren Buffett has profited mightily from having GEICO as a cornerstone of his investments. There's a lot to be learned from that. When an increasing number of people need insurance, there's money to be made. In China, cars and homes are not yet owned by enough of the population to make insuring them a viable investment consideration. However, there are more than a billion real live people in China, and millions of them are looking to acquire life insurance for the first time.

If I took a random poll and asked people to name the most explosive sectors in Asia, I doubt many would put insurance on the list. Yet in China, the insurance industry is growing a solid 15 percent a year. Even more important to the long-term potential, just 2.7 percent of the people there had insurance at the end of 2005. That's far below the levels in other Asian countries and in the United States, and about half the global average of nearly 5 percent.

As the Chinese middle class expands and people there take charge of their own destinies, more people will purchase insurance. In the coming years, I look for China's insurance industry to grow rapidly and eventually become the largest insurance market in the world.

There are several important factors that make China's insurance market a great opportunity for investors: (1) a huge and aging population base; (2) soaring economic growth, improving income levels and affluence, and a growing middle class; (3) the dismantling of the government-provided social safety net; (4) an increasingly educated population; (5) urbanization; and (6) lack of attractive investment alternatives. Most of these have been key elements in the creation of the China Miracle.

I've already explained how the Chinese people are excellent savers. Yet, as China moves away from its socialist ideals, public retirement and health plans have deteriorated. This has generated high demand for personal retirement accounts and protection vehicles such as life insurance.

Over the past decade, China's life insurance business has grown about 30 percent each year, twice the rate of the insurance sector as a whole, making China the world's fastest-growing major life insurance market. Rapid growth is expected to continue for at least a couple of years, and by next year China will likely exceed $100 billion in premiums, surpassing France and Germany.

The life insurance industry in China is heavily protected from foreign and private sector competition, so the top three Chinese insurance companies have a combined market share of 70 percent. But 70 percent of the current market barely covers 2 percent of the potential market. With more than 95 percent of the market still untapped, there is an incredible amount of room for growth.

Because competition is limited, you have to look at which companies inside China stand to profit from a business that still has barely dipped into the pool of potential customers. In this regard, you need to find the companies that have already staked a substantial claim to market share—nascent as it is—and can build on established performance. In this case, I found market leader China Life (NYSE: LFC) particularly appealing. While it happens to be an SOE, it is one of those select SOEs that meet my criteria of being well-managed, operating in a high-growth and heavily regulated industry, and enjoying special support from the government in Beijing. Beyond that, it also happens to be the largest insurance company in China, with a dominant market share of 51 percent. And after its highly successful IPO on an American exchange, it is now the world's top insurer by market value, ahead of American International Group (NYSE: AIG).

According to a recent survey, China Life is a brand name recognized by 92.6 percent of the people in China. That's the highest recognition among its insurance peers and clearly gives the company an edge in attracting investors. In addition to creating brand recognition, China Life excels in other key areas necessary for insurers to succeed. It has the biggest nationwide distribution network in China, owning more than 3,600 branches and 12,000 field offices, with 90,000 *bancassurance* outlets (banks that sell insurance) and 650,000 sales agents as of last count.

Not surprisingly, about 70 percent of its network is located in major cities, which is where wealth is growing most rapidly. This means there is still a huge opportunity in the rural areas and second-tier cities. China Life has plans to open another 15,000 branches, and I believe expansion into the rural areas will be a key to the company's growth as it capitalizes on its first-mover advantage in these areas. I also expect it to take full advantage of local expertise to enhance its brand image in China.

China Life's growth will come primarily from expansion in its fast-growing sector, but changes in some recent regulations should add to the company's bottom line. Here's why: In addition to insurance premiums, China Life also grows its profits the same way you and I do—by investing. At the moment, fixed income securities and bank deposits are the company's main investments. These are not high-growth investments, but the Chinese government recently allowed insurance companies to invest more of their assets in the stock market. The company has already started to take advantage of the new rules (and its government-backed status) by acquiring shares in some of the hot oversubscribed Chinese IPOs, often earning returns of 20 percent or more on the first day of trading.

China Life is gradually becoming involved in larger direct investments. It bought a 31.9 percent stake in Southern Power in December, 2006 and before that, China Life joined Citigroup's (NYSE: C) consortium to acquire a 20 percent stake in the Guangdong Development Bank. It also bought 500 million shares of Citic Securities, one of China's major brokerage firms, for $582 million, making it Citic's second-largest shareholder.

China Life is using its ample cash to extend its business to other financial sectors like banking and securities. Specifically, the Chinese government approved the creation of a joint venture asset-management company formed by China Life with global investment firm Franklin Templeton. As a result, China Life is transforming itself into a diversified financial holding corporation with mixed operations in the banking, insurance, and securities industries. I believe this is an excellent diversification strategy that will be great for the company over time and will increase its earnings by producing higher returns on investments.

Of course, China Life's true potential lies in its ability to offer a product that will be of increasing value to millions of potential customers. As Chinese people seek to place their money in life insurance and other financial plans that will pay off for them personally, China Life will prosper from having the strongest presence in the marketplace. And while that position will be attractive to those looking for insurance coverage, it will be even more attractive to investors who pay close attention to how it grows and expands its business over the next few years.

The investment opportunities I've addressed in this chapter—credit card purchases, health care, life insurance coverage—are all based on the potential that comes with millions of people, even hundreds of millions of people, starting to exert personal control over their daily lives in ways that have long been commonplace in Western countries. We think little of having to spend money for life insurance or using credit cards to buy groceries or DVDs. But these are brand-new experiences for many Chinese, and I expect that the Chinese population will—en masse—come to view these experiences the same way we do in the West, meaning that ultimately most Chinese people will accept them as facts of life.

Growing Fast in Food

I want to close this chapter by talking about one other uniquely Western invention that the Chinese are beginning to embrace with fervor. It's as much of a staple in our culture as credit cards are, and the Chinese people view it as an inexpensive way to experience a part of

American culture. It's far removed from the cost of life insurance or health care, but it is something that has seen tremendous growth due to the increasing disposable income of people in every region of China. What is it that is so uniquely American and so affordable that nearly everyone in China can get a piece of it? Well, it's one of the best investment opportunities in the China Miracle, and it's one of the most surprising: fast food.

With more money in their pockets, many people in China now take eating out seriously. Dining with extended families and friends has always been an important Chinese tradition, but leaving the home for meals has for a long time been prohibitively expensive. The options were few and far between, consisting of either (1) overpriced high-end restaurants that catered to bureaucrats and foreigners or (2) restaurants for locals that were little more than storefront operations serving slightly better versions of dishes that Chinese were making for themselves at home.

As I've frequently pointed out, times have changed. Most popular magazines in Shanghai, Hong Kong, and Taiwan now have several sections devoted to food and restaurants. The Chinese are getting the opportunity to sample cuisines that were unavailable to them, including food from other regions of their own country.

While there are four popular types of regional Chinese food—Guandong (Cantonese), Zhejiang (Shanghainese/Hangzhou), Shandong, and Sichuan—Americans are most familiar with Cantonese-style food because Cantonese dominates the offerings of Chinese restaurants in the United States. This is the Chinese food we typically get from our local Chinatown, served up quickly and inexpensively—and we think of it in terms of "Chinese fast food."

Once you get beyond Cantonese cuisine, it is fairly difficult to find authentic dishes from other regions of China outside of China, at least in the Western world. And, truth be told, most native Chinese would not even recognize some of the staples from Chinese take-out restaurants as they are served up in the United States or Canada, for instance. The Western desire for fast and tasty Chinese food has resulted in some decidedly non-Chinese dishes, like chop suey in the United States.

All across the United States, Canada, and Europe—even in major cities without a Chinatown or a significant Chinese population—Chinese food has long been a fast-food staple. Yet, being able to get American fast food in China is a very recent phenomenon. China's isolation has kept this unique element of American culture from permeating China to the same degree that it has many other countries. But, like many things for the people of China, that is changing rapidly.

A survey by Horizon Research Group found that spending on food grew faster than any other expense among the people in Shanghai in 2004. As incomes rise, eating habits change, and consumers are willing to try new foods. Over 100 million Chinese families that survived on hand-to-mouth subsistence as recently as 15 years ago can now afford to dine out at least once a week at a midpriced family restaurant.

More and more, this means going to an American fast food restaurant. For decades, American restaurant companies have invaded (for lack of a better word) foreign markets with incredible success. You can get Big Macs in Moscow and burritos from Taco Bell in Ecuador. A lot of this is due to the simple fact that the world likes American brands and American culture. Another reason is that these companies spend a lot of advertising and marketing dollars in these new markets.

Yet convincing the Chinese people to eat American food—especially when they are quite happy with their own dining traditions—has been a tough go for many U.S.-based purveyors of fast food (or "quick service restaurants," as the industry calls itself). Most of the major chains have entered China, and you can find recognizable fast food restaurants in every big city. But not all of them have been successful, primarily because they don't understand the Chinese people.

For instance, Howard Schultz, Starbucks' (NASDAQ: SBUX) founder and CEO, has declared that China will eventually become the company's second-biggest market. While that is entirely possible, I am personally not convinced. For Starbucks to truly succeed there, the company will need to transform itself from a coffee shop into a lifestyle company. Most Chinese do not yet drink a lot of coffee, and certainly nothing on the order of what Americans and Europeans drink. Affluent Chinese in certain regions are beginning to view Starbucks as a trendy place to go, but not necessarily as a place to get their coffee fix.

One of the major restaurant chains that has already figured out what it takes to compete and succeed in China is Yum! Brands (NYSE: YUM), parent company of Kentucky Fried Chicken (KFC), Pizza Hut,

Taco Bell, Long John Silver's, and A&W. Unlike many companies that claim to have a China strategy but not much business to show for it, Yum! has become the number-one restaurant chain operator in China. The first Kentucky Fried Chicken opened in 1987, and today KFC is the preferred restaurant of choice for many Chinese families on their weekly night out.

As the leading restaurant company in China, Yum! is opening the equivalent of three new restaurants a day. This is an impressive feat for a company that is best known for selling American staples like chicken and pizza. However, I believe its success is due primarily to its ability to create localized variations of chicken and pizza that suit Chinese tastes. For example, at Pizza Huts throughout China you can order toppings like sea eel, crab sticks, and tuna. KFC restaurants offer a chicken wrap in Peking duck sauce, one of the most popular menu items in China.

Yum! is successful in China because it combines a willingness to adapt to local tastes with the speedy efficiency, cleanliness, and trendy image of Western fast food. It is committed to serving local Chinese people exactly what they want. Yum! has taken localization a step further by opening six actual Chinese restaurants, called East Dawning, in China. These are based on the KFC business model of service, and are more spacious and open than typical Chinese restaurants.

Fast food icon McDonald's (NYSE: MCD) is a distant number two in China, and has been trying desperately to catch up to Yum! for years. Whereas McDonald's dominates in most fast food markets, in China it has less than one-third the number of outlets that KFC has. Because McDonald's is perceived as a hamburger place, its attempts to offer localized fare have not been nearly as successful as Yum!'s. You can do only so much with a hamburger, so the company has recently changed its tactics in China. But get this: Instead of changing the menu to include food more suitable to local tastes, McDonald's has embarked on a marketing campaign focusing on the benefits and masculinity of eating beef. How's that for not understanding what people want?

The jury is still out on the new McDonald's strategy, but I'm skeptical that it will achieve the desired results. The Chinese people have long enjoyed chicken as part of their diet, but hamburgers are something different altogether. Ground beef patties in a sesame seed bun are not part of the cultural vernacular.

Yum!'s rapid growth in China and other parts of the world is nothing short of astounding. Thus, it is worth noting that the biggest drag on its fiscal performance is its flat domestic operation in the United States, which still accounts for 60 percent of total sales. While Pizza Hut and Taco Bell are holding their own in the United States, KFC is losing market share to healthier and tastier fast food offerings. The long-revered Colonel Sanders just doesn't have the same marketing appeal to Americans anymore.

In contrast, according to an ACNielsen survey, KFC is the top consumer brand in China, ahead of Coca-Cola (NYSE: KO) and Nike (NYSE: NKE). That's a ranking you're not likely to find in any other country. But KFC is ubiquitous across China with 2,800 restaurants. The average Chinese KFC outlet produces $1.2 million in sales each year, more than the $900,000 posted by U.S. outlets.

A large part of KFC's success is due to the early decision to offer menu items popular with local Chinese customers. While we think of KFC as a brand that serves Southern-style fried chicken, in China its menu includes sides of bamboo shoots and lotus roots in place of coleslaw, which never caught on in China. Soup and rice porridge are offered during the winter months. There is also a twister sandwich based on Peking duck, blending chicken with scallions and plum sauce. All in all, the menu at KFCs in China is 80 percent different from its American menu. While those who want the Colonel's nine-piece Original Recipe can certainly find it, most Chinese customers opt for lighter offerings.

Like KFC, sister company Pizza Hut has also adapted to local consumer taste. For instance, it offers imitation crab as a pizza topping choice. That might not sound overly appetizing to you or me, but it works on the Chinese Mainland. Because of this strategy of localization, Pizza Hut is gaining widespread acceptance in China as a popular midpriced, Italian-style, Western-themed family restaurant chain.

The underlying factor in Yum!'s success in China is that the company realizes that the fast food experience is about more than just the items offered on its menus. The company is well aware that its restaurants symbolize America . . . even Americana. My six-year-old daughter, Rachel, who grew up on food from exceptional Italian restaurants in the United States, usually isn't interested in eating at Pizza Hut. While visiting the ancient Chinese city of Xi'an, however, she asked me to take her to the Pizza Hut near our hotel. She wanted to eat there because it represented a familiar piece of life back home.

Pizza Hut is viewed as emblematic of the American consumer lifestyle that the emerging middle class in China aspires to. For many, eating a meal at Pizza Hut is the closest they will get to experiencing the "good life in America" that they read about or see in movies. This has become so true that for affluent urban customers, Pizza Hut is often the restaurant of choice to celebrate Western holidays such as Christmas and Valentine's Day.

Today, there are close to 300 red-roofed Pizza Hut restaurants in Mainland China, and it's not unusual to see long lines outside the entrances in the major cities. In fact, the average wait for Pizza Hut customers in China last Christmas was more than two hours!

While Pizza Hut is not known for stellar cuisine, it is often the best bet for pizza in second-tier Chinese cities, which is Yum!'s next great growth market. Having conquered Beijing and Shanghai, both KFC and Pizza Hut are expanding rapidly into roughly 30 second-tier Chinese cities—the ones that have larger populations than Chicago. Yum! plans to open at least 250 KFC and 80 Pizza Hut outlets in second-tier Chinese cities on an annual basis.

The success of KFC and Pizza Hut propelled Yum!'s operating profits in China over $200 million in 2004, accounting for over 15 percent of its worldwide earnings. Since 1998, the company's profits in China are already up an amazing 1,000 percent, growing from 2 percent to 16 percent of total operating profits. That number will increase in the coming years as the fast-growing Chinese market will more than offset flat sales in the United States. Assuming the current trend continues, China will become Yum!'s biggest and most important market in the next 5 to 10 years.

Yum! shares are up over 200 percent during the past six years, a solid testament to the company's strong fundamentals and solid earnings growth. The stock's great six-year performance becomes even more pronounced when compared with those of archrival McDonald's, which doubled while Yum! shares more than tripled. The greatest difference between the two companies' performances is the China factor;

being successful in China has a direct effect on the bottom line. Yum!'s successful Chinese growth strategy simply left McDonald's in the dust. It has profited from the China Miracle, and will continue to do so.

There will be many businesses in the coming years that service the everyday needs of the Chinese people. Like fast food or better medical service, these businesses will identify the natural evolution of China as it becomes a nation of spenders, typically by using Western models of consumer behavior. While this is an acceptable jumping-off point, only those companies that tailor their offerings to China's unique culture will succeed on a level that is meaningful to investors. This includes a vast range of businesses that, again, Americans think of as being part of the bare essentials of consumerism. Cosmetics, clothing, specialty foods, home furnishings, and personal electronics will all be welcomed in China, but their purveyors will have to customize elements of their marketing in order to ease the Chinese people into buying what they have to offer.

The companies noted here have all set the standard for reaching the Chinese people and rewarding American investors. When exploring other opportunities related to China, it's important to look beyond the obvious. Conventional wisdom tells us that McDonald's does fantastically well almost everyplace it goes, so that will be true in China. However, the company's failure to understand that the Chinese aren't fond of hamburgers—and prefer chicken because it is a staple of their diet—would raise a warning sign that we shouldn't be so quick to believe that its history of success is guaranteed in China.

And while we might dismiss KFC in the United States as a fast-food also-ran, we'd miss an opportunity by not taking into account China's penchant for chicken and American brands.

I can't emphasize this enough: When looking at potential investments, consider those things that Westerners take for granted but still place great value on: cheap, fast food; easy access to credit; life insurance from a corner broker; quick lab visits thanks to advanced medical equipment. We don't give these a second—let alone a first—thought.

Now, as you go through your day, imagine if these goods and services—and countless others—were to disappear. Estimate how much value you put on them. Then make one final leap: Imagine if these were all available to you pretty much for the first time. This will get you thinking about what the Chinese people are buying right now and will focus your investments on businesses that will become indispensable to the Chinese people. It's not ice cream parlors and stationery stores; it's pharmacies, specialty stores, home improvement centers, restaurants, insurance brokers, and other businesses that millions of Chinese are just now able to appreciate—and afford.

Chapter 12

Danger Signs

The Proverbial China Shop

As with anything of value, the savvy investor has to beware of the potential downsides in China. Many investors have already been burned by putting their trust in financial advisers who do not understand the unique dynamics of investing in China, including the role of the government, access to the markets, lack of shareholder rights, and the myriad cultural differences. Understanding the culture is important in identifying what will and what will not work in China.

By this point in our journey through the China Miracle, you've no doubt gained an understanding of those elements that will make investing in China successful. You know to avoid lumbering state-owned enterprises (SOEs), you know to beware of trying to navigate China's exchanges, and you know that Chinese manufacturing is—for all its efficiency—not the path to investor profits.

These are some of the lessons that will be true for years to come, and they are easy to apply. However, some pitfalls are not related to making specific investments. We encounter these every day in investing: wild mood swings on Wall Street, knee-jerk reactions to everything from a Federal Reserve chairman's comment to an unexpectedly high consumer confidence index. Usually, these correct themselves quickly, and you can easily weather these temporary roller-coaster rides.

Other factors outside of the investment community, however, should be paid attention to when they have the potential to affect your investments directly or the economic climate in which they are traded. There are several factors of which investors looking to profit from China need to be acutely aware. They include inflation, overheated exchanges, and overzealous pitchmen, to name just a few.

But let's start by looking at the big "X" factor when it comes to investing anywhere: the economy. When the National People's Congress (NPC) convened in March 2007, it addressed many of the issues facing China's economy and its unparalleled growth. In his closing speech to the NPC, Chinese Premier Wen Jiabao stated that China's current growth rate is "unstable, imbalanced, uncoordinated, and unsustainable." This didn't come as much of a shock; Chinese officials have been saying that repeatedly for the past several years. In fact, Wen himself expressed the same concerns as far back as early 2006, saying that China's double-digit growth is unsustainable and potentially dangerous.

Opening the Gates

China's private sector is growing much faster than the government-controlled economic sectors, and that worries China's leaders, who are used to controlling the economy. This free-market growth may frighten the government, but it's clearly a good thing for us as investors. Planned economic coordination from government bureaucrats doesn't work as well as the market's so-called invisible hand.

Despite the fears, China has achieved over 10 percent gross domestic product (GDP) growth for each of the past three years. I believe that growth is sustainable, but anytime a major economy is growing that fast, it will be unstable by definition. That doesn't necessarily make the growth dangerous, but it does mean that it can be buffeted unduly by external forces that are magnified simply by being associated with such phenomenal growth.

Beijing's highest priorities right now are holding on to what China has achieved and consolidating the huge gains made in both stocks and real estate. High housing prices, especially in coastal cities, have become a source of public resentment in Mainland China. The average housing price is roughly 20 times the average annual household income in many cities. By comparison, in U.S. cities where property values are inordinately high, such as Los Angeles and San Francisco, the average home costs less than 12 times the average household annual income.

What has caused this incredible run-up in Mainland China real estate? The Chinese are turning to real estate because of the lack of other good investments in the country. The $3 trillion in China's banking system cannot get inflation-beating returns from the 2 percent to 3 percent yield offered by bank deposits. This is the money that has fueled the dizzying rise of the Mainland exchanges and the extraordinary valuation of A-shares over the past two years. But real estate and A-shares are about the only investment games in town for Chinese citizens.

Quite simply, China needs to make more good investments available. Limiting investment options will funnel too much money into the exchanges and into real estate, inevitably driving prices for both up to price levels completely out of sync with actual value. And once other opportunities become available, as they always do, these initial investments will come crashing back to Earth.

One way for China to lessen the strain on real estate and Mainland exchanges is to allow investment abroad. Recently the Chinese government permitted select institutions to buy publicly traded stocks of Chinese companies listed outside of Mainland China. Soon we'll see more Mainland Chinese institutional investors putting money into Chinese companies listed in Hong Kong and New York. These other exchanges will help to serve as a release valve for China's investment dollars.

Another way to handle excess liquidity is to increase consumption— encourage people to spend more and save less. To that end, China's consumer financing industry is getting a jump start. Since 2006, Beijing has been pushing state-owned banks to hand out credit cards to anyone who has a job. The number of credit cards in China doubled in 2006 and 2007, from 25 million to 50 million. All these cards in the hands of Chinese citizens are another reason I believe domestic consumption in China will continue to increase as it becomes the most important investment theme in the world.

Keeping domestic property and stock markets in check is only part of what China needs to do to protect its economy. Fortunately, it hasn't stopped there. The Chinese government is planning to invest in economic development across the country. The intention is to spread the wealth, so to speak, such that there is a more equitable distribution of resources and development throughout the nation.

These investments are designed to accomplish several goals, not the least of which is economic and social stability. The three main areas targeted for investment by the government are: development in western China, improvement of rural farming villages, and primary education for children.

Development in Western China

The overwhelming majority of China's population—a staggering 90 percent, to be exact—lives in the eastern half of the country. Not surprisingly, this is where the biggest cities and ports are located. Western China, by contrast, consists of several poor rural provinces and ethnic territories, such as Xinjiang (Eastern Turkestan), and lags far behind the rest of the nation in economic development. In order to improve the social and economic balance within the country, China needs to invest heavily in the underdeveloped western half.

It has begun by making the western regions more accessible to commercial and vacation travel. The Qinghai-Tibet Railway, which links Beijing with Lhasa and is also the world's highest rail line, was completed in 2005 to boost tourism and investment in western China. Reaching out to the region will be important for years to come (think of the westward movement in the United States in the mid-twentieth century after the Depression) and will benefit companies that jump on it. A good example is oil and gas refiner Sinopec, which has already begun developing natural gas reserves in the large western region of Xinjiang.

Improvement of Rural Farming Villages

China is intent on creating economic balance between urban workers and rural farmers. Leaders in Beijing are urging local governments and companies to invest in farming infrastructure to bring the standard of living of rural citizens closer to that of suburban and even urban areas. A substantial part of this plan involves bringing villages into the Information Age with access to a wide range of telecommunication and Internet services. If this effort is successful, it will ensure continued, and dramatic, increases in Chinese consumption for at least a decade.

China Mobile (NYSE: CHL) has been playing a big part in developing wireless communication infrastructure and offering cell phone service in rural areas. In fact, the world's largest wireless operator is seeing its largest growth rate from rural China and not from saturated coastal cities.

Primary Education for Children

A poll taken in 2005 concluded that the two greatest household financial concerns in China are health care and education. In addition to paying for school tuition and books, most parents enroll their children in pricey extracurricular tutoring so they can keep pace with China's ultracompetitive, exam-driven education system. This is why New Oriental Education & Technology Group (NYSE: EDU) is one of the most successful private tutoring operations in China.

Yet poor farmers and rural migrant workers simply can't afford to pay for tutoring classes for their children. Thus, when it comes to competing with more affluent urban students, kids from rural areas are at an enormous disadvantage. To ease the burdens of schooling, Beijing has ordered rural schools to waive tuition and book costs for underprivileged children. This is a very smart move. By improving educational opportunities for the poor, China is not only shrinking its huge socioeconomic gap, but it is also cultivating its most valuable asset: future leaders and entrepreneurs.

The investments that the government is making will be a boon to a nation that has already seen hundreds of millions of people rise out of poverty in the past decade. But along with China's higher standard of living has come a problem that we're very familiar with in the United

States: inflation. And this is another potential pitfall that investors need to keep a close eye on.

Prosperity and Inflationary Pressures

It is no secret that China, along with most of Asia, is experiencing inflation as one of the downsides of its newfound prosperity. Inflation is one of those terms that economists and the media talk about as if it were simply a concept, but it is very real to those people who feel its effects. Inflation is hitting Asian consumers who buy everything from staples to luxury goods.

I saw this in a most unexpected setting on a recent visit to Seoul, South Korea's capital and its largest city. The purpose of my trip was to investigate several extremely promising investment opportunities. Since I was going all that way—and staying for several days—my wife Yvonne, who takes Korean ginseng root as a health supplement, asked if I could pick some up in Seoul in between meetings.

In traditional Chinese medicine, aged ginseng root is prized as an energizing herb. High-end Korean ginseng is especially popular among Chinese consumers because of its excellent quality, successful branding, and attractive packaging. Millions of ethnic Chinese around the world, like Yvonne, regularly take ginseng as part of their health regimens. But lately it has become difficult to find premium-quality Korean ginseng in the United States.

When I located ginseng at a specialty store in Seoul, I was surprised by the price on the package. The ginseng root cost more than I had ever seen. I chatted with the store manager, and she confirmed my suspicions: Prices have shot up 40 percent in just the past two years. The reason? Chinese herb and medicine shops in Mainland cities have locked up most of the available supply of aged Korean ginseng roots. As recently as 10 years ago, very few Mainland Chinese had the means to spend money on a box of high-priced ginseng that weighs less than a pound. Today, a huge number of increasingly wealthy Chinese citizens can easily afford to spend their cash on such goods.

Prices for items across the board are rising. Everyday items like rice and milk are becoming more expensive as well. In 2007, Premier

Wen Jiabao stated that his dream is for every Chinese child to be able to drink a half-liter of milk each day. That may happen, but Chinese parents are going to pay a higher price in the process. During the course of 2007, milk prices jumped by more than 30 percent. Pork prices increased even more, by 50 percent. Other staples such as rice and instant noodles have also become more costly. In Beijing, a recent price increase by two of the largest ramen noodle companies in China caused a widespread consumer backlash. As a result, the price increase has been nixed for now, but the reality is that prices will have to rise eventually.

Food prices in China have been climbing for two main reasons. First, more than 200 million rural farmers have left the fields and have entered the cities to try to grab their share of wealth available there. According to official statistics from the Chinese government, 75 percent of China's total population lived in rural farming communities 20 years ago. As of last year, only 49 percent of the people in Mainland China still lived in rural areas. This means that there are one-third fewer farmers to produce food for Chinese citizens.

Even though that is a dramatic statistic, I think the government has underestimated the true number of workers who have moved into the cities. The Chinese government based its calculation of the rural population on census data from village households. I don't believe these census numbers are accurate, because a large percentage of farmers who moved to cities are still registered as residents of the rural villages that they left long ago. The numbers show that perhaps six or seven out of 10 employable workers have moved away from rural locations. This urbanization trend will continue until farming becomes an economically viable alternative to moving into the cities. Until then, farm production will suffer.

The cost of food is also climbing because of the increasing deregulation of food prices. For decades, the Communist government used price controls to keep food prices low, maintaining social stability at the expense of rural peasants. Over the past four years, however, food prices have been allowed to move up to meet free-market supply and demand. And as Chinese citizens have earned more money, they have gained the means to buy more and better-quality food. This is driving up the price of food on the demand side.

Boosted in part by increased wealth, Chinese demand for a wide range of goods has caused huge price spikes around the world. This is evident, for instance, in the cost of natural resources from oil to iron ore. During the past four years, largely because of demand from China and other emerging economies, prices of oil and industrial commodities have increased by an average of 100 percent to 200 percent. As crude oil prices approached the previously unthinkable level of $100 a barrel, prices of agricultural commodities started to play catch-up to industrial commodities.

This is creating a second wave of commodities inflation, led by agricultural commodities such as wheat, soybeans, and corn. Here are some examples: During the summer of 2007 alone, wheat prices shot up more than 50 percent. Over the course of the year, soybean prices went up by a whopping 75 percent. Corn went up less, but still jumped nearly 40 percent more than its price a year earlier.

This inflation of agricultural products is becoming a problem for many countries, but the effect is especially pronounced in China. The central bank in China raised interest rates six times in 2007 alone to fight inflation. And yet there's no sign that commodities inflation will decline anytime soon.

When a government raises interest rates to counter inflationary effects, it naturally decreases demand for loans. Yet most of the private sector economy in China does not depend on bank loans, so these rate hikes have a limited effect on curbing the country's increasing money supply. Another factor working against government actions are the increases in China's foreign reserve from foreign investment. Coupled with its trade surplus, these economic conditions have forced the Chinese central bank to grow its money supply rapidly and continue the cycle of inflation.

Because of its incredible economic growth, China can afford to raise interest rates. The United States, however, is a different story. Slowing economic growth related to the U.S. housing bubble prevents the Federal Reserve from increasing interest rates. In the past, low-cost China exports countered inflationary pressures in the United States. But now prices of Chinese goods are starting to creep up. Between May and July 2007, the cost of imports from China climbed a worrisome 4.2 percent.

To help homeowners fight foreclosures and to stimulate the economy, the Fed lowered interest rates throughout 2007 and allowed the U.S. dollar to further weaken against other major currencies. Like throwing gasoline on a fire, these moves will further intensify inflationary pressures in the United States because a weak dollar will make imports more expensive and generally erode the purchasing power of the currency. Since 2002, the U.S. dollar has lost 40 percent of its value against other major currencies, and as long as the Fed maintains a low-interest-rate monetary policy, the devaluation will continue. The Chinese yuan, in contrast, rose 7 percent against the dollar in 2007, and more appreciation will likely continue, making Chinese stocks even more attractive.

However, there is another way that inflation could cause Beijing to take action. Inflationary pressure could force the Chinese central bank to allow the yuan to appreciate much faster than the planned rate of 5 percent per year. If the Chinese yuan appreciates faster, prices of Chinese exports will shoot up and increase the inflation rate in the United States. If this happens, I wouldn't be surprised to see the annual inflation rate shoot back up to the double-digit levels last seen back in the 1970s. Should that occur, Chinese exporters would be hurt, yet companies that sell products domestically in China would benefit.

I believe that, going forward, inflation will spread globally beyond basic commodities and affect a wide variety of goods. This new wave of inflation will create huge changes that will facilitate a worldwide transfer of wealth. That is because wealth will shift from consumers of commodities to producers of commodities, much like it did in the 1970s when members of the Organization of Petroleum Exporting Countries (OPEC) saw huge inflows of cash from rising oil prices. Holders of assets denominated in weak currencies such as the U.S. dollar will lose out, and holders of assets denominated in strong currencies such as the Chinese yuan will win. As an investor in China's leading companies, you will be on the winning side of this massive transfer of wealth.

I've been very mindful of the effects of inflation, and in fact, many of the companies and industries I've discussed in this book are well positioned to benefit from this wave of inflationary pressure. In general, you should keep the following three guidelines in mind when attempting to benefit from increasing global inflation.

1. *Stay away from dollar-denominated assets.* It is clear from the 2007 rate cuts that the Fed is willing to let the dollar fall in order to stimulate the U.S. economy. In an environment where the U.S. dollar is dropping, investors need to invest in assets denominated in undervalued currencies (like the Chinese yuan) or in inflation hedges (like gold). Investors in Chinese companies are already positioned for a rapid rise in the Chinese currency.

2. *Invest in companies that benefit from industrial commodities inflation.* In a rising commodities environment, companies involved in the production and processing of natural resources will benefit. In particular, foreign companies that produce commodities benefit from both a stronger currency and rising commodity prices.

3. *Invest in companies benefiting from increased demand in agricultural commodities.* As agricultural commodity prices rise to unprecedented highs, I expect demand for fertilizers and other farming essentials to go up sharply. Investors paying attention to specific agriculture-related commodities will profit from the explosive demand for agricultural products both in China and around the world.

Inflation, commodity pricing, and interest rates all exert economic pressure on the stock market, and their cumulative effect can drive stock prices down. While that can make investing riskier than we'd like it to be, these aren't dangers inherent to individual stocks. In fact, they are probably less dangerous to your specific holdings because you can see that inflation, for instance, affects an entire industry as opposed to an individual company. You can measure inflation's overall effect when you compare the various players in a given industry.

The more insidious dangers that you have to watch out for are those that come from within the companies themselves. And because so few people understand how the China Miracle has really developed, companies with astounding potential for wealth creation stand side by side with hollow investments that are billed as "can't miss" vehicles by less-than-knowledgeable stock analysts and advisers. To separate one from the other, you have to look for the dangers in a potential investment, just as you look for the profit potential.

Case Study: Baidu and JA Solar

There are times when you'll find unexpected momentum in China stocks. I've identified the places to look for these stocks in each chapter, from buying what China needs to capitalizing on the buying power and trends of Chuppies. But momentum is about timing and jumping in after you identify a company or an industry that has started on an upward trajectory.

There are times when momentum comes from unexpected sources, and you have to be ready to move quickly in order to stake a position. In China, momentum can evolve from situations we're not typically familiar with in the United States. I'm talking about those occasions when the Chinese government gets involved in the market. The government can open the door very quickly on opportunities, and it can also slam that door just as quickly. When buying into this kind of momentum, you have to be vigilant in monitoring your stocks.

I experienced this scenario at the end of 2007. There were two stocks that I bought in mid-2007 to take advantage of the growth in Internet use and solar power in China: Baidu (NASDAQ: BIDU) and JA Solar (NASDAQ: JASO). (See Figures 12.1 and 12.2.) Internet use was escalating throughout the country, and solar power—although a crowded market with lots of second-tier plays—has been mandated by the government.

One of the reasons I looked at these stocks was that the Chinese government was about to expand its pilot program for allowing Chinese investors to put money in nondomestic financial markets. This program, which included both institutions and individuals, was called the Qualified Domestic Institutional Investors (QDII) program. Implementation of the program meant that money from China could be invested directly in Hong Kong or in the United States. Institutional investors would have greater freedom in their investment choices, while individuals would be limited to Hong Kong.

(Continued)

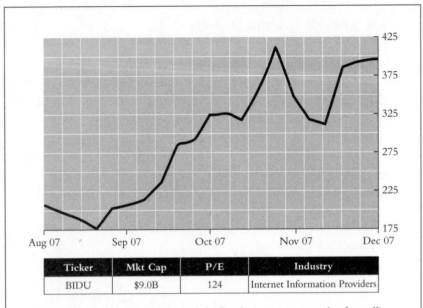

Ticker	Mkt Cap	P/E	Industry
BIDU	$9.0B	124	Internet Information Providers

Figure 12.1   Baidu (One month before buy to one month after sell)
SOURCE: InvestorPlace Media, LLC.

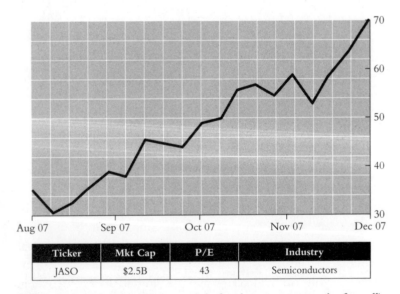

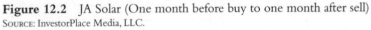

Ticker	Mkt Cap	P/E	Industry
JASO	$2.5B	43	Semiconductors

Figure 12.2   JA Solar (One month before buy to one month after sell)
SOURCE: InvestorPlace Media, LLC.

Either way, homegrown companies listed on those exchanges were certain to benefit.

Baidu and JA Solar were both popular companies within China and were both trading in the United States, and they both stood to benefit from institutional and individual investment coming out of China.

Some of the newly created mutual funds were allowed to buy Chinese stocks listed in the United States. The impact the program would have on American depositary receipts (ADRs) had the potential to be astounding. Plus, Baidu.com and JA Solar were among the first to be accumulated by several Chinese mutual funds.

You are probably familiar with Baidu. It's known as the Google of China, and its initial public offering in 2005 made one of the biggest IPO splashes of this century. When Baidu went public on the NASDAQ on August 5, 2005, its shares opened at $66, more than double its $27 subscription price. It finished the day at $122.54, accumulating gains of 354 percent on its first day of trading.

The company was established in 2000 by two Silicon Valley software engineers, Robin Li and Eric Xu. Headquartered in Beijing, Baidu was funded by initial venture capital totaling $1.2 million. Both its cofounders are Chinese nationals who studied and worked overseas before returning home to China.

Since its inception, Baidu has emerged as China's most popular web site and the fourth-largest web site worldwide. The company is also dominating China's growing online ad market. In 2005, China had very little in the way of e-commerce, but online ad revenue jumped an impressive 54 percent in 2006 to $508.3 million.

Baidu in 2007 accounted for 24 percent of China's online ad sales. Google, Baidu's largest rival, had only 9 percent. Baidu controlled 58 percent of China's paid search market, while number two Google had only 23 percent. Beyond basic search,

(*Continued*)

Baidu offers services including image and video searches, plus searches for MP3 music files, which make up almost one-third of its traffic.

According to investment bank Credit Suisse Group, sales of search-linked ads in China will more than quadruple by 2009, averaging more than 40 percent growth per year. By then, Baidu is expected to have grown its revenue fivefold to 4.24 billion yuan ($561 million).

The magazine *ComputerWorld* conducted a survey in Beijing, Shanghai, and Guangzhou. Results showed that nearly 80 percent of respondents used Baidu. Google was a distant second place with 17 percent. That's a very strong market share for Baidu.

I avoided Baidu when it went public, but over the course of two years it proved itself to be the dominant player in one of China's fastest-growing industries. When the company was started, e-commerce in China didn't exist. But Baidu has taken this concept and run with it. The company is now a leader in its field, and its strong market position helped entice companies like Motorola (NYSE: MOT) and Alibaba.com (Hong Kong 1688.HK) to buy more search-linked ads on Baidu's site. The company was in a great position to cash in on paid search advertising, the fastest-growing segment of a fast-growing online advertising market.

On the solar front, I had to be very selective in this sector. As I've said in other parts of this book, solar is a growth industry, but it is extremely crowded with competitors throughout China. After analyzing multiple solar makers, I chose JA Solar as one of the best candidates to play the solar boom.

The Chinese company, founded in 2005, was launched by former senior executives from Suntech Power Holdings Co., Ltd. (NYSE: STP). JA Solar's focus is on producing high-quality solar cells that it sells to major solar module makers. One advantage of specializing in solar cell production is that the company has lower general and administrative expenses, and lower sales costs, than some other parts of the supply chain.

The company also has lower manufacturing costs, making it more competitive than solar cell producers in Europe and the United States. This cost advantage helped JA Solar maintain a profit margin of 20 percent.

Access to supplies of silicon wafers, the most important raw materials for manufacturing solar cells, is crucial to the success of solar cell manufacturers. JA Solar enjoys a strong relationship with big polysilicon supplier Jinglong Group, one of the largest producers and suppliers of solar wafers in China. Actually, Jinglong Group is also owned by JA Solar's chairman and largest shareholder, Baofang Jin. JA Solar gets its polysilicon from Jinglong at a discount that's 5 percent below spot market prices.

The stock was trading at about 25 times the following year's forecasted earnings, which was cheap for a solar company with over 50 percent earnings growth potential. I expected JASO's strong momentum to continue because of the company's rapid growth, its competitive profit margin, a hot solar market, and a secure supply of raw materials.

So I had two positions, one in Baidu and one in JA Solar. The first wave of QDII mutual funds investing in stocks outside of Mainland China was launched in mid-2007. More than $15 billion was raised for these mutual funds, and demand continued to be strong for new funds.

As part of the pilot initiative, Chinese citizens would have invested in the Hong Kong–listed shares of stocks traded on American exchanges (ADRs). At the last minute, however, the government decided to restrict domestic investors from investing in non-Mainland markets, saying it needed to do a more thorough review of the program.

Because of the change mandated by the government, Chinese investors would instead be buying the exact same ADRs that U.S. investors own (through mutual funds, of course). This was bound to have a bigger effect on U.S. stocks, as Chinese investment money from individual investors would be coming straight to the U.S. exchanges.

(Continued)

There was a quick run-up in both of these stocks through the late fall of 2007. But in November, both stocks fell off sharply and suddenly, with very little bid underneath them indicating that the first wave of buying might already be over. That also meant that momentum had most likely stalled.

I believe that in a defensive environment, traders should not hold positions that have already experienced big run-ups in speculative sectors like the Internet and solar energy. While both Baidu and JA Solar were doing well, they were also trading at very high valuations after big rallies. Chinese solar and Internet companies tend to perform very well in up markets but do very poorly when markets are selling off.

With no momentum to push the stocks higher, I took my gains: 68 percent in Baidu and 44.5 percent in JA Solar. And both of these occurred in less than 90 days. Again, I was able to tap into the momentum generated by the QDII program, and then pulled back when that same program was changed.

For me, this was further proof that paying attention to China as a culture, as an economy, and as a nation is crucial to understanding exactly how to reap windfalls from the China Miracle's unique investment opportunities.

Self-Proclaimed Experts

You can protect yourself from the outset by ignoring much of the rhetoric offered up by China know-nothings. Let me give you an example. When I speak at conferences or attend financial events, I'm always thrilled by the incredibly strong interest in China and its investment offerings. Such interest bodes well for those who are willing to understand the market and invest their money wisely.

Unfortunately, I am equally amazed by the huge number of China-related vendors who show up at these events and have absolutely no understanding of what China is other than where it is located on a map. Many of these opportunists can't even speak, read, or write Chinese. A lot of them have sprung up overnight, claiming to be China experts just to take advantage of the hype surrounding China investing. The worst part, however, is that investors who listen to many of these so-called experts often get burned.

These self-proclaimed China gurus usually direct investors toward the biggest SOEs and the most highly publicized China IPOs—the companies that get all the media attention. Because of the size and notoriety of these companies, they are easy for the media to cover, and many advisers lazily point their clients to them as great China investments. But as you well know, that is not the case. SOEs, with just a few exceptions, are bad investments because they don't have dominant market positions, are poorly managed, are rarely profitable, and have very opaque accounting practices that make it difficult for investors to really see what they're investing in.

Yet, the supposed experts throw these stocks around as having great potential with little regard to the reality of their positions. I can't tell you how often investors ask me about highly touted China stocks and all I can do is tell them to stay as far away as they can.

One stock I get asked about all the time is China Medical Technology (NASDAQ: CMED), which develops, manufactures, and markets medical devices to treat cancer and benign tumors. CMED's products are used almost exclusively in Mainland China.

I view CMED as more of a cancer cure story than a play on China's growth, and I've heard mixed results on the effectiveness of the company's technology. Developing a successful cancer treatment would be great for CMED and cancer sufferers around the world, but many companies have tried and failed. If you're going to put money into China, you need to put it into companies with a more certain future and products that deliver as promised.

Another stock I often get asked about is China Yuchai (NYSE: CYD), a diesel engine maker in the city of Yulin in Guanxi province. Chinese investors from Singapore privatized the company, transforming it from an SOE controlled by the city of Yulin. While I like it better as a private company than an SOE, there are several reasons why I don't like it as an investment.

First, diesel engine manufacturing in China is a highly competitive industry with shrinking profit margins. Investors too often forget that, even though China is the world's biggest potential market, it is also the world's most competitive market. Chinese companies, especially SOEs—like China Yuchai used to be—often lower their prices to grab market share. That is rarely a good long-term strategy.

Also, profit margins in China's auto parts industry have shrunk *dramatically* during the past five years as money-losing SOEs entered the business. You're better off investing in industry leaders with strong competitive advantages that prevent others from entering their businesses . . . and China Yuchai fails on that account. Although China Yuchai is the largest diesel engine company in the country, net income shrank by a whopping 85 percent between 2004 and 2005.

Second, China Yuchai has questionable corporate governance. The company paid its board members and parent company $5.2 million in 2005, a significant amount when you consider it made only $8.6 million that year. There are also ongoing disputes between China Yuchai's state holding company, which is controlled by the city of Yulin, and its Singapore-based majority shareholders. As with most SOEs, I recommend you stay away from it.

Sometimes I don't invest in a popular China stock simply because there are better picks in the same industry. You should always strive to invest in the best of breed, not the also-rans. For instance, the industry leader in China's online gaming sector is Netease (NASDAQ: NTES), a solid company. I didn't recommended it to investors, however, because I believed The9 (NASDAQ: NCTY) was a much better opportunity back in 2006 when I recommended the latter stock. The9's CEO, Zhu Jun, understands that his company's strength is in distributing and operating the games, not developing them. As a result, top international game developers like Blizzard and Microsoft teamed up with The9 as their exclusive distributor in China. Netease, by contrast, focuses on being a domestic developer and is therefore constrained by the size of China's market.

So there are times when the trade-off in what to buy and what not to buy comes down to the better long-term momentum play. Two stocks in the same business may both have value, but going with the best strategically placed player in the market will assure you of less risk when buying into that particular industry.

Getting Out

Speaking of risk, knowing when to sell a stock is usually much more difficult than knowing when to buy. When investing in China—the world's fastest-growing, fastest-moving, and most dynamic economy—this is especially true. Today's market champion can quickly become a has-been tomorrow.

China is the world's most competitive market because it is constantly changing and adapting. One of the reasons for this is that Chinese businesses are very good at copying products and duplicating services, so maintaining a unique business there is challenging. Everything from product lines to store designs, business models, brand names, and trademarks is vulnerable to copycats.

I always try to invest in industry leaders with strong competitive advantages that can defend their market position—thus making them best-of-breed buys. Leading companies doing business in China can usually stay on top if (1) they can establish a strong brand name, (2) there is a strong barrier to newcomers entering the market, and/or (3) the company possesses unique technological or intellectual property advantages. However, even with all of these characteristics, it's often only a matter of time before copycats come in and start taking big pieces of the market share pie.

Not only that, but competitors wage price wars whenever they can, causing profit margins to shrink sharply. Therefore, the biggest problem for businesses in China is maintaining a strong profit margin in an extremely competitive marketplace. When making an investment decision about whether to buy or sell positions, I analyze revenue and earnings growth as well as the story behind the company, but deteriorating margins are usually the biggest reason that I recommend selling a Chinese stock.

There are few warning signs that indicate "sell" as obviously as when a company's profitability starts to deteriorate. When I see that occurring, I will typically decide to get out of a China position. Then I look at which company is most directly responsible for eating into the leader's position and determine whether that should be the new play. This happened when I was holding shares of Motorola. As we discussed in Chapter 8, after introducing its RAZR cell phones in China,

Motorola had a strong market position. But the company rested too long on its laurels, allowing a slew of competitors to come in and grab the interest of Chinese consumers looking for newer and more feature-laden phones that cost less. Motorola's position was no longer defensible, and it reacted too slowly in introducing radically new and upgraded phones. That's a tough position from which to recover, and I wasn't willing to wait and see whether Motorola could pull it off. My money belonged in stocks where there was momentum, not regrouping.

Sometimes the best investment decisions are the investments I don't make. This means avoiding some of the obvious plays and letting other investors take their chances with them—even if it feels like I'm standing on the sidelines. My rationale for taking this stance in some cases is due to the fact that the market is full of hot companies that have not been able to execute a successful plan for growth in China. Most U.S. companies touted as China plays derive fewer than 5 percent of their business from China. These companies include Wal-Mart (NYSE: WMT), Coca-Cola (NYSE: KO), Starbucks (NASDAQ: SBUX), and McDonald's (NYSE: MCD). There are many Chinese companies that fall short in China as well, such as Acorn International (NYSE: ATV).

When Acorn, China's version of the Home Shopping Network, went public on the New York Stock Exchange, I will admit that I was very interested in it. On the surface, Acorn seemed like a good bet: The network was a play on China's booming consumer market, its business was growing rapidly, and even though the stock was a bit pricey, the numbers led me to believe that there could be a viable investment opportunity here.

Naturally, my next move was to get research that would validate the buy. I read all the appropriate filing documents, and then called my research team in China to ask them what they thought about the company and what consumers were saying. To my surprise, I learned that Acorn was developing a bad reputation among local shoppers for selling shoddy products. That was enough for me to not recommend the stock. And then, during a visit to China, I went ahead and checked out the network's programming for myself. I was not impressed by the snake-oil salesmanship I saw. Seeing it firsthand, I knew that Acorn was a company that had no business being in my portfolio.

My decision to avoid the company was confirmed by the stock's poor performance. Since its IPO, the company's stock has sold off and is down 55 percent since its first day of trading. This is the advantage of having boots-on-the-ground intelligence and getting information directly from China and from qualified sources. It reinforces the need for thorough research and understanding of both the market and the culture.

Case Study: Nvidia

Nvidia Corporation (NASDAQ: NVDA) is a computer graphics company headquartered in California (see Figure 12.3). Its Taiwanese-born founder, Jen-Hsun Huang, is another great example of the entrepreneurial spirit that is driving much of the spectacular growth in Asian economies. Huang's father was a chemical and instrumentation engineer, and his mother was a homemaker who insisted that her children learn English even though she couldn't speak it herself. The family eventually moved from Taiwan to Oregon, where Huang started playing table tennis nearly every day after school at a club in downtown

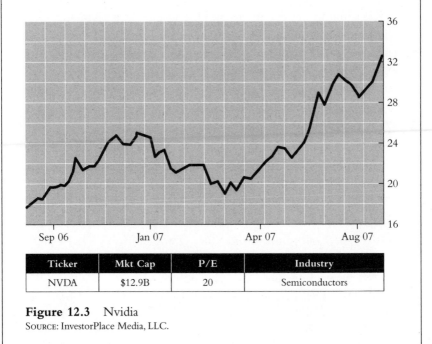

Ticker	Mkt Cap	P/E	Industry
NVDA	$12.9B	20	Semiconductors

Figure 12.3   Nvidia
SOURCE: InvestorPlace Media, LLC.

(*Continued*)

Portland. He became an accomplished player, placing third in junior doubles at the U.S. Nationals at age 15.

Huang learned an important lesson about success early on. It occurred three decades ago on the streets of Las Vegas. He was a bright-eyed 13-year-old scheduled to compete in the U.S. National Ping Pong Tournament, and the glitz and glamour of Las Vegas made it hard for him to focus on the match. The night before the tournament, instead of getting a good night's sleep, he stayed out late walking up and down the Strip, mesmerized by the bright lights and hustle and bustle surrounding him.

Huang didn't win the tournament, but he did learn from the experience: In order to succeed in life, he needed to maintain a laserlike focus on his goals. Thirty years later, he has taken that approach in making his Santa Clara firm one of the biggest graphics chipmakers in the world, with annual sales of more than $2 billion.

After earning his bachelor's degree in electrical engineering at Oregon State University, Huang moved to Silicon Valley and got his first job at Advanced Micro Devices. In 1993, he and two engineers from Sun Microsystems decided to start their own graphics chip company, and Nvidia was born.

Today, Nvidia is the world leader in computer graphics technologies and one of the semiconductor industry's largest fabless companies (a fabless company designs its chips and outsources its manufacturing operations to companies like Taiwan Semiconductor). Nvidia designs, develops, and markets graphics processing units, media and communications processors, wireless media processors, and related software. Its products play a vital role in PCs, laptops, workstations, personal digital assistants (PDAs), cell phones, and video game consoles. That covers just about every hot high-tech segment.

Nvidia's chips are used by industry stalwarts like Dell (NASDAQ: DELL), Hewlett-Packard (NYSE: HPQ), Microsoft

(NASDAQ: MSFT), and Apple (NASDAQ: AAPL). In fact, when I bought its stock in 2006, Nvidia's chips were slated to be the key components of two widely anticipated new products: Sony's (NYSE: SNE) next-generation PlayStation 3 console and an updated version of Apple's video iPod player.

The company's mobile graphics chips were also on track to provide cell phones with the ability to display smooth, high-quality video. It is estimated that around 24 million U.S. mobile users will pay for some form of video content and services on their mobile devices by 2010, which would be a 200 percent increase from today.

So I bought Nvidia because it had two exceptional elements contributing to its momentum. First, the company's chips were slated to be used in several widely anticipated new products, and second, I wanted to take advantage of the company's growing communications market.

I had the stock for 10 months before I saw that much of the good news related to Nvidia's chips—such as stronger PC sales and the continued increase in video game console sales—had been priced into the stock shortly after these events had transpired. With the introduction of the iPod and the PlayStation 3, along with chip orders from cell manufacturers, I didn't see any additional near-term catalysts on the horizon that would boost Nvidia's shares in the immediate future. I decided to lock in gains of 43 percent before the stock's momentum slowed, and was extremely pleased with my return.

Identifying a Bubble

There is one more red flag in this China shop that I want you to be aware of. That is the growing concern among investment advisers over the rapid growth of China's Mainland exchanges. Although I've warned you away from the markets in Shanghai and Shenzhen (regardless of your ability to actually invest in them), these exchanges are important to the Chinese government. Anything that might radically upset the machinations of its upward-trending markets could result in Beijing stepping in and trying to artificially protect or realign the marketplace.

Right now, the high valuation in Mainland China's domestic market is prompting many, including Premier Wen Jiabao, to publicly talk about the risks of a stock market bubble. With all this speculation, people wonder if there are warning signs of impending correction or collapse. And because of my success, I'm regularly asked to identify major tops in a stock market run-up. While there are no crystal balls to predict the way the market will behave, there are some historical factors to look at. Of course, every speculative bubble is different, but whether it was tulips in Amsterdam during the seventeenth century or Internet stocks in New York at the turn of the millennium, the mass psychology behind bubbles remains the same.

Personally, I have lived through and studied two stock market bubbles in my life: the Taiwanese stock market bubble of the late 1980s and the tech-stock bubble of the late 1990s. Because I was still in college in the United States when the Taiwanese bubble occurred, I didn't get to financially participate in it. Nevertheless, I studied the Taiwanese bull market very carefully because its collapse—a 75 percent decline—wiped out my father's fortune.

By the time the tech-stock bubble came about in the late 1990s, I had both the capital and the professional expertise to take full advantage of the market conditions. I did well on the way up and avoided most of the damage on the way down.

After giving it some serious thought and looking at the history of both exchanges, I identified three major signs of impending market tops in both the Taiwan and NASDAQ exchanges. Given the right circumstances, these can be applied to almost any exchange.

1. *Significant rally of speculative money-losing companies.* Highly speculative companies that are losing money tend to move up sharply during the final leg of a major bull market. In Taiwan, shares of many money-losing, debt-ridden manufacturing companies shot up in the final leg of the rally. These companies always claim that they can close their factories, sell their land, and turn themselves around. Likewise, money-losing technology companies on the NASDAQ

outperformed profitable technology companies by three-to-one in 1999. Money-losing companies selling hype tend to be the last ones to move up in a bull market.

2. *Uninformed public investors making a killing.* My childhood nanny recklessly plunged her entire savings into the Taiwanese stock market in 1988. At the market peak 18 months later, her investment was up 400 percent. During the tech bubble in 1999, many young and inexperienced retail investors quit their low-paying jobs and made six-figure incomes from day trading. My nanny lost everything. She had no retirement funds left, and my family has been helping her ever since. Ultimately, most of these investors gave back their gains and more. When too many unsophisticated investors make a killing, it's time to watch out.

3. *Excessive and extravagant spending.* During the peak of Taiwan's speculative bubble, nightclub valets often received hundred-dollar tips. Professional stock operators in Taipei frequently and famously ran up bar tabs over $10,000 at trendy clubs. Similar levels of excess were common in Silicon Valley during 1999. Many companies burned through millions of dollars each month without ever having made a dime. They thought that the party would never end and that corporate profits would catch up to stock valuations. In most cases, profits never did.

Each of these conditions, or signs, played out for 12 to 24 months before the market actually topped out. The Mainland Chinese market has started to exhibit some of these signs, but at a very nascent level, so there is still plenty of room to run up. The higher the stock valuation, however, the more vulnerable share prices are when a sell-off occurs.

I tell you this because as an investor in China, you should be aware of what is happening across a wide and related range of investment venues—even if you're not personally committed to them. Should some of the air get sucked out of the Mainland Chinese markets, however, you won't have to worry because you already know to stay away from Shenzhen and Shanghai. And by investing in strong stocks on the U.S. exchanges, you've avoided much of the danger that you might conceivably encounter while profiting from the China Miracle.

By using this information—and paying attention to the market—you will never be gored by the proverbial bull in the China shop.

Chapter 13

China's Political Place in the World

As investors, we've seen how betting on the growth of the Chinese economy can lead to huge wealth. As consumers, we've experienced firsthand how inexpensive Chinese imports have driven retail costs down and allowed us to buy more in our stores for less money. These are both exceptional economic benefits that we've derived from the developed world's relationship with China.

But we have to stop and consider China's political place in the world. China is still a Communist country in name, and its ideals run counter to those of many other countries. As a nation still not comfortable with democracy in all its forms, China controls the media and censors those who speak out against the government. It repeatedly tells the rest of the world to mind its own business when it comes to domestic politics.

At the same time, China's wealth is allowing it to buy resources and commodities to which the West has always had a proprietary attachment. As China purchases more and more of the world's oil, metals, timber, and other raw materials, prices are driven up and China is competing with nations long accustomed to getting everything they need on the open market.

The question that arises from these conflicting states of affairs, and one I get asked virtually every time I discuss China's potential, is whether the nation of China is ultimately a friend or a foe.

This question has several answers, all of them multilayered but not very complicated. I'll address the foe answers first, because—while they are important—there are fewer of them than you might think.

China remains the only large Communist country in the world. Just the mere mention of the word *communism* causes many in the United States to flinch, especially those who came of age during the Cold War. But the United States' antagonist during the Cold War was the Soviet Union, not China. It's now a very different world. Today, what remains of the Soviet Union—in the form of Russia—is an important U.S. political ally. In contrast to Russia, China's brand of communism was not trotted out for global political power so much as it was applied to its own people.

The changes that Deng Xiaoping set in motion roughly 30 years ago have changed China mightily. Its government is still Communist in name, but with a pragmatic market orientation. As Deng famously said, "It doesn't matter if it's a white cat or black cat; as long as it can catch mice, it's a good cat." The late Chinese leader believed that labels such as communist or capitalist were not important; allowing the people to create jobs and wealth was what mattered.

Ever since then, the country has raced to catch up with, and even outpace, every capitalist nation on the planet. From the perspective of finance and commerce, China actually has some policies that are more friendly toward capitalists than those in the United States. For example, there is no capital gains tax for investors in China; people making millions of dollars on China's exchanges don't pay a dime in taxes. There are quite a few U.S. investors who would leap for joy if that policy were in effect in our country.

China watchers regularly cite the potential for national unrest as its citizens demand more of the freedoms enjoyed by the West. The reality is that over the past few decades there has constantly been some level of unrest. People have demonstrated, protested, and rioted against the government over any number of policies and procedures. Most recently, the government has employed the rule of eminent domain to confiscate land for everything from commercial development to the 2008 Summer Olympics. Public outcry has been steady and constant across the country as millions of people have been displaced.

But in a land where more than a billion people are packed into a geographic space roughly equal to the 50 United States, political skirmishes and even small-scale riots go unnoticed at the national level. I've seen estimates that tens of thousands of demonstrations occur every year, usually by peasants protesting against land grabs or poor wages. However, since they occur in villages and towns—and not the national stage, like Tiananmen Square in Beijing—they have negligible impact on the behemoth that is the nation of China and its economy.

In the same way that protests at a courthouse in New Jersey against a local tax hike are not going to affect the gross domestic product (GDP) or political focus of the entire United States, regional protests in China are not going to affect the country's growth going forward. So China watchers who worry about social upheaval are not looking at the big picture. Barring something on the scale of a full-blown revolution, which is unlikely to happen in a country whose citizens are benefiting from unprecedented economic growth, China's future looks to be quite stable by any measure.

While China's domestic social and political policies will be watched intently for years to come, they currently have little impact on China's status as one of the United States' most important trading partners. China's massive production has been a boon to the U.S. economy in the form of low-priced merchandise, and I don't believe anyone can logically argue against that point. However, there are several negatives associated with China's production, each of which has served to heighten levels of animosity over doing business with China.

The first is outsourcing. As I described earlier, outsourcing is the process whereby American goods are manufactured in China and then shipped back to the United States for sale over here. The rationale for the practice is simply to reduce costs; Chinese labor and parts cost a fraction of what they do in the United States. As a result, American workers who have lost their jobs to outsourcing view China as a foe—a country that is stealing their jobs.

Anytime workers find themselves unemployed, it is a huge concern for all citizens of that country. The United States, in particular, has a heavily consumer-based economy relying on having as many of its citizens working as possible; there is also the social belief that everyone who is capable and wants to work should be able to. China, as we've mentioned, is not the culprit behind lost jobs. Like other countries that offer low-cost manufacturing (especially Mexico), China is being hired in aggregate by U.S. corporations to provide a service. Manufacturing is a low-skill, labor-intensive process and as such has always been an area in which business has sought to keep costs as low as possible.

Because we live in a global economy, international businesses can cross borders to find the lowest costs in regional labor markets. Those low costs are no longer in the United States or Europe or Japan; they are in emerging economies like those in Southeast Asia and Central America. The job trend in the United States, Europe, and Japan is toward higher-paying jobs that involve innovation and intellectual capital. Outsourcing to China does not change that elemental fact of production and labor.

More relevant to evaluating any negative aspect of China's manufacturing are the dual concerns of piracy and tainted products. China's greatest threat to the Western economies in general and the U.S. economy in particular is actually intellectual property theft: counterfeit goods, software piracy, and other copyright violations. In addition, its reputation has been hurt by the outsized number of product recalls that occurred in 2007, especially toys and food products.

Looking first at piracy, the software and entertainment industries have claimed for years that the Chinese authorities ignore the widespread copying and selling of illegal versions of books, software, CDs, DVDs, and video games. The Motion Picture Association of America states that less than 10 percent of the DVDs sold in China are legitimate, and that film companies lose several billion dollars each year to pirated versions of their movies.

After repeated complaints to the World Trade Organization (WTO) from the United States and Europe, the Chinese government is beginning to understand that it cannot be a true global economic power without dealing with the problem of piracy. Over the past couple of years, government authorities have cracked down on software piracy by declaring that all PCs manufactured in China must come with a preloaded legal operating system, such as Microsoft's Vista or Windows XP.

The government has begun to regularly raid shopping centers such as Beijing's Silk Market that are infamous for selling counterfeit goods. Steep fines have been imposed, and while this is a good start, more action needs to be taken, and the United States is demanding it. While the U.S. government acknowledges that Beijing is making a modicum of effort, it argues that not nearly enough is being done, and has asked the WTO to take the lead on cracking down on Chinese piracy.

As I discussed in Chapter 9 on manufacturing, one of my key strategies for profiting from the China Miracle is to never invest in businesses or products that can be easily copied. They're just too risky. Perhaps at some point China's copyright protection laws and enforcement may match what we enjoy in the United States, but that time is still a long way away.

Piracy adversely affects U.S. businesses, but unless you work in an industry affected by China's counterfeit goods, you're probably only aware of it in a peripheral sense. More important to you and me as consumers is the rise in products coming out of China that contain toxic material. Toys, pet food, vitamins, and toothpaste topped the list of items that were recalled in 2007 as consumers and the media seemed to uncover an unending stream of tainted or dangerous products from China. Reading the stories about these items, you'd think that everything manufactured in China was defective or deadly.

China acted quickly to quell fears of tainted products by participating in the recalls and revamping many of the organizations that oversee or are involved in product safety. It also shut down factories and arrested managers. And while the contamination was very real, there was more to the story than rogue manufacturers. Mattel, which recalled nearly a million toys, ultimately apologized to China and took the blame for one of the recalls, stating that the problems lay with its product design and specifications, not the manufacturing process.

According to the Chinese government, the number of products affected by recalls and safety concerns amounted to only 1 percent of its exports. I haven't seen any reports that contradict that number, either. One percent, no matter how you want to view it, is a tiny fraction of China's products, and puts the recalls in a more accurate context. Yes, tainted goods are a concern to every consumer and more regulations should be put in place. But the overwhelming majority— 99 percent—of China's goods are safe and we use them every day. As investors, our concern over the impact of recalls on China's overall economy should be weighed against the facts. And the facts are that most of China's products are perfectly safe.

Piracy and contamination are the two leading business issues Americans have with China. Its huge trade surplus with the United States is a key political and economic issue—especially during election years—but is a result of trade policies created by our elected officials. The only way we can have any direct effect on trade is if we all decide to stop buying clothes, electronics, and appliances en masse. That, obviously, is never going to happen. Besides, no one can blame China for selling everything it can to U.S. consumers. After all, that's the goal of every one of us who has ever been in business—sell as much as you can. Trying to pin our surplus problems on China's trade policy is a nonstarter.

The Currency Conundrum

China has replaced Japan as the nation with the largest trade surplus with the United States. As a result, demand for the Chinese yuan is surging, which benefits those companies getting paid in the yuan, as well as investors who track the currency. The Chinese government is letting the value of the yuan float within a defined range, and it continues to appreciate slowly and steadily against all other major currencies. I expect the yuan to keep appreciating 5 percent to 10 percent a year for at least the next three to five years. If you invest in companies with significant operations in China, they are likely to enjoy extra profits just from currency gains, which should help their stock prices.

But the value of the yuan is of huge concern to the United States, especially as the dollar plummets ever downward. The dollar has lost 40 percent of its value against other currencies since 2002—another reason investors seeking to build their wealth should be looking past the dollar to invest in companies doing business in China. The dollar's fall has prompted Treasury Secretary Henry Paulson, who was head of Goldman Sachs, to visit China no less than five times since 2006 without stopping in Japan even once. This demonstrates that Paulson believes—correctly, I might add—that China is more important to U.S. interests and has greater economic potential than Japan, even though Japan is the second-biggest economy in the world.

Paulson has asked China to be a "responsible partner" by cleaning up piracy and pollution problems and by allowing the yuan to be valued by the market instead of being pegged to the dollar. He is certain to get a positive response to his insistence that China get tougher on the dual scourge of piracy and pollution. China is already cracking down on intellectual property piracy, and is already spending billions on environmental cleanup. This is great news, because both are serious problems.

Any efforts to protect intellectual property are welcome, but true progress will take time. As far as the environment is concerned, I've mentioned the severe pollution problem in some of the major cities. Beijing, for example, is clouded by smog on a regular basis, and it affects your ability to breathe when you walk down the streets. The world's most polluted cities are in China, and that is because China's rapid growth has forced the nation to consume traditional energy resources like oil and coal at a literally breathtaking rate.

It is the reason why the government has mandated that the amount of clean, renewable energy like solar and nuclear power more than double to 15 percent of the country's output in the next three years. But China is aiming to make progress before then, partly because of the Olympics in 2008, which the government has dubbed the "Green Olympics." Companies that can help the government meet its goals, like solar cell manufacturer Suntech Power Holdings Co., Ltd. (NYSE: STP), are in a great position to benefit. Suntech (which I described in Chapter 7) was chosen to supply a solar system for Bird's Nest Stadium, the main stadium for the Olympics.

Getting back to U.S. concerns, I must say that I have great respect for how Henry Paulson dealt with China while he was there. I believe his strategy of asking China to be a responsible partner rather than demanding action is a subtle but important shift that will be well received over time by China's leadership. However, I don't expect Paulson to be successful in getting China to revalue the yuan quickly. He has met with continued resistance, and I don't see that changing anytime soon.

China doesn't want to let its currency rise sharply and quickly for two main reasons: (1) Most Chinese exporters are in low-margin contract manufacturing, and rapid currency appreciation could put them out of business because a more expensive yuan would eliminate China's low-cost advantage, and (2) China's biggest competition in the export business, Japan, spends billions each month buying U.S. Treasury securities to keep the Japanese yen artificially low.

That said, China is loosening its restrictions and letting the yuan float more than it used to, and I expect it to continue appreciating steadily for the foreseeable future. A stronger yuan automatically boosts the profits of companies paid in that currency—businesses based in China or with significant operations there—which is good news for almost all significant investments in China-related companies. Companies that sell to China will also benefit.

Gold prices are also important when discussing the problems of currency. Chinese central bank chief Zhou Xiao-chuan has made it a goal to diversify the world's biggest foreign reserve away from U.S. dollar-denominated assets. I expect that to mean that China will buy more gold for its gigantic $1.3 trillion foreign reserves. Gold prices shot up over $20 immediately after the announcement, and I recommend to all investors that they find a good strong gold position and stake it out. One way for investors to invest in gold without actually taking physical possession of the shiny metal is through the StreetTracks Gold Shares ETF (NYSE: GLD). This exchange-traded fund (ETF) is backed by gold bullion and tracks closely the price of physical gold.

We also have to consider China's consumption of gold, which increased an impressive 17 percent in 2006. The Chinese people love gold, and as the middle class builds wealth—and credit cards become widely available—consumption should remain strong.

China has used its increased buying power—built up through its trade surplus and its foreign reserves—to acquire a larger share of commodities than it ever has in the past. Not only can it afford more energy and more raw materials, but it needs them to sustain its growth. This puts it in competition with the United States, much of Europe, Japan, Canada, and other industrialized countries for commodities that are increasingly hard to come by. But we have to remember that many of the resources China currently consumes are used to make low-cost goods for consumers in the United States and Western Europe. Despite higher raw materials costs, Chinese factories have kept prices of finished goods low so millions of American and European consumers can afford to buy them and enjoy a higher standard of living.

Returning to the China watchers for a moment, many of them question whether China will content itself with just being the highest bidder. "Isn't it possible the country could decide to forcibly take control of commodities it wants but may be unable to get?" they ask.

Again, when I hear this sort of talk, I have to shake my head. There has never been a time in China's history when it has sought to build empire outside of its geographic region. Unlike most global powers in history, China has never invaded any country outside of its own continent. The country has always shielded itself from the outside. It is simply not in China's history or its nature to seek out confrontation with other countries far away from its homeland.

Part of this is because China, unlike European countries, has both a huge expanse of interior land and thousands upon thousands of miles of coastline. When the English, Spanish, Dutch, Japanese, and Portuguese sought to expand their empires, it was because they had been surrounded by neighboring countries and had run out of land (which is a requisite for natural resources), or they were hemmed in by the sea, requiring that they set sail to find new regions in which to settle a growing population and develop outlets for commerce.

The Chinese perspective has always been that of a regional power, primarily a self-contained and self-sustaining power. The speed at which its economy has grown, however, has required that China reach out to countries that can provide it with the additional resources it hasn't been able to provide for itself.

Something that has been pointed out to me by my European friends is that China has been cultivating these international relationships by respecting the sovereignty of the nations with which it wants to do business. Not that there is a right way or a wrong way, say these

European colleagues, but they invariably point out that respecting sovereignty is often not the way the United States does things. Then again, I counter, neither does Europe. This always makes for long and interesting arguments.

My European friends, whom I respect for their straight talk, marvel over how China has managed to make inroads into these countries without antagonizing the rest of the world. Their point is that Western countries still rely on either military or police action when they need oil, or they give aid to countries with strings attached, such as food for oil. China typically gives aid to generate goodwill, and hopes (rather than demands) that this goodwill will be returned in kind.

While my friends are making a sweeping generalization—the United States gives more in foreign aid than most of the other nations in the world combined—there is evidence to back up China's goodwill efforts. The Chinese government has offered to pay part of the cost of the reconstruction of Ethiopia's roads and has donated all the funds to build a new conference center for the African Union in Addis Ababa. It has set up similar programs in Angola and Sudan, where it is helping to underwrite the costs of building everything from schools to stadiums.

China is investing in Africa; of that there's no doubt. Whether there is a quid pro quo is anybody's guess. But right now, many African countries are selling a great deal of their oil and iron ore to China. And African nations like dealing with China, because they are not being told that they should change their way of life or system of government.

By leveraging its newly gained economic power as a tool of diplomacy, China is also gaining popularity throughout East Asia. China has built highways and railways connecting it to neighbors in the south, such as Vietnam, Laos, Burma (Myanmar), and Thailand, and sells billions of dollars' worth of low-cost merchandise to them. Increasing economic integration with China is helping these countries prosper.

The Asian Coattails Effect

In fact, many of China's neighbors have ridden on the coattails of the China Miracle for just over a decade. But it required weathering a significant financial upheaval to ultimately bind these countries together.

The upheaval began immediately after the United Kingdom transferred control of Hong Kong to China in a ceremony at midnight on July 1, 1997. The very next day, July 2, marked the start of a two-year-long incident called the "Asian contagion." Traders waged a speculative attack on Thailand's currency, the baht, and over the next six months, it lost more than 40 percent of its value against the U.S. dollar.

Other Asian countries in the region with large foreign debts and small foreign reserves also succumbed to speculative attacks against their currencies: Malaysia, Indonesia, South Korea, and the Philippines all followed Thailand's currency collapse. The worst-hit currency was the Indonesian rupiah, which lost nearly 80 percent of its value over the next 10 months, eventually culminating in the overthrow of the longtime Indonesian dictator Suharto.

This financial crisis in Asia was sparked by a combination of factors such as slowing exports, overdependence on global speculative capital, rapid capital flight from foreign investors, excessive real estate speculation, and large foreign debt in the region.

The problem even spread to economically powerful Japan. The Land of the Rising Sun took a hit because it was still mired in recession, suffering from the fallout of its speculative bubble during the 1980s.

At the time, several of my former colleagues at Goldman Sachs made a killing from short positions in Asian currencies. One trader, my friend Will Peters, shorted the rupiah in a big way and made impressive profits of 150 percent in 1997. By early 1998, the Asian contagion had spread throughout the entire Asia-Pacific region, with only China, Hong Kong, and Taiwan left unscathed. Will then decided to short the Hong Kong dollar and the Taiwan dollar, the only two major currencies still left standing in Asia.

I advised Will not to sell short the currencies of Hong Kong and Taiwan, because both central banks, especially Taiwan's, held huge foreign exchange reserves. Also, both Taiwan and Hong Kong had relatively little outstanding foreign debt. I also knew that Mainland China, a country immune to speculative currency attacks, would do everything in its power to defend Hong Kong now that it had been restored to the Motherland.

A big clash developed with hedge funds, Wall Street investment banks, and emerging-market mutual funds all siding against the central banks of China, Hong Kong, and Taiwan. Global speculators shorted both the currencies and the stocks of these regions, while U.S. and European emerging-market funds liquidated their Asian stock portfolios in a hurry.

Then, in a controversial move that was widely criticized by Wall Street, the Hong Kong central bank stepped in and bought $15 billion in stocks at the height of the crisis to defend its falling stock market. Supported by the Chinese central bank's increasingly deep pockets and political resolve, Hong Kong successfully fought off the global speculators. A few years later, the Hong Kong central bank liquidated the stocks it bought during the currency crisis, making over $4 billion in gains. As the second-largest holder of foreign reserves in the world, Taiwan's central bank also managed to emerge from the Asian financial crisis relatively unharmed.

Will got out of the short trade without making a profit. Chastened, he came away very impressed by China's growing financial and economic might, as did I. More than any other single event that I had witnessed, the Chinese central bank's strong performance during the Asian crisis changed my perception of Mainland China. I knew right then, back in 1998, that China's economic emergence was for real, and every serious investor and business executive in the twenty-first century needed to develop a China strategy.

Fast-forward to the present. It has been just over 10 years since the Asian financial crisis first erupted in Thailand. Led by China's economic miracle, Asia has made a remarkable recovery. Stock markets hit hard during the financial crisis, such as those of South Korea and Hong Kong, managed big comebacks by piggybacking on China's success, significantly leapfrogging past the peaks they made before the crisis. The stock markets of Malaysia, Thailand, Singapore, the Philippines, and even Indonesia came back strong as well, also trading above the highs made before the crisis.

As a rule of thumb, smaller Asian countries that integrated themselves into China's economic emergence prospered the most. The countries that didn't follow China grew at a much slower rate. Ironically, the only two major Asian stock markets still trading below their old highs in the 1990s are Japan and Taiwan, the two countries that held up relatively well throughout the disaster.

Japan has structural demographic problems holding it back, but Taiwan is a different situation. The Taiwanese stock market has lagged other Asian markets because of its government's reluctance to come to terms with China. Despite this, many Taiwanese companies have significant operations in Mainland China, and they will help the Taiwan exchange play catch-up to Hong Kong and Shanghai's stock markets— both of which have experienced huge run-ups over the past few years.

Taiwan won't be the only economy playing catch-up to China. I believe other Asian peripheral stock markets with exposure to China will also make an effort to catch up to China's massive run. That's why so many of the Asian ETFs—like iShares MSCI Taiwan Index, the iShares MSCI Singapore Index, and the iShares MSCI Hong Kong Index—have become so popular. These markets are also helped by the fact that they are much more reasonably valued than the shares on the expensive Chinese exchanges.

The Rise of a Superpower?

Some may interpret China's aggressive rise in prosperity to a desire to become a dominant superpower. But, as I said, China does not harbor any ambition for world domination. The Chinese do want to become a major regional power in Asia, and have formulated their foreign policies to promote that goal. China has always been focused on its position relative to its neighbors, not on what takes place in faraway lands dominated by other major powers.

China typically does not get involved with the politics of other governments. The one exception is Taiwan.

I have a strong personal interest in Taiwan because I was born in Taiwan. As long as I've been alive, the relationship between Mainland China and Taiwan has been a complicated one. However, from a business perspective, it has never been better.

The People's Republic of China and Taiwan are still living on opposite sides of a civil war that was over many years ago. The split occurred in 1949 when Chinese Nationalist troops suffered defeat at the hands of the Communists and retreated from the mainland to the nearby island of Taiwan. Ever since, both sides have rattled their sabers at each other, each claiming to be the rightful heir to China's heritage.

But since Mainland China opened in the 1980s, a tremendous reverse migration has occurred: Nearly one million of Taiwan's most affluent, resourceful, and ambitious citizens and their families have moved to the mainland, investing $200 billion to participate in and prosper from the China Miracle.

Businesses controlled by Taiwanese entrepreneurs account for nearly 20 percent of China's total exports. Because these entrepreneurs had capital and expertise—not to mention proximity—they had a head start in entering and profiting from the China Miracle, and many amassed immense fortunes as a result. Companies like Quanta and Foxconn have become enormously successful not simply because they are Taiwanese companies, but because they are Taiwanese companies that have built manufacturing empires in the Chinese Mainland.

Businesspeople have long understood the benefits of a positive relationship with Mainland China, yet Taiwan's politicians are often determined to undermine that relationship at any cost. Chen Shui-bian, Taiwan's president, has long been an advocate of moving the island's interests further away from those of China. Chen is losing his influence, however, as a result of low approval ratings, corruption charges, and the country's economic decline. To add to his troubles, his son-in-law was arrested on insider trading charges, and the U.S. State Department sent 300 people to investigate (a good friend of mine was one of the leaders of that group of investigators). To top it off, the deputy U.S. trade representative called on Taiwan to end trade restrictions with China, saying the country was putting its own businesses at a disadvantage, which is true.

Since Chen rose to power in 2000, the Taiwanese government has gone out of its way to cut itself off from China's economic emergence. Such recalcitrance did not stop smart Taiwanese entrepreneurs and investors from participating in the China Miracle, though. Over one million Taiwanese, half of them in Shanghai, now spend more time in Mainland China than in Taiwan. The $200 billion that Taiwanese businesses have invested in China over the past two decades is more than any other country in the world has invested there. Despite his best efforts, Chen's government didn't stop Taiwanese businesses from moving to China; it only made the process more inconvenient and expensive.

How inconvenient? Try this: Because of political tension, there is currently no direct flight between Taiwan and the Chinese Mainland. Passengers need to stop over in Hong Kong, which makes a two-hour flight between Taipei and Shanghai into a six-hour slog that eats up the better part of a business day. At an extra cost of $150 per flight, Taiwanese travelers to China pay an extra $9 billion a year—and yet there are over six million trips made annually.

Chen will be out of office when his term ends in May of 2008. I believe the ruling Democratic Progressive Party will be out as well. The embattled Chen currently has an approval rating of 6 percent, making him the most unpopular elected head of state in the world. It's hard to believe that in this day and age any elected official could actually sink into single-digit approval, but it has happened in Taiwan. As a result, I expect Harvard-trained, pro-China opposition party chairman Ma Yin-jo to prevail in the 2008 presidential election.

For all the economic benefits that the two share, Beijing still considers Taiwan a renegade province that should be returned to the Mainland, and I believe it would go to great lengths to take back the island. For example, if Taiwan declares formal independence, the risk of war would escalate. Chen has made the situation worse by doing things that antagonize the Mainland Chinese government. For instance, he terminated the island's National Unification Council with China. Though largely inactive, the council was symbolic of Taiwan's ties to Mainland China, and terminating it served to distract voters from his administration's poor record with the economy and government corruption.

This political maneuver may have distracted voters, but it also served to irritate Beijing. President Hu Jintao of China called Chen's move a "grave provocation" that threatened stability in the region. Likewise, senior Chinese military leaders announced their willingness to "defend the unification and sovereignty of the motherland." In other words, they would launch missiles at Taiwan if they felt justified.

The United States, Taiwan's main military ally, has long attempted to rein in Taiwanese moves toward independence and saw this as a bad situation. Though it supports Taiwan in its policies, Washington needs Mainland China's help in dealing with North Korea and Iran, and

Wall Street looks to China for increasing investment and deal-making opportunities. When Chen terminated the council, the U.S. State Department "encouraged" him to change his wording. He wound up rephrasing his position, saying the council would "cease to function" instead of being "abolished."

All of this has had a more profoundly negative impact on Taiwan than on Mainland China. Although many Taiwanese investors are highly successful in China, Taipei's pro-independence government makes it difficult for money to flow back home from the mainland. The huge capital flow between Taiwan and China is a one-way street, with money going to China and not coming back. As living conditions have improved in China, more and more Taiwanese have decided to move their entire families to cities on the mainland. Increasingly, people in Taipei are mortgaging their homes to take out loans in order to buy condos in Shanghai.

This financial malaise is reflected in the country's economy. Taiwan's annual GDP growth has declined from 6 percent to 4 percent in the past two years. For the first time in recent history, Taiwan may run a trade deficit against its major trading partners. Unemployment rose sharply as entire industries were transplanted to Mainland China.

In the past, I've enjoyed visiting Taipei because I have friends and relatives living there; plus, I've always reveled in the city's hustle and bustle. But now, in contrast to the confidence and energy of Beijing and Shanghai, Taipei is filled with gloominess. Unless Taiwan finds a way to participate in China's economic emergence, the island will become increasingly isolated in the global community.

The risk of military conflict between China and Taiwan is slim, because the reality is that they need each other. They might not like each other's policies or leaders, but businesspeople are reaping benefits while the politicians battle it out. China likes getting investment money from Taiwan, and Taiwanese businesses are capitalizing on the Chinese Mainland's proximity, shared language, and cheap labor. And if the two were ever to join forces, China could absorb Taiwan's economy and they both would prosper.

Nonetheless, the situation between Taiwan and China needs to be watched carefully. If the political tension between the two can be resolved, I believe Taiwan will be ripe with exciting turnaround stories. I hope for both that better times lie ahead.

For investors, the better times are right now. China's role in the world is changing, but it is changing in ways that have been hugely positive for its neighbors, its trading partners, and its citizens. China has good relationships with most of the rest of the world.

Today, China and the United States are economic allies; they depend on each other for trade, investment, and mutually beneficial business relationships. Their politics are not always aligned, but their goals of economic development and prosperity are. Outside of political posturing, there is very little that can happen that would upset this state of affairs. And both countries—and their respective investors—will benefit from their continued cooperation.

Chapter 14

Your China Strategy

This is the final and most important chapter of our exploration of the China Miracle.

I've talked to you about how to follow trends and how to avoid pitfalls when buying into the China Miracle. Now is the time for you to put it all into practice. To assist you in doing that from this moment forward, I've created an outline of the steps that are essential to successfully building your portfolio and creating serious wealth. If you use this as a guideline—and apply some thoughtful research along with a little common sense—you will be on your way to getting rich from the China Miracle.

Here's how to start.

Step 1: Gather Accurate Information about China

Too many investors overlook this critical first step, which in my opinion is the most important part of buying a stock. If your information is flawed, your investment will be, too.

I've given you a great deal of information on China in these pages, which has provided you with the fundamentals you need in order to understand what's going on and how you can profit from it. Going forward, you need to continue getting information in order to select the stocks and track the trends that best suit your personal investment strategy.

To accomplish this, you should keep up with news coming out of Mainland China on a regular basis, at least once a week. Pick a day that you can dedicate to spending an hour reading about current events in China. I recommend the following sources:

The *Economist* is an excellent magazine and web site (www.economist .com) that provides up-to-date analysis of social and business events around the world. Its reports are among the most objective and insightful you will find anywhere.

The BBC is an international news icon that is available on many cable TV networks and has a web page dedicated to Asia-Pacific news (http:// news.bbc.co.uk/2/hi/asia-pacific/default.stm). It's a great resource for daily news as well as for investigative pieces on everything from national politics to corporate behavior.

The *South China Morning Post* is Hong Kong's leading English news-paper and has always been a good source for tracking news in and around Asia, especially the Chinese Mainland. You won't find it readily available on U.S. newsstands, so I suggest visiting its web site (www.scmp .com/portal/site/SCMP/).

The *China Daily* is the Mainland's primary news outlet to the rest of the world. While it won't give you much objective insight because it's produced by the government, the web site (www.chinadaily.com.cn) will provide you with a great deal of information about what the government is doing, and it does report on many of the positive economic trends occurring in the country.

By visiting a variety of China-related web sites over time, you'll get a strong sense of the current political and business climate and will be able to pinpoint relevant news stories and potential investment opportunities.

Investor's Business Daily is a daily newspaper that I find to be an invaluable source of information for all my investments. It's pricey, but it contains excellent analysis and news. The *IBD* web site (www .investors.com) has many free areas that are updated throughout the day.

Of course, it would be disingenuous of me not to point out that I think my newsletters and my weekly dispatches contain the best investment information about China available anywhere. You can find out more about them at *China Strategy* (www.chinaprofitstrategy.com) and *Asia Edge* (www.asiapacificedge.com). Both newsletters cover the most recent happenings and feature my insight into what's happening now and how to profit from it.

I have also set up a web site for *China Fireworks* at www.chinafire worksbook.com so that you can check out some of my latest thinking on what's going on in China today and how you can take advantage of market trends.

Step 2: Identify Industries That Are Growing

After you've familiarized yourself with current business events in China, identify those industries that are enjoying growth. Of course, right now almost every industry in China is growing, but you should focus on areas that I've outlined in this book. Consumer trends, demand for services, and commodity requirements will provide the bedrock for your portfolio. Once you've picked the industries, select companies within those industries that are selling into China, not necessarily Chinese companies selling domestically. For instance, China is producing more and more of its own steel, and you don't want to invest in Mainland Chinese steel companies.

Instead, consider the global mining industry. International mining giants are selling heavily to China and are benefiting from higher world prices brought about by strong Chinese demand. I feel the same way about energy companies. Most U.S.-based multinational companies don't get enough of their business from China for it to really make a difference in their bottom lines. This may change in a few years as China's consumer market grows.

Step 3: Pick Industry Leaders

After you've determined which industries offer the best potential and best fit for you as an investor, identify the companies that are dominating that industry or are at the leading edge of innovation. But before you jump in,

I have some criteria for identifying those leaders that are most worth buying. Buying the leaders is not simply buying the biggest one you can find.

- The company has to have a sustainable competitive advantage not easily copied by competitors. I've already identified the most important of these, which are size (an established operation that is large enough so its business can't be easily eaten into by newcomers or copycats); brand recognition (a business or product that is perceived as being unique and desirable over the competition, even lower-priced competition); and technology (innovators that have intellectual capital that is not easily duplicated and is substantially ahead of the competition).
- The company must be growing. Earnings growth should be 20 percent year-over-year, or consecutive quarter-to-quarter growth should be 10 percent over two quarters. These aren't hard-and-fast numbers, but you certainly want to ensure that the company has quantifiable (and qualifiable) growth. If there isn't a lot of growth, but the company is a demonstrated leader—using the criteria listed—examine its market share and determine if it has a position in the industry that significantly exceeds it competition.
- Because I'm a momentum investor, I invest in companies that are making higher highs rather than higher lows. A company that is regularly reaching higher highs is growing and its stock has momentum; the rising share price reflects this. Conversely, stocks that are just climbing out of their lows (i.e., only reaching higher lows) don't have the dynamic growth that I want to see from my holdings. That doesn't mean that they won't eventually gain traction and become attractive, but when they're hovering around their lows, I know that their payoffs are in the far distant future.

I don't put as much weight in some of the investing matrices and numbers that many investors live and die by, like price-earnings (P/E) ratios. A demonstrated history of high growth and the potential for continued growth are at the core of what I look for in every company.

You can find out how stocks fit into this growth matrix by doing some strategic Web surfing. Go to the company's web site and visit its investor relations section. There you will typically find several years of annual reports as well as the most recent quarterly filings. Then check sites that offer comparative and competitive data, including Hoover's (www.hoovers.com), the investment section of Yahoo! Finance (http:// finance.yahoo.com), and Google's iGoogle Finance page for investors (http://finance.google.com/finance). If you're not already using these as investment tools, you'll be surprised by how detailed and extensive their information is. Plus, they make research easy, very fast, and most of the time free.

Step 4: Make Your Buy

If you've done your homework well, you're ready to invest. I don't need to tell you how much to invest or what percentage of your portfolio should contain which holdings.

Step 5: Be Ready to Get Out and Collect Your Profits

In momentum investing, the market typically determines the length of your hold. This means that you hold your stocks until they start losing value. That can be a short time or a long time, but you have to be prepared.

If you follow growth stocks, you should take your profits when the growth rate in your holding slows down. To put an even finer point on it: When the company stops growing, get out. If there is no growth from one quarter to the next, your stock no longer has momentum. Even if you're a patient investor, you need to get out after two quarters of no growth. The only exceptions to this are when your stock has acceptable one-time charges, incurs expansion and investment expenses, or experiences a seasonal downturn—which I've seen in strong companies like New Oriental Education & Technology Group (NYSE: EDU), which has fluctuating revenues and enrollment based on the school year.

Getting out of a stock quickly requires discipline. A lot of people get attached to their stocks, even when they start dropping, in hopes they'll play out over time. That's not a wealth-building strategy; that's a waiting game. It is the same strategy that sank so many investors in the dot-com bubble. They were waiting for the market to come back around instead of taking the gains that were right there on the table. Many of them lost everything waiting for a turnaround that never happened.

My advice to investors when stocks stop advancing is to get out while you can still take profits. If the stock has the potential for future gains, then you can always get back in. Personally, I look for new companies to buy and usually don't look back.

Step 6: Keep Your Eyes and Ears Open

Once you become attuned to your investments, you will look at stocks in an entirely new way. You'll be able to integrate news about trade and oil prices and retail expansion into your understanding of China. Trust me—it will almost become second nature. If Apple (NASDAQ: AAPL) opens one of its hugely popular stores in Beijing or if KFC expands into western China or if Citicorp (NYSE: C) introduces a new credit card targeting Chinese consumers, you'll start evaluating each event as the basis for a potential China play.

In addition, watch the news, read company announcements specific to China, and look at and listen to advertisements. Advertisements may seem like a strange addition to your investing strategy, but one of my best stock moves was based on seeing some TV ads. It was several years ago, just as companies and countries were beginning to talk about the need to "go green." It was obviously a groundswell, and it led to decisions like Australia's plan to eliminate incandescent lightbulbs. In particular, I remember seeing a report that several dealerships around the United States had started waiting lists for hybrid cars.

As all this was transpiring, however, I was seeing TV commercials during sporting events for General Motors' (NYSE: GM) Hummer, which was regarded as the single biggest gas-guzzler on the road. And as I watched the ads, I couldn't help but think how out of touch General Motors was with the way people were thinking, and how that would translate into the way people would buy. It became apparent that instead of momentum, the company was heading for a brick wall. I sold short GM just before the stock took one of its worst hits.

If you think about building your wealth—and you should always be thinking about it—then more and more of the things you see, hear, and experience will be valuable in helping you make informed decisions about your money. Do it enough that it becomes automatic, and you'll be open to more investment opportunities than you ever before realized.

When it comes to the investment opportunities in China, you've already made the first part of your journey. You've learned that there is vast potential, and you've learned how to take advantage of that potential. My wish for you is that going forward you are able to reap the same benefits that I, along with the thousands of investors whom I advise, have enjoyed by building our wealth on the China Miracle.

Bibliography

Barboza, David. "Beijing Moves to Boost Confidence in Its Products." *New York Times News Service*, September 8, 2007. www.taipeitimes.com/News/editorials/archives/2007/09/08/2003377819.

Business Standard. "Aluminum to Rise 30% on China Imports." October 22, 2007. www.business-standard.com/common/storypage_c.php?leftnm=10&autono=301926.

China Daily. "China to Approve Bankruptcy of Over 500 SOEs." December 6, 2006. www.chinadaily.com.cn/bizchina/2006-12/06/content_751692.htm.

Forbes.com. "Hong Kong Nov Exports Up 6.6 Pct on Yr by Value vs +9.8 Pct in Oct—Update." December 28, 2007. www.forbes.com/afxnewslimited/feeds/afx/2007/12/28/afx4478750.html.

Gong Zhengzheng. "Iron Ore Import Rules Tightened." *China Daily*, December 29, 2006. www.chinadaily.com.cn/cndy/2006-12/29/content_770325.htm.

Hale, David. "China's Growing Appetites." *National Interest*, Summer 2004. www.thefreelibrary.com/China's+growing+appetites.-a0119572861.

Jao, James. "Healthy Growth of Cities." *China Daily*, November 5, 2005. www.chinadaily.com.cn/english/doc/2005-11/05/content_491585.htm.

Loyalka, Michelle Dammon. "A Chinese Welcome for Entrepreneurs." *Business Week*, January 6, 2006. www.businessweek.com/smallbiz/content/jan2006/sb20060105_926372.htm.

Mahr, Krista. "Selling Steak to China." *Time*, September 27, 2007. www.time.com/time/printout/0,8816,1665979,00.html.

MarketWatch. "China Oil Imports Soar." October 7, 2007. www.marketwatch .com/news/story/china-says-oil-imports-soar/story.aspx?guid={EFEC3 C0F-BADB-493E-B726-9168305BFC40}.

McKinsey Quarterly. "Spurring Performance in China's State-Owned Enterprises." November 4, 2004. www.mckinseyquarterly.com/article_abstract.aspx? ar=1492&L2=19&L3=69&srid=27&gp=0.

PricewaterhouseCoopers. "China's Impact on the Semiconductor Industry: 2006 Update," February 7, 2007. www.pwc.com/extweb/pwcpublications.nsf/ docid/180B20958CDFFE4F8525727300701687.

2003 Human Development Report (HDR), commissioned by the UN Development Programme (UNDP), for "Millennium Development Goals (MDG): A Compact among Nations to End Human Poverty." http://hdr.undp.org/en/ reports/global/hdr2003/.

"QA: Claude Leglise," January 29, 2006. Red Herring, Online Edition.

About the Author

Robert Hsu is the founder and president of Absolute Return Capital Advisors LLC, a private client money management firm. His firsthand knowledge of Chinese culture, business, and government, combined with his phenomenal track record as an investor, make him a popular speaker on investing in China. Formerly a hedge fund trader with Goldman Sachs, Robert earned average annual returns of more than 20 percent as a private money manager (and retired as a millionaire at age 30).

Robert has long been in an exceptional position to profit from the events shaping the unbelievable growth in China. Born in Taiwan and fluent in Mandarin, he maintains an organization of analysts in China who research and report firsthand on cultural, corporate, and governmental shifts within the country.

Robert also has two investing services, *China Strategy* and *Asia Edge*, which have become two of the best-selling and fastest-growing financial newsletters in the United States. Each service provides investors with weekly updates on his recommended companies, shares the details of his research team's latest findings, and provides commentary and advice for taking advantage of market trends.

Index